Jewish Law In The Diaspora:
Confrontation And Accommodation

Jewish Law
In The Diaspora:
Confrontation
and
Accommodation

A study of the development, composition and
function of the concept of *Dina D'Malkhuta Dina*
—the law of the kingdom (the state) is the law.

By

LEO LANDMAN

THE DROPSIE COLLEGE
FOR HEBREW AND COGNATE LEARNING

PHILADELPHIA   1907 — 1968

Dedicated to

MY WIFE, SHIRLEY

הנך יפה רעיתי, הנך יפה

Song of Songs IV:1

CONTENTS

PREFACE

I take this opportunity to express my appreciation to the Dropsie College for giving me the scholarly tools necessary to produce a work of this nature and for publishing this book. I am also grateful to Yeshiva University for providing the rabbinic training which proved invaluable in preparing this book.

This work was initially presented in partial fulfillment of the doctoral requirements at the Dropsie College under the guidance of my revered teacher and friend, Professor Solomon Zeitlin. I can never repay my indebtedness to him for sharing his knowledge and wisdom with me. His stimulating suggestions, his skilled supervision, and his constant guidance were of immeasurable help to me in preparing my doctoral dissertation and in readying it for publication. I deeply appreciate his writing the foreword to this volume.

It is with pleasure that I express my thanks to the members of Beth Emeth Congregation and especially to Norman Cristol for his unstinting encouragement and friendship and to Harold Kline, Milton Jacobs, Harold Fink and Jack Shachter for their understanding and helpfulness; to the librarians at the Dropsie College who put at my disposal much of the source material required to research this book; and to Dr. Harold Goldfarb, the Executive Director of the Board of Rabbis of Greater Philadelphia for his helpful suggestions.

I make special mention of Mr. Louis Gritz and his entire family and the Oxford Bookbinding Co. who were so generous in binding this book.

I am grateful to my wife who urged me to undertake this project and was most helpful during this time, to my parents whose love for learning permeated my home, and to my children, Dina, Chana, and Dovid who showed a sympathy far beyond their years and an understanding deeply rooted in love.

LEO LANDMAN

FOREWORD

The prophet Jeremiah, in his epistle to the Judaeans who were taken captive to Babylonia, wrote: "Seek the peace of the city whither I have caused you to be carried away captive, and pray unto Yahweh for it: for in the peace thereof shall you have peace." In the long history of their dispersion, the Jewish people followed the principle laid down by Jeremiah. They were always loyal citizens of their adopted countries when they were not persecuted and when they were treated equal to the rest of the population.

After the Restoration, the Persian king, Artaxerxes, vested in Ezra the power to appoint judges who were to instruct the people and who were to be given the authority to punish by death, by confiscation of goods, or by imprisonment those who did not follow the laws of God and the laws of the king. During the entire Persian period, the high priests had the right to supervise the laws of the State and the religious laws. The Jews of Palestine and their coreligionists in Babylonia were politically and religiously united. Both Jewries were united under the Persian flag. When the Persian Empire was conquered by Alexander, both Jewries continued to be united under his flag. After the death of Alexander, his empire was divided. Palestine was conquered by the Ptolemies and Babylonia came under the rule of the Seleucids. For the first time since the Restoration, the Jews of Babylonia were separated from the Jews of Palestine. Later, when the Seleucids conquered Palestine, the Jews of Alexandria became separated politically from their mother land.

When Simon the Hasmonean declared Judaea an independent state, the Jews of Alexandria and the Jews of Babylonia were not politically united with their brethren in Judaea. During the period of the Second Commonwealth, the dispersion grew and there were great Jewish settlements not only in Alexandria and Babylonia but also in Antioch, Rome and in the many islands in the Mediter-

11

ranean Sea. The Jews of Alexandria called themselves Alexandrians. They had their own Council called *Gerousia* and their leader was called *Alabarch*. The Jews who lived in Babylonia called themselves Babylonians and those in Antioch called themselves Antiochans. The Jews living in Rome called themselves Romans. While the Jews were politically loyal to their adopted countries, they cherished great affection for their motherland Judaea. Religiously they were dominated by the Bet Din, later called the Sanhedrin, of Jerusalem.

After the destruction of the Temple, particularly after the collapse of the Bar Kokba Revolt, the influence of the Judaeans over their brethren in the Diaspora began to diminish. Babylonia now became the center of the Jewish people. Samuel, a native of Babylonia, who was one of the disciples of Rabbi Judah the Prince, returned to his native land and became one of the great architects in building the center of Jewish learning in Babylonia. He was famous for his decisions on civil law while his colleague Rab specialized in ritual law. The Talmud states that with regard to civil law, the law is always to be decided in accordance with the opinion of Samuel.

Samuel laid down the principle that *Dina D'Malkhuta Dina,* the law of the kingdom (the state) is the law. This principle only referred to civil matters, the laws promulgated by the state. It did not refer to religious laws. During the history of the Jewish dispersion, the state generally did not interfere with the observance of the Jewish religion. During the Persian period, the religious authority over the Jews was vested in the high priests. In the Hellenistic period as well, the high priest was the spiritual leader of the Jews. When the Romans annexed Judaea, they appointed procurators, civil authorities, who did not interfere with the religious life of the Jewish people.

After the year 70, particularly after the collapse of the Bar Kokba Revolt, the Jews regarded the Romans as conquerors of their country and considered that they were ruled by force, not by right. Thus the principle of *Dina D'Malkhuta Dina* was not applicable to the rule of the Romans. That is the reason that this principle never occurs in the Palestinian Talmud.

At the end of the tenth century and the beginning of the eleventh, the Jewish center in Babylonia began to decline and then disappeared. In its place there arose two great Jewish communities, one in Spain and the other in Franco-Germany. Hitherto the Jews had been controlled by one center of learning—first Palestine and then Babylonia. Now Jewry became divided with two Jewish centers of learning. Each had its history and individual development. The history of the Jews in Spain differed from that of the Jews in France. The Jewish population of Spain had been predominantly of Babylonian origin. Many Jews who lived among the Arabs and Berbers in Babylonia and Africa migrated with them to Spain. The Jews of France were of Palestinian origin. Thus these two Jewish centers molded their religious and social life after the institutions developed in the lands of their origin. The Spanish Jewish community was molded in accordance with the Jewish institutions of Babylonia while the Jewish community in France molded its institutions in accordance with the mode of life of the Palestinian Jews.

In Spain, the spiritual and secular leaders were appointed by the king. In France, the spiritual leaders, rabbis, were elected or appointed by the Jews. These Jews never accepted any spiritual leader who was appointed by the government. The principle of *Dina D'Malkhuta Dina* was applied by the two countries in various ways, and different explanations were given for this principle in its application as a part of Jewish law. There was also a difference in the organization of the government of Spain and that of France. In the former, there was a centralized government which was lacking in the latter. Recognizing the differences inherent in these two countries, we can better understand the necessary variegated applications of the principle of *Dina D'Malkhuta Dina*. The Jews of France strove with all their strength to limit the authority of the government over the rights of their community. The rabbis of France invoked *Herem Hayishub*. In Germany, too, since no

13

central government existed, the Jews, in order to prevent unwelcome migrants from entering their city, invoked the *Herem Hayishub*. This *Herem* was introduced to give the inhabitants of a city the right to prevent the entry of a newcomer. With great zeal they opposed the government's attempts to void this *Herem*. In the Spanish Jewish community there was no such *Herem* since the whole country was controlled by one central government.

The application of the principle of *Dina D'Malkhuta Dina* during the Middle Ages is very complicated. Only one who is well versed in rabbinic literature, particularly in the Responsa, can throw light on its development and application.

Dr. Leo Landman, in his book *Jewish Law in the Diaspora: Confrontation and Accommodation,* shows his mastery of the Responsa and skill of interpretation. It is an admirable piece of work, full of new insights and ideas. The book will be indispensable for historians of the Middle Ages. At the same time it is a valuable book for the intelligent layman who wishes to learn about the Jews and Judaism of the Middle Ages. It is a remarkable accomplishment.

SOLOMON ZEITLIN

Dropsie College

CHAPTER I

The Talmudic Period

A principle of Jewish law set forth in the Talmud is "the law of the kingdom is the law"—*Dina D'Malkhuta Dina*. The Talmud attributes this principle to the Babylonian sage Samuel (3rd century C.E.), and it is quoted in his name a number of times.[1]

The reference to it in the Talmud Gittin is the only direct statement made by Samuel himself. In all other cases concerning his law, we find that it is others who quote the law in his name.[2] The Talmud is troubled by the Mishneh[3] which validates any document issued by a Gentile court and witnessed by Gentiles with the exception of a divorce and a bill of manumission. Apparently no distinction is made between a bill of sale, which serves merely as proof that a sale occurred, and a bill certifying a gift, in which case the deed actually accomplishes the transference of the gift from the donor to the recipient. The Mishneh validates both types of documents issued by a Gentile court. In the latter case, the Talmud[4] questions the validity of such a document. Two solutions are proposed. One is by Samuel, that "the law of the kingdom is the law" and that therefore it is by the king's law that such documents are to be considered valid. The second solution states that a document whose legal status is similar to a divorce is also excluded by the Mishneh.[5] Accordingly, if a gift is transferred by a document issued by a Gentile court and witnessed by Gentiles, the document would have no more value than a blank piece of paper.

While discussing yet another statement made by Samuel, namely, that the property of a Gentile has the status of a desert,[6] the Talmud finds this conflicting with the idea that "the law of the kingdom is the law." Jewish law stipulates that a Gentile relinquishes his rights to property upon receipt of the purchasing price, while a Jew who buys such property cannot acquire it until the deed comes into his hands. In the interim, the property remains without title. From the time that money changes hands until the deed is in the hands of the Jew, anyone may acquire this parcel of land.[7]

Abaye properly questions R. Joseph: "Is it possible for Samuel to maintain such a position? Did not Samuel state that "the law of the kingdom is the law"? And the law of the king is that title to any property can only be transferred by means of a written deed." If the law of the kingdom is to be followed, then there exists no interim stage during which the Gentile's property remains without title.[8]

The Talmud also cites a case of a Jew who bought land from a Gentile while another took possession of the land. R. Judah ruled that the one in possession of the land is now the rightful owner but the original purchaser may demand his money back. This decision also contradicts Samuel's law.[9]

The Talmud arrives at no solution for this problem. Actually there is no contradiction at all between the two principles set forth by Samuel. An older law, which originated during tannaitic times, states that real-estate may be acquired in one of three ways, i.e., with money, by means of a deed, or by actual possession.[10]

Samuel amended this law with regard to the property of a Gentile. In order for anyone to acquire land, actual possession is necessary. Samuel did not introduce a new law, but rather amended the old tannaitic law. When taxes are to be levied on properties, there must first be possession. It is for this reason that Samuel compared the property of a Gentile to a desert.[11] The property does not become *res nullius*; rather, just as *res nullius* is acquired by means of possession only, so a Gentile's property may only be acquired by actual possession. Consequently, the two principles of Samuel not only do not contradict each other, but rather support each other.[12]

The sages of the Talmud, although they accepted Samuel's law, nevertheless found it a most difficult and puzzling legislation. They saw a number of apparent contradictions to the principle that "the law of the kingdom is the law" from earlier, tannaitic sources.

In a Mishneh,[13] we find that when a tax collector wished to appropriate fruits for the king's taxes, the Jew was permitted to make a vow rendering this fruit *Terumah,* even though afterwards, the fruit did not assume the sanctity of *Terumah.* The Mishneh apparently gives Jews permission to evade payment of taxes by means of this ruse.[14] The Talmud wonders if the maxim which Samuel had proposed, namely, that "the law of the kingdom is the law," is not contradicted by this Mishneh? If Samuel's law held true, then no Jew would be permitted to evade his obligations to follow the law of the kingdom. The Talmud concludes that Jews may evade payment of taxes [15] whenever an unlimited tax is placed upon Jews by the government or else in the case of a powerful self-appointed tax collector [16] who has no authority from the king. In such cases, "the law of the kingdom" does not apply.

Similar is the instance related in the Mishneh [17] which forbids the exchanging of coins from a collector's purse. The Mishneh implies that the tax collector possesses stolen monies of which no Jew ought to make use. Once more the Talmud queries, if Samuel's law is valid, then the law of the kingdom gives the tax collector the right to appropriate these funds. They should not be considered stolen monies.

The Talmud makes the same stipulations as were made in the tractate Nedarim; namely, that "the law of the kingdom" does not apply where an unlimited tax or a self-appointed collector is involved.

The Talmud also lists three cases, wherein Samuel's law is further developed by the later sages of the Talmud.

Rabba (Rava), in the name of the Exilarch, Ukbah, refers

17

to three things which were handed down to him in the name of Samuel concerning the principle of "the law of the kingdom is the law." [18]

A. *Arisuta d'Parsai ad mem Shnin*—Parthian law required that a period of 40 years of unchallenged possession elapse before anyone might claim title to land. R. Samuel b. Meir, in his commentary,[19] explains this in two ways. If anyone retains land for a period of 40 years, according to Parthian law he becomes its rightful owner. Since "the law of the kingdom is the law," no Jew may later claim that this property was stolen from him. Secondly, despite the fact that Jewish law demands only three years for "possession," Parthian law supersedes it and requires the Jew to wait for 40 years.[20]

B. *Hani Zeharurei de'zavin Ar'oh le'tasko Zevinhu Zevinei*—This is another instance where *Dina D'Malkhuta* applies. Anyone who redeems land which was forfeited by the poor through failure to pay taxes, becomes the rightful owner of the property since "the law of the kingdom is the law." Whosoever pays the taxes on the land, becomes its owner.

C. *Hani Mili le'taska Aval le'Harga lo*—The third situation merely qualifies the above mentioned precept. Only property for which land taxes were not paid may legally be confiscated by the king. However, land may not be taken away because of the failure to pay a head tax. In the latter case, "the law of the kingdom" does not apply.

It is readily understandable that as long as one pays the tax on his land, so long may he retain it. The ownership of the land and the payment of the tax are linked together. Failure to pay the tax renders the land forfeit. However, where one omits payment of a head tax, the confiscation of the land is arbitrary. Any sort of fine could have been imposed. It is, therefore, outside the scope of *Dina D'Malkhuta*.

Rava further develops Samuel's law in the following instance. If a king demands that trees be supplied for the building of a bridge, he may confiscate anyone's property for this purpose. The method by which the necessary materials are acquired is left in the hands of the king's agents whose authority is equally recognized with that of the king on whose behalf they act. Consequently, even if the king demands that an entire group supply the needs for this project, the agents may confiscate all supplies from one individual and that person has no recourse since "the law of the kingdom is the law." [21]

Yet another reference to Samuel's law occurs when the Talmud speaks of a Gentile who failed to pay his head tax and was required to work for a Jew who paid the head tax for him. R. Papa[22] wonders whether the Gentile is subject to all the laws of a slave so that when he is to be emancipated he would require the customary bill of manumission. Rava, in the name of R. Sheshes, replies that it is the law of the king that he become the slave of the one who pays his head tax. "The law of the kingdom is the law" and as such requires the Gentile to become a slave.[23] Should he wish to marry a Jewess, he would have to receive a writ of manumission and undergo conversion rites before he may do so. Should a Jew redeem the head tax of a fellow Jew, the latter would also require a writ of manumission. He could not be released by mere verbal emancipation.[24]

Finally, although the principle itself is not mentioned, Samuel states that the acquisition of land bordering a river is governed by Parthian law.[25] Obviously, the same principle is involved.

These sources tell little concerning Samuel's motivation for his principle. Actually, there appears to be but one direct statement made by Samuel himself.[26] The other references are either statements made by others quoting Samuel[27] or else are statements made by the sages of a later date attempting to reconcile Samuel's law with earlier mishnaic precepts.[28]

However, one theory [29] implies that Samuel was prompted to assert that "the law of the kingdom is the law" because of his great love, loyalty, and devotion to the Persian king, Shabur I.

19

The proponents of this theory claim that this is the reason why Samuel was called *Shabur Malka*.[30] They also assert that the name *Aryok* given to Samuel alludes to his close relationship to the Persian government,[31] the word *Aryok* referring to *Aryok,* king of Ellosor and having the connotation of one who is close to the king. Finally, the proponents of this theory claim that Samuel's great devotion to Persia was also demonstrated when he refused to mourn for the 12,000 Jews of Caesarea who opposed and were killed by the Persians.[32] The resulting picture is of a man who had become so close to the Persian government that he allowed his loyalty to Persia to supersede his love for his own people. Every instance, they would have us believe, confirms this fact. All references tend to show that Samuel was motivated by a desire to increase the harmony between the Persian government and its laws, and Jewish life in that country.

It seems that far more was at stake and a far broader scope was encompassed in Samuel's law. It was more than the immediate devotion to a particular government which prompted Samuel.

It is difficult to determine to whom and, precisely, to what the term *Shabur Malka* refers. Rashi [33] noticed this difficulty and pointed to two different interpretations. Five references are made to *Shabur Malka* in the Talmud. Three are made in connection with Samuel.[34] However, in two places they cannot refer to Samuel. One is clearly indicated by Rashi at the end of the tractate Babba Metziah and the second is found in connection with Hermes (?) the mother of *Shabur Malka*, referring to a mythical god and certainly not to Samuel.[35] The writer is inclined to agree with the view of Rashi and the Tosafists [36] that the name merely implies authority and explicit knowledge rather than devotion to Shabur I. Samuel's position is paralleled to the position of the king. His authority concerning Jewish law is equal to that of the king.

Similarly, the references to Samuel as *Aryok* [37] are not to denote his close relationship to the Persian kings but again to show that he was like a king in the realm of Jewish law whose laws are obeyed.[38] The reference in the Talmud makes absolutely no sense if *Aryok* denoted close relationship to the Persian king. If the theory that *Aryok* was given to Samuel because he was so influential a person in the king's court were true, why, then, would Levi say to Samuel that he would not sit down, i.e., that he would remain with him until the latter explain a certain law to him? The reference to remaining with him cannot be associated with the awe or respect due to Samuel's position as the king's confidant. In fact, the expression[39] *lo tetiv a'kareih ad demefareshet li le'ho milta* was used by Samuel himself when he wanted an explanation concerning a point in Jewish law from Abuah Bar Ihi.[40] *Aryok* refers to Samuel's position as a scholar and the authority which was his to decide Jewish law. That is why Levi, impatient to hear Samuel's explanation, threatened to remain with him until such a time when that explanation would be given him.

Finally, the assertion that Samuel, by refusing to mourn for the Jews killed by the Persians, showed that his loyalty to Shabur superseded even his love for his people, is not borne out by the sources. It was Samuel's contention that *KERIAH* (the rending of a garment) is not to be performed when evil tidings are heard unless it involves the majority of Jews.[41] Furthermore, in this particular case, it was the rebellious spirit of his people which brought the attack upon themselves. The Romans were fighting the Parthians, and the Jews of Caesarea joined the Roman forces but were defeated in battle. Naturally Samuel, who lived under Parthian rule whose armies also contained Jews in their ranks, looked upon the Jews of Caesarea as members of a foreign army. This does not show a lack of love for his people at all. During World War I, when Jews fought on the sides of both the Allied forces and the Central Powers, the Jews of America or England did not mourn over the loss of Jews who fought on the German side and were killed in battle. They fought for their adopted land just as American, English, and French Jews fought for theirs. No pe-

21

riods of fasting or lamentations were in order as they were during the atrocities committed by Nazi Germany.

Samuel occupied an important position in the king's court. However, the principle of "the law of the kingdom is the law" had little to do with that position. It is based upon Samuel's knowledge and understanding of the difficulties encountered in diaspora life. It provided the Jewish people with a *modus vivendi* in the exile. Cultures differing from each other, when confronted with each other, are likely to clash. Jewish law and the law of the kingdom wherever Jews might reside, might differ and be antagonistic to each other. Samuel tried, by his very flexible principle, to solve this problem. He tried to provide the Jews of all ages, all countries, and all environments with a tool to operate, a principle which would allow existence to a "people scattered and dispersed among many nations."

As can readily be seen, it was Samuel who was given credit for this law. Since it also is obvious that this law was an essential factor allowing for the existence of the Jews in the diaspora, one would assume that the idea of this law preceded Samuel. After all, Jews lived in exile before his period—in Babylon, Antioch, Egypt, Rome, and elsewhere. Jewish law, civil or religious, must have come into conflict with the secular governments then as well. In fact, some maintained that Samuel merely articulated a law which had been in existence for many years, even centuries. Ezra and Nehemiah, during the period of the Restoration, were appointed to office by Darius of Persia to rule in Judea, signifying that the authority of their rule stemmed from King Darius. It was thought by some that their decisions were accepted and their power considered final by Jews because "the law of the kingdom is the law." In this case, it was the edict of Darius that established the law of the kingdom.

It must be stated at the outset that this concept is found nowhere in any form whatsoever prior to Samuel. Biblical and tannaitic sources are silent on this issue. As far as Ezra and

22

Nehemiah are concerned, there is no doubt that their authority was derived from outside sources. However, it must be clearly understood that the concept of "the law of the kingdom is the law" never determined or regulated such authority. The foreign powers ruled by sheer force of conquest. Their decisions were followed because of the power which they wielded. The choice was never left in the hands of the Jews. Whether or not "the law of the kingdom is the law" applied to any particular situation or not had absolutely no bearing upon the decisions of any foreign king. This was true later on during the Gaonic period, the Middle Ages, or even modern times. While Jews lived in the diaspora, the principle of "the law of the kingdom is the law" had no influence upon the laws and edicts issued by these monarchs. Why then worry about such a concept? "The law of the kingdom is the law" was a concept which operated within Jewish law. It governed the internal affairs of Jews in so far as their relationship with the outside world was concerned. If "the law of the kingdom is the law" was applicable, as interpreted by Jews, then a particular edict was considered lawful. Similarly, if the king or his deputy was recognized as having legal authority, then his decisions would be considered as binding even by Jewish law. Any property which would change ownership as a result of such an edict would legally change title. Any evasion or violation of such an edict would be punishable by Jewish law as well. Contrarily, when "the law of the kingdom is the law" does not apply, then Jewish law does not recognize the authority of the monarch; neither are his decisions considered valid by Jewish standards, while properties involved are considered as stolen goods. If a fellow Jew acquires them, he is the recipient of stolen goods.

The authority of Ezra and Nehemiah or of the other kings was derived from foreign powers. This in no way proves that the concept of "the law of the kingdom is the law" was the principle under which they operated. On the contrary, although Ezra was appointed by Cyrus, it was only after a long struggle that the

23

Sadducean view prevailed and that Judea became a theocracy headed by Ezra. The victory of the Sadducees decided the issue for the time being. The struggle was never given up by the Pharisees. If the principle of "the law of the kingdom is the law" was involved, the Pharisees hardly would have opposed Jewish law.

Again, in later years, the only group which acquiesced passively to any monarch in power was the Essenes. They believed that no man attains such an exalted position as the king of a state without the Divine Will. Opposing a monarch was tantamount to rebellion against God.[42] The Essenes were the only ones with this attitude. Once more, if the principle of "the law of the kingdom is the law" applied to all kings of the second Temple who were appointed by foreign powers, the Pharisees would not likely have been the ones to oppose them. As much as they might have been at variance with the kings' policies, they would have accepted their edicts as binding.

It was Samuel who not only articulated the principle of "the law of the kingdom is the law," but it was he who originated it as a means for Jewish survival in diaspora life.

What, then, may we say concerning the maxim "the law of the kingdom is the law" as it was known and applied during the talmudic period?

First of all, it was Samuel who originated the law. He did so not to be loyal to a particular government of a particular time, but to propose a *modus vivendi* for the Jew. He applied it to civil matters, such as deeds of sale or documents transferring a gift from the donor to the recipient that were issued by Gentile courts and witnessed by non-Jews. It did not apply to a bill of divorce or to a writ emancipating a slave. A century or so later, it was expanded to apply to regulating methods of sale with regard to the sale of properties. It also applied to the duration of *hazakah* necessary for the acquisition of land as well as to taxes and other essential necessities required for the successful operation of any government. Finally, the concept was extended to include all

24

agents of a monarch so that they would have equal acceptance by virtue of the monarch's authority in whose behalf they acted. In fact, the details and methods by which the king's orders were to be carried out were left entirely to the discretion of the agents. This held true, even when they changed the edict of the king somewhat.

It is from these cases enumerated in the Talmud that tremendous development ensued and from which the concept was expanded during later ages. It is to these developments that we now turn.

CHAPTER II

The Gaonic Period

Samuel's principle, "the law of the kingdom is the law," is mentioned only a few times in the Gaonic literature. There was little, if any, further development of this concept during this period. The fact that it is referred to so infrequently shows the insignificant role it played in the life of Jewry during the centuries known as the Gaonic Age. There was little need for the Geonim to invoke Samuel's law. A prefatory analysis of the extensive influence upon diaspora Jewry exerted by the scholars comprising the Gaonate enables us to understand more clearly why this was true.

The Gaonic period, stretching over five centuries, plays an important role in the history of the Jewish people. Information concerning this period and the life of the Jews during that time is derived from the responsa written by the Geonim. At the outset of this period, the influence the Geonim wielded was limited to Babylon alone. Perhaps, because of this, we find only a few responsa written by the early Geonim. With the conquest of large expanses of land by the Arabs, reaching as far west as Spain, the sphere of influence of the Geonim was also extended. As the authorized leaders of the Jews, their influence held sway over a great number of countries. Their responsa were sent to the cities of Babylonia, Asia Minor, and North Africa. Some even were sent as far as southern France and Germany. Sura and Pumbedita, the headquarters of the Gaonate, became the spiritual center for all the communities where Jews resided. The outside communities continued to cement their ties with the academies. These ties reached their maximum intensity with the last [1] of the Geonim, R. Hai (998-1038).

The centuries between the close of the Talmud and the reappearance of intense Jewish culture in the western countries is probably the most obscure stretch of time encountered in the history of the Jews. The Gaonate, with the exception of a handful of men, was not made up of top calibre scholars. Yet, the Geonim wielded great influence upon Jewry of many centuries.

We now ask, "From where did their power stem? What was the source for their authority?"

In early amoraic times (c. 3rd century), the Exilarch was the temporal, as well as the spiritual, head of Babylonian Jewry.[2] It was within his power to set standards for weights and measures.[3] He was able to order the arrest of anyone on various charges, even on apparently minor ones.[4] The Exilarch had the right to appoint judges for the communities of Babylonia. A judge who did not wish to be held personally responsible in case of an error of judgment would have to accept his authorization from the Exilarch.[5] However, the heads of the academies were not appointed by the Exilarch. On occasion, the Palestinian sages were asked for advice in the matter of choosing these men, but never the Exilarch.[6] The heads of the schools of Sura and Pumbedita were selected by the members of the academies themselves, and it was they who ordained their students.

These offices, the office of the Exilarch and the heads of the academies, with their separate powers, caused constant strife.[7] Each vied to gain power for their respective office. Towards the end of the amoraic period, almost all authority was snatched away from the Exilarchs. Civil authority was claimed by the heads of the schools by tracing their lineage directly to R. Judah, the Prince.[8] Religious authority had gradually become theirs. In fact, the sages of that period ignored the Exilarchs. Only a few of the names of the Exilarchs are recorded in the Talmud, which tends to show that the sages tried to minimize their importance.

When the Arabs conquered Babylonia, new life was given to the Exilarch. He now received complete authority to govern the Jewish community. He appointed the Geonim as the heads

27

of the academies and was able to dismiss them whenever he so desired.[9] In one instance, the Exilarch disliked Rab Aha and refused to appoint him to the Gaonate. Instead, he appointed Rab Natronoi, although he was far inferior in scholarship to Rab Aha. In anger, Rab Aha left for Palestine where he remained until his death.[10] Rab Natronoi maintained his position for 13 years, showing that even though he was second in scholarship to Rab Aha, he nevertheless held his own.

During the early days of the Goanate, only the head of the academy of Sura carried the title, Gaon. When he addressed the head of the academy of Pumbedita, he used the lesser titles of Resh Metibta or Rosh Yeshiba.[11] However, the head of Sura was required to be addressed as Gaon even by the head of Pumbedita. As the power of the Gaonate gained, while the power of the Exilarch waned, the heads of the two schools both bore the title Gaon. Nevertheless, Sura still maintained its superiority. It became the right of its Gaon to appoint the head of the academy at Pumbedita.[12] The title Gaon was not an empty one. In case the Exilarch died, and until another took his place, the Gaon of Sura held all powers.[13] It is interesting to note that Sherira Gaon was silent concerning the superiority of Sura. Since he came from Pumbedita, he obviously wished to glorify that academy.[14]

By the eighth century, the Gaonate had gained sufficient authority to block the appointment of an Exilarch whose religious policies conflicted with theirs.[15] In the tenth century, after the dispute between the Gaon of Sura and the Exilarch, the Exilarch's power was almost gone.[16] No longer was it his prerogative to authorize judges. This power was now vested in the Gaonate. The Gaon, in the name of his court, gave authority to individuals to assume the position of judge.[17]

Thus, we find that in the early days of the Geonim, when the Exilarch was appointed (approved) by the caliphs, he did not require anyone's consent for his decisions.[18] He was an officer of the king. His position was fourth in the royal hierarchy.[19] His word was law. Anyone who violated his decisions was considered equal to one who disregarded or rebelled against the word of the king.[20] His authority lay in "the law of the kingdom." Although, as a descendant from the House of David,[21] he controlled the appointment of judges and thus, indirectly, controlled religious law as well, nevertheless, decisions of Jewish law were in the hands of the heads of the academies. In fact, a number of the Exilarchs were not learned individuals.[22] These judges derived their authority from the Exilarch's official position. Their decisions in law were considered binding not only because they were the sages of their day or because their decisions were based upon the *halakah,* but more so because legal authority was bestowed upon them as appointees of the Exilarch. However, even though the authority of the Exilarch [23] had its source in "the law of the kingdom," he could not appoint judges who were not excellent scholars. Scholarship was an essential prerequisite.[24]

At the end of the Gaonic period, the Geonim usurped almost all the powers of the Exilarch.[25] Sherira and Hai emphasized their descent from the family of David in order to elevate their leadership and maintain and develop their position of supremacy over the Exilarch. They claimed to possess all the essential and traditional requirements of the Exilarch and could easily fill his office. In fact, they so overemphasized their claim that the authorities arrested them. It was a group of Jews, obviously their enemies, who informed against them.[26] The arrest was caused when their enemies, who were followers of the Exilarch, informed the government that the Geonim were rebelling against the official status of the Exilarch. The official position of the Exilarch was the last vestige of power left to him. The power struggle between the Exilarch and the Geonim dated back many years. When the Geonim had almost all authority in their hands, how natural for them to deliver the *coup de grace* to an institution already standing on its last legs. The Geonim, Sherira and Hai, bitterly complained

29

of the corruption found in that office[27] and consequently desired its abolishment.[28]

The general status of the Jews towards the end of the Persian rule was precarious. These were the days of persecution and suffering.[29] Magians made life unbearable for them. A tax was placed upon every home. Jews had to contribute to the Persian fire temples.[30] When the Arabs came to power, the situation changed. The religious persecutions stopped to a great extent and the Jews fared far better. Jews gained influence in the court of the caliph and many rich men were able to intervene on behalf of their coreligionists.[31] With the rise of Arab power, the ecclesiastical authority, the Bet Din, which was found in most communities and whose members were appointed by the Exilarchs or later by the Geonim, had full autonomy and were able to decide and to rule in accordance with the *halakah.* To be sure, there were occasional exceptions to this rule. At times the Moslem rulers invaded the privacy of Jewish law which they otherwise respected. The Gaonic responsa show that the rulers were extortionate with regard to the taxes which they imposed upon Jews.[32] Often Jews were driven to take drastic means in order to avoid the exorbitant fines levied upon them.[33] At times they were arrested and could not leave the town. Consequently, a man would issue a bogus document of divorce to his wife so that she would be able to assume possession of her husband's property in lieu of her dowry (*Ketuba*) and at the same time provide the means for her husband's escape.[34]

The fact that the authorities did not confiscate the estate left by the husband upon his exit from the town points to the legal recognition the divorce had in the eyes of the secular government. The wife was permitted to hold on to the estate even above the claims of the secular rulers.

In general, the Gaonate and the individual ecclesiastical courts enjoyed complete autonomy.[35] They strongly disliked any attempt on the part of Jews to bring their disputes before non-

Jewish courts. Jews who voluntarily testified before non-Jewish courts were excommunicated.[36] They vehemently opposed such moves although exceptions were made when circumstances warranted it.[37] On the whole, the vast majority of Jews obeyed the injunction of the Geonim and preferred to settle their cases before a Bet Din. The Jews did not look favorably upon secular courts.[38] The Geonim would not recognize the courts because these courts were not to be trusted. This decision resulted not from blind prejudice but rather because of the corruption found. Wherever the courts were known to be honest and reliable, the Geonim recognized their decisions.[39]

Whenever the Bet Din saw that their decisions were ignored or disobeyed, they would readily avail themselves of the power of the secular government.[40] However, this was used only as a last resort. In order to enforce its own decisions, the Bet Din, in Gaonic times as well as long afterwards, had a number of means at its disposal. Among these penalties were excommunication, flogging, and the disqualification from testifying before a Bet Din.[41]

Excommunication included two forms, a lighter, temporary exclusion for 30 days (*Niddui*) and the more severe form of *herem*.

Corporal punishment (*Malkot*) consisting of 39 lashes could no longer be applied by the courts of the Gaonic period. In order for a court to administer this punishment, *Semikha* was required, which the rabbis of this period did not possess. Instead, they utilized *Makot Mardut,* corporal punishment which consisted of lashes, the number of which was to be determined by the court.[42]

Many communities had a prison to detain persons awaiting trial at the Bet Din. (*Bet ha-Sohar*).[43] Public disturbances, physical violence resulting in damage, defamation of character, etc., presented a problem to the Geonim. These offenses belong to the category called *Dinei Kenasot* (fines) and according to a talmudic decision, these fines could only be imposed by the courts in Palestine.[44] Were such offenders allowed to go unpunished,

31

chaotic conditions would result.[45] The peace of the diaspora communities would be threatened. If something were not done to curb such offensive activities, the victims might very well look elsewhere for protection and the authority of the Gaonate and their appointed courts would be weakened. Consequently, the Geonim searched for some means whereby they could circumvent the talmudic principle of *Ein Govin Kenasot b'Bovel.* The Geonim found a way. Under the threat of excommunication they forced the guilty parties to compensate and conciliate their victims. The Bet Din still could not levy a fine, but at least they could suggest a settlement and coerce the offender to abide by it or else remain excommunicated.[46]

It now becomes clear that the Geonim were almost never in need of Samuel's law. They possessed almost complete authority to govern the religious, civil, and economic life of diaspora Jewry. We have seen how they exercised this authority in all fields. They jealously guarded this autonomy. The non-Jewish courts were considered off-limits for Jews. The Geonim were able to deal with all offenders within the scope of Jewish law and in the courtrooms of the Bet Din.

With the exception of taxation, which by its very nature involved the secular government, and to a certain extent trade between Jews and non-Jews, there were but a few occasions where *Dina D'Malkhuta* could apply. In fact, in one instance where *Dina D'Malkhuta* is mentioned, it was to restrict and to limit its scope rather than to develop it. In a responsum attributed to Saadya,[46] the Gaon refused to validate a writ of transference of a gift issued by a non-Jewish court and witnessed by non-Jews. The Gaon ruled in favor of the opinion stated in the Talmud which equated such documents with divorces, where Samuel's law does not apply.[47] The Gaon ignored the opposite opinion recorded in the Talmud,[48] validating such a writ, because such validation would have recognized the authority of the non-Jewish courts in yet another matter and would have given greater leeway to the concept of

32

Dina D'Malkhuta. It simply did not concur with their contemporary outlook which shied away from extending secular authority.[49]

The Geonim could not help but recognize the authorities with regard to trade. The maritime laws of salvage declared that the rescuer of property from a sinking ship may only demand payment for the salvage operation. He does not assume ownership of the articles rescued. Despite the fact that this did not follow Jewish law,[50] "the law of the kingdom is the law." No Jew was permitted to purchase the rescued cargo from the salvager.[51]

This position did not conflict with the general view of the Geonim concerning the authority of the State. They were willing to grant the authorities the final say in such matters. The abandonment of the hope for recovery of the property (*Yi'ush*) is dependent upon the state of mind of the original owner. The court, in such matters, must determine whether or not the owner relinquished his possessions. Varied circumstances could alter the owner's hopes of recovery and consequently determine the court's decision. In the case where the law of the kingdom protects the original owner from salvage crews, no man would be ready to give up hope for the recovery of his goods. To be sure, "the law of the kingdom" is used, but merely because it affects the owner's state of mind.[52]

We have, therefore, seen the very lukewarm attitude of the Geonim towards Samuel's law. They recognized the need for this principle but enjoyed enough power so that they were rarely forced to resort to it and avoided doing so.

During the talmudic and Gaonic periods, as well as long afterwards, the prevailing opinion was that no king could come to power unless God so willed it. Any individual who ascends the throne, does so by Divine Will. An edict issued by the king expresses the desire of the king, and since the king himself is sanctioned by God, his laws have authority.[53]

On the basis of this theory, the Geonim justified Samuel's law. Just as God rules over the kingdoms of the world, so it is

33

the right of a king to rule over the property of man and to do with such properties as he pleases. He acts according to his will and his subjects must obey.[54]

The Gaonic theory appears to be in contradiction with their practice. We have seen how indifferent they were to Samuel's concept, and how at times they ignored it. How can this be justified with the theory to which they subscribed, namely, the "divine right of kings"?

Actually there is no contradiction. The Geonim had no need to relinquish their autonomy. The kings, to a great extent, allowed them self-government. They were permitted to live according to the dictates of Jewish law. Consequently, their theory never came into conflict with life. They recognized only the need to support governmental law when it involved the welfare of the State and the welfare of the public.[55] Towards this goal they wholeheartedly subscribed.

CHAPTER III

Rabbinic Attitudes Toward Government

In the previous chapter we discussed the Gaonic attitude toward government. We determined that they saw the power of the king as emanating from the power of God. They believed in the theory of the "divine right of kings."

During the early part of the 12th century, R. Samuel b. Meir (RaSHBam 1080-1158) issued the following statement: "All regular and special taxes, and all decrees promulgated by the kings are the law, because all the people of the kingdom willingly accept the statutes and ordinances of the king. These are therefore binding. No man may be accused of robbery if he holds money given him by "the law of the kingdom." [1]

In a handful of words, R. Samuel expresses an idea which appears far too sophisticated for the 12th century, namely, rule by the consent of the people. R. Samuel enunciated the concept that a king's authority is based upon the acceptance of his reign by his subjects. It is government by the will of the people.[2] It is the theory of government based upon the idea of the "social contract." [3] The free will acceptance of the citizens, so basic to the theory of the social contract, does not demand that this be a formal declaration and neither does it require anyone to be present when a king assumes the throne. Whenever an individual takes up residence within the domain of a king, he does so with the express understanding that he must accept the authority of the king and will act in accordance with the prevailing laws.[4] Maimonides also accepted the theory of the social contract as the basis for government.[5] In order to determine whether or not a king has been voluntarily accepted, we merely must determine whether or not his currency is utilized throughout the land. The fact that coins issued by a king are used by the citizens of a nation in their business affairs was "proof positive" that the king's authority is recognized. This was a well known and accepted method dating from antiquity and was still employed during the Middle Ages. It even found its way into the codes of Jacob b. Asher (1269-1340) and Joseph Caro.[6] Conversely, a lord who conquers a neighboring land and rules it with an iron fist and is not accepted by the conquered people, is not considered the rightful monarch of that land. His laws are not valid since neither his coins nor he are accepted.[7]

A third theory of government, as articulated by the Tosafists,[8] states that "the law of the kingdom is the law" applies only to non-Jewish kings because the land is their property. It is within their power to demand obedience to the law. Defiance would be met with expulsion. This privilege is denied to Jewish kings since the Land of Israel is owned by all Jews in a partnership.[9]

Most modern scholars agree that the Tosafists took a dim view of Samuel's law. It expresses the thought that there was no other choice but to accept "the law of the kingdom." Refusal to do so would mean expulsion. However, this interpretation does not take into consideration and does not explain the various limitations which the Tosafists put upon the concept of *Dina D'Malkhuta*.[10] The fear of expulsion would have demanded that they accept the laws of the kingdom without any reservations. It is the writer's opinion that the Tosafists did not base their theory on an attitude of bowing to their overlords. It was not fear which led to the acceptance of the secular laws. Were it so, they would not have dared to circumscribe the authority of the king. The Tosafists recognized that the power of the king stems from the fact that he owns the land. The land belongs to the king and he may do with it as he chooses. He rules by right of ownership. However, ownership is determined by the power of expulsion. Non-Jewish kings may expel anyone and therefore they own the land. Just as an individual who owns a parcel of land has the right to make any decision with regard to that land, to permit or to prohibit its use by others, so it is within the right of the king to rule over an entire nation, over the inhabitants of land which he owns.[11] However, ownership grants such rights to the king only as long as he acts within legal bounds. It does not grant him the authority to overstep legal boundaries.[12]

According to this theory, ownership is also determined by conquest. When a king invades another country, he becomes the owner of enemy territory by virtue of his conquest. The law demands that the property of those executed by the crown be forfeit to the crown. The conquered people deserve to be killed for their opposition to the king. It is only by the grace of the king that they are spared. The fact that he spares a political criminal does not deny the right to the king to assume possession of the criminal's property.[13]

Before an analysis of these three theories is offered, one other point of view must be presented. We refer to R. Tam who states that "the law of the kingdom is the law" because the Jewish court was given the express power to declare anyone's property *res nullius*.[14] Just as the rabbis of the Talmud instituted various *takkanot* by declaring property *res nullius,* so authority was granted to the kings as far as Jews were concerned to alter property rights. The Jewish courts were able to allow this because of their power to declare property *res nullius*. Thus, "the law of the kingdom is the law" is based upon the principle of *Hefker Bet Din Hefker.*

The above is not a justification for Samuel's law; it is merely a method whereby the laws of the kingdom may be enforced.[15] There is considerable doubt whether the assumption of R. Tam regarding the concept of *Hefker Bet Din Hefker* is operative when there is no prior justifiable claim. Many authorities ruled that the concept of *Hefker Bet Din Hefker* can only be utilized by the courts when an already existent legitimate claim must be enforced. In cases of a debt, or the collection of a dowry (*Ketuba*), or forcing a husband to sustain his wife, all of which are legitimate

37

obligations in themselves, the court may coerce the debtor by means of *Hefker Bet Din Hefker*. However, without a prior justified claim, the courts have not this power. *Hefker Bet Din Hefker* does not justify a claim; it merely justifies a court action. It would then follow that "the law of the kingdom is the law" cannot be explained by *Hefker Bet Din Hefker*. The case must first possess a legitimate reason for the courts to be able to enforce it by means of *Hefker Bet Din Hefker*. The method whereby something is implemented is not the same as the justification for its origin. The views of the Geonim, R. Samuel, and the Tosafists explain the origin of government and thereby its authority. R. Tam merely points to a method by means of which the ordinances of a king may be carried out.[16]

One other distinction is to be made between the theories of the Geonim, R. Samuel, and the Tosafists on one hand, and R. Tam on the other. R. Tam's approach incorporates *Dina D'Malkhuta* into Jewish law. It becomes part of the Jewish legal system. However, the other theories regard *Dina D'Malkhuta* as law for Jews, but not as Jewish law.

The Gaonic theory follows the idea of the "divine right of kings." This is not a legal justification that is found within Jewish law. It explains that the source of a king's authority rests with God. It is supra-legal. Jews, as subjects of a king, must abide by the king's decisions for such is the Divine Will.

Samuel's theory was that Jews, together with all the people of the nation, by their free acceptance of the ordinances set forth by the king, allow the government to do with their property as governmental law demands. This opinion is based upon the right of every man to do with his property as he chooses. Jews may accept the decisions of any power they select.

Similarly, the right of a monarch to do with his lands as he pleases, which is the view of the Tosafists, is based upon the rights of ownership. Again, it is not the *halakah* that determines this authority.

38

It is only with R. Tam's theory that "the law of the kingdom" actually becomes part of Jewish law. On the one hand, the *halakah* provides the secular government with the right to make any decision for its citizens. However, it is by means of Jewish law that these decisions are carried out for Jews. By means of rendering property *res nullius,* the Jewish court may grant the property to the king. He may then dispose of it in any way he cares to. *Dina D'Malkhuta* becomes part of Jewish law.

In fact, the entire question of whether or not royal decrees become incorporated into Jewish law as part of the Jewish judicial system or whether they remain merely laws for Jews, has been debated by many rabbis of different eras. Does a violation of a law of the kingdom automatically imply a violation of Jewish law? If the answer to this question is in the affirmative, does it then follow that the Bet Din must enforce these laws?

The consensus of opinion among rabbis throughout the ages has been that "the law of the kingdom is the law" does not imply that such laws enter the Jewish legal system. The laws of any nation must be obeyed, but they do not assume the status of Jewish law.

A few illustrations will demonstrate the extra-legal nature of Samuel's maxim.

In accordance with the views of a goodly number of rabbis, the Bet Din was required to enforce the law of the kingdom and to recognize documents issued by Gentile courts only when an explicit decree of the king demanded such procedure. Should Jews be given the choice to follow either system of law, then the law of the kingdom was to take second place. Only when there exists a requirement that the royal decrees be obeyed to the exclusion of all other systems must the Jewish courts follow the secular ordinances.[17] This can only be possible if *Dina D'Malkhuta* is not part of Jewish law; otherwise, the courts would have to follow the king's decisions at all times.[18]

Furthermore, various documents issued by a notary public

appointed by the government were validated by Nahmanides. They were acceptable if they contained the signature of the royal appointee even if they lacked the signatures of other witnesses. This is not in accordance with Jewish law. Nevertheless, the documents are valid because "the law of the kingdom is the law." Again we see that the specific regulations of the kingdom are extra-legal and are not part of Jewish law, but must be obeyed by Jews.[19]

Finally, in civil matters, even in instances where Samuel's law would not be cited,[20] it is within the rights of the parties concerned to subject themselves to the laws of the kingdom. In money matters, every man may make his own decisions or let any other authority decide for him. Consequently, if a document issued by a Gentile court is not recognized by the Bet Din,[21] if it is the express desire of the individuals involved to accept the law of the kingdom, then these documents are binding upon them even though Jewish law denies their validity. Once again, this can only be possible if the concept set forth by Samuel is law for Jews. It cannot be so if it were part of Jewish law.[22]

One exception might be cited to disprove the above thesis. A provocative phrase occurs in a responsum of the 19th century paralleling a decision rendered by Ibn Adret. A distinction was made between the decrees of a monarch recorded in the chronicles of the kingdom, and decisions handed down by an individual Gentile court. It was said that the royal decrees have biblical sanction (*Med'uraita*) based on the principle of *Dina D'Malkhuta,* whereas the decisions of Gentile courts cannot be invested with greater authority than the decisions of the Bet Din.[23]

It is obvious that the term *Med'uraita* was not used to imply that the concept of *Dina D'Malkhuta* is biblical. Furthermore, it ought not to be construed to mean that the concept of *Dina D'Malkhuta* is part of Jewish law. It merely signifies the greater authority vested in the king's ordinances. The term *Med'uraita* lends emphasis to the greater power given to the king, above and beyond the authority of the courts of the land. The king's regulations supersede even Jewish law. The decisions of the courts are no more binding than those of the Bet Din.

Having stated the three basic theories for the origin of government and thereby the reasons for the concept of *Dina D'Malkhuta,* and having analyzed their relationship to Jewish law, we might now endeavor to find the political and social forces which inspired these theories. Nothing is formulated in a vacuum. The political and social status of the Jews in various countries of Europe caused certain definite reactions. Samuel's law, which deals directly with the relationship of Jews to their adopted state, must be affected by the status of Jews.

During the 12th century, Jewish culture in Spain had reached its highest level. The Jews were able to consider Spain as their home. Even while the Almoravides were the masters, they permitted the Jews to live in security and in peace. Only on rare occasions did the reigning powers attempt to interfere with their liberties or try to coerce them away from their faith. In these instances, numerous influential men were always able to intercede on behalf of Jewry and by offering bribes were able to avert all evil decrees.[24]

In France, the liberal reigns of Louis VI and VII of the House of Capet (1108-1180) were favorable to Jews. The Jews lived in ease and in comfort. They prospered and soon owned large tracts of land, homes, and gardens. These were mostly cultivated by Christian servants, only rarely by themselves.[25] The Jewish communities were recognized as independent entities. Their own chosen leaders had complete authority over the Jews and were even granted the power to arrest Christians who failed to pay their Jewish creditors and compel them to pay that which they owed.[26]

The very same held true for Germany, at least until the time of the Second Crusade. The political and social status of the Jews was drastically altered by the Crusade. From this time and with increasing intensity, the Emperor was regarded as the protector of the Jews.

In northern France, it was the last part of the 12th century that marked the change in the political position of the Jews. The monarch Philip Augustus had little land of his own. Ile de France and a few other provinces constituted his entire estate. The rest of the land as controlled by powerful noblemen. Philip, a very ambitious man, planned to gain control of all land for the crown. For this purpose, he needed money, money for troops and their upkeep.[27] The obvious solution to his problem was the wealth of the French Jews. He plotted all sorts of ways to extort money from them and ended by expelling them. Fortunately for the Jews, the properties of the king and the provinces he controlled were few. The Jews thus expelled from his lands were permitted to settle elsewhere in France. Philip soon realized what an economic loss he had sustained when the Jews were driven out. The king and the noblemen then changed their attitude toward the Jews. Suddenly they developed an extraordinary fondness for them. They treated them as if Jews were so dear to them that they could not exist without their presence. The lords would not allow Jews to leave one province to settle in another. They began to place Jews under oath not to emigrate beyond the borders of their province.[28] Consequently, the Jews lost a most precious right, freedom of motion. From the Roman period until then, they had been permitted to move about at will from one place to the other. Now they were forced to remain stationary just like the serfs.

The Jews fought this status. Isaac b. Samuel of Dampierre (Ri) stated: "For we saw throughout the country that the Jews had the legal right, similar to the rights of the knights, to live wherever they wanted to; and the law of the kingdom provided that the overlord should not appropriate the Jew's property after he had moved away from his town. This was the custom throughout Burgundy." [29]

The same held true for Germany of that period, where the

attitude also was that when a Jew had moved away from his town, the overlord of that province did not possess the right to appropriate the estate the Jew left behind. Every Jew had the inherent right, according to the law of the kingdom, to leave his home town at will and freely move from place to place. Any ruler who violated this right did so not in accordance with the law, and was guilty of "royal robbery." [30]

Even in earlier centuries, when an occasional attempt had been made by local rulers to subjugate the Jews and to deprive them of the right of freedom of motion, stern measures were taken to combat this attempt to enslave Jews. A *takkana* was promulgated that forbade any Jew from becoming the surety for another in order to guarantee that the latter would not emigrate from the province. [31]

From the Franco-German centers, the same view was brought to Spain by Asher b. Yehiel at the end of the 13th century. "It is the custom in all lands and it is the legal right of Jews, granted to them by kings and princes, to live and to migrate to any place they desire. No lord may deprive them of any of their belongings." [32] The right to freedom of domicile was stressed by many Spanish rabbis. [33]

It was stated above, that the kings often resorted to placing Jews under oath not to forsake their lands. The Jews took the pronouncing of an oath seriously. Nevertheless, when they were forced to take an oath not to leave the province of a particular nobleman, the rabbis permitted them to silently add the word "today" (*ha-yom*); that is, they qualified their oath to restrict their migration for that day only. Of course, this was only permitted when the oath was taken under duress. [34]

Similarly, in the 14th century, when Marranos were forbidden to leave their places of residence in order to return to their faith, or when other regulations were set that were designed to provide the government with a vehicle to confiscate Jewish property if they emigrated from their province, the kings were

43

denounced. It was proclaimed that if such illegal ordinances were enacted, the Jews might utilize any means at their disposal to prevent the loss of their property or their freedom of domicile. They declared that Samuel's law does not apply to such high-handed and inequitable laws just as it does not apply when extortionate taxes are levied.[35] However, it must be understood that these declarations were proclaimed for internal application only. The kings did not pay heed to, if indeed they were even aware of, these Jewish regulations and sentiments. The legality and enforcement of a particular royal edict did not depend upon the Jews' stamp of approval. Such declarations served but as guidelines for the Jewish courts in internal Jewish disputes.

The political position of the Jews of Spain during the 13th century, especially in comparison with other European lands, was quite tolerable. Indeed, nowhere in Christendom did they enjoy better treatment. However, the status of the Jews of Spain began to assume different characteristics. The dense, dark clouds which were to engulf Spanish Jewry two centuries hence could already be noticed in the distant horizon.

The 13th century played an important role in the political status of the Jews. It marked the dividing line between almost complete freedom and their status as servants to the king. This was certainly true as far as the Jews of Germany and France were concerned. In Spain, the signs of decline were now visible.

In this setting, we may now better understand the views of R. Samuel b. Meir and the Tosafists. Up until the 13th century, we have seen that the Jews of Europe lived in freedom. They were treated well. Although their taxes were always exorbitant, nevertheless, their economic status was not impaired. Whenever an individual nobleman mistreated the Jews of his domain, it did not alter the economic and social status of the Jews. These were momentary incidents. By and large, the Jews fared well. In consequence thereof, the Jews recognized the "social contract" of kingship. It was the theory of R. Samuel which prevailed and was accepted, not only in France and Germany, but in Spain as well.[36] When a turn of events altered the status of Jews, the Jews of Germany and France reacted to it. They no longer saw the relationship between themselves and the king in terms of a "social contract." The king became the owner of their land. He had the final say and the power to expel them. The "social contract" no longer had validity. It was the rule of the despot that now controlled their lives. Thus, the Tosafists' theory became prominent. The first mention of the Tosafist theory in Spain is found at the end of the 13th century expressed by Ibn Adret. It is fully accepted by Nissim Gerondi in the 14th century. Ibn Adret still wavers between the two theories, but as the conditions of the Jews became more desperate, the Tosafists' theory seemed more accurate and in keeping with the times.

As the noose slowly tightened about the Jews and as the pressures of the outside world became more severe, the concept of "the law of the kingdom is the law" underwent a great metamorphosis. It was broadened or narrowed as the living conditions demanded. Safeguards had to be placed. These will be discussed in the next chapter.

CHAPTER IV

Safeguards to Samuel's Law

The very nature of Samuel's law serves, as well as threatens, Jewish jurisprudence. On the one hand, it provides for the establishment of relations between Jews and non-Jews. It offers the method whereby Jews living among non-Jews may observe their own law without defying secular law. On the other hand, the authority which is thereby granted to the kings and the secular governments of the diaspora might endanger the very existence of the Jews. Investing the king with powers which allow him to enact laws that also become the law for Jews, not only compromises the sole sovereignty of Jewish law, but also threatens the welfare of Jewry. Restrictions and safeguards to Samuel's law had to be placed in order to keep the powers of the king in check and to circumscribe such powers lest Jews commit judicial, social, religious, and economic suicide by means of their own principle.

We already encounter stipulations meant to curb the authority of a monarch in the talmudic period. The king's powers were enumerated and limited to the matter of improving the welfare of the State.[1] The king could not be extortionate in his demands for taxes.[2] Only properly authorized tax-farmers appointed by the king could collect taxes. Otherwise, it was royal robbery.[3] In Gaonic times, further limitations were imposed. The Gentile courts could not issue writs for all matters. Only deeds of sale were recognized. A gift could not be transferred by a writ issued by a Gentile court and witnessed by Gentiles.[4] These restrictions were by no means sufficient to restrain the kings who ruled in a predominantly Christian Europe. A new series of safeguards had to be erected.

A minority opinion, ignored by many medieval rabbinic authorities, stated that "the law of the kingdom is the law" applies only to matters involving real-estate and taxes. The land belongs to the king and he may keep or dispose of it in any way he desires. He may regulate all transactions concerning the land.[5] The king may refuse entrance to his land or even refuse to allow anyone to traverse his land unless a tax is paid. Since the land belongs to him, it is legal for him to demand such taxes.[6] He may expel anyone for refusal to pay such a tax.[7] Samuel's law was not to apply to anything else. In all intra-Jewish disputes, the Jewish courts felt that the king has no right to regulate other matters, such as commerce, loans and debts, etc.[8] The fact that the king owns all land, and merely permits his subjects to till it or to build upon it, also gives the king priority to foreclose on property upon which he has a lien.[9] This right was not extended to a commoner. If a Jew claimed that a Gentile had a lien against all his property, it did not grant priority to the Gentile so that the Jew could evade other creditors.[10]

In Turkey, a king's daughter wanted to buy a number of houses in Constantinople, but the owners refused to sell. The court ruled that the entire land belongs to the king, and the permission to use the land which is given to the people is not sufficient cause to prevent the king's daughter from demanding these houses.[11] Here, as in similar decisions, Jewish law did not affect the king. The rule was intended to guide the Jewish courts in internal Jewish affairs.

Similarly, regulations concerning building and construction are to be governed by the State and such laws are binding upon Jews. As in all such matters, the law of the kingdom supersedes Jewish law.[12] Certainly when such construction jutted out into the thoroughfares, the law of the kingdom prevailed.[13]

In a certain community, the *juderia,* the Spanish Jewish quarter, was separated from the rest of the city by gates and fences. These were not considered sufficiently secure since an alley (*Mabui*) opened directly into the city proper. At a meeting, some of the homeowners, with the approval of the king's agent, put a

47

gate in the center of the alley which inconvenienced the other members of the alley. They argued that the barrier would inflict hardship upon them. They were hindered from conveniently reaching their synagogue and ritual bath. They felt it was against Jewish law to erect the gate without the unanimous consent of all householders who were affected by it. However, since the king owns the streets, highways, and market places, it is within his, or his agents', power to erect such a gate. It is by his command that streets are opened and closed, or that streets are repaired or improved. These are considered every day occurrences. The right to erect such a gate was granted to those who so desired it.[14] Thus, a group of Jews were able to make use of the law of the kingdom for their own purposes. If the law of the kingdom supports a Jew he may make use of it, either to build or to prevent others from building.[15]

Soon more restrictions came into being. A king's decree, which is considered theft or robbery when enacted for an individual, becomes law when it is common practice for all subjects. When a king, without cause, demands a share of an individual's income, it is robbery. Once he demands a share of every subject's income, it becomes a justifiable tax and is no longer robbery.[16]

The authority of the king was not challenged when a legislation involved everyone. Any decree becomes law when it concerns and encompasses all citizens.[17] Confiscation of an individual's property without just cause is regarded as robbery. When enough people are involved, it becomes the law of the land.[18] Finally, there emerged the theory that equality in law is required before any royal decree is recognized by Jews. They were willing to invest the king with power. They understood the necessity for a government to maintain full authority. However, they also were wary of such centralized power. They were fully cognizant of the terrible results of discriminatory laws. Consequently, they demanded that any law that is to be accepted by Jews must first be a law that is applied equally to all subjects of the land.[19] A law is not valid, even if it be applied equally to all people of one province. It must apply to the entire land or else it is not acceptable.[20]

Despite the king's right of taxation, he could not impose a head-tax upon rabbis. It was accepted law that the clergy be exempt from such taxes. Any change constituted a discriminatory law and was void.[21] Local governments could not impose laws which were discriminatory either. Their laws, like the ones issued by the king, must encompass the entire population.[22] Some rabbis pointed to the very words of Samuel's law—*Dina D'Malkhuta Dina*—"the law of the KINGDOM" and stated that it was only law when it became the law for the entire kingdom.[23] Laws which were placed against any minority group, e.g., people belonging to one trade such as money-lenders, are not valid.[24]

When a law includes all people, then full authority is granted to the king. No one may accuse the king, or anyone who purchases from the king, of theft.[25] A community that rebelled against their king or displeased him, could be punished by force. All property confiscated by the king at such a time is rendered *res nullius* and those who purchase such articles from the king become the legal owners. The king acts according to accepted procedure and his method of meting out punishment is a method which would be applied equally to all citizens who rise up against him. Consequently, it is not the duty of those who redeem such confiscated items, be they even sacred articles such as a scroll of the Torah, to return them to those who by chance escaped the wrath of the king.[26]

That the demand for "equality in law" was based on the fear of discriminatory laws is best expressed in a responsum dealing with a *Ketuba* (*dowry*). The government demanded that certain conditions with regard to dowries be met by husbands (Jew or non-Jew), conditions which were not required by Jewish law. The rabbi to whom this responsum was addressed ruled that the government's demands must be fulfilled, since these demands were required of all people residing in their country. The rabbi stated: "Nevertheless, we may deduce that in such matters (dowries) we follow the accepted custom, and the decisions of the king's judges do not matter unless it is established law of the kingdom for the entire nation, *including the Jews,* since "the law of the kingdom is the law."[27]

The phrase toward the end of the quotation is of importance. The law is recognized only when it is "established law of the kingdom for the entire nation, including the Jews." The law must be promulgated for the entire nation. It cannot be issued for Jews alone. The *Ketuba* as a document was no different from other documents, such as bills of sale or promissory notes, that were valid when issued by a Gentile court. They were recognized provided all regulations that the law required were regulations applicable to all subjects alike.[28] However the *Ketuba* was a document for Jewish women only, and any secular law governing the *Ketuba* would be a law directed to Jews alone and to no one else. Such a law would not be considered binding, for it is a law discriminating against the daughters of Israel.[29]

Of special interest is the ruling attributed by Moses Isserles to Joseph Colon, namely, that special taxes levied specifically for Jews are within the rights of the government and must be paid.[30] This ruling appears to contradict the prerequisite of "equality" to which everyone, including Colon, agrees and demands in order for any royal decree to be valid on the basis of the concept of *Dina D'Malkhuta Dina.* Perhaps Colon, who lived in 15th century Italy, at a time when Jews had been barred entree in many countries of Christian Europe, felt compelled to accept the premise that Jews may be taxed more heavily in order to find a haven of refuge. Else, he recognized that Jews had been forced to pay exorbitant taxes everywhere, by everyone, and in every century. As such, it had become the accepted norm and no longer was considered as discriminatory by him. Exorbitant taxes had become a prerequisite for Jewish existence in the diaspora so that Colon no longer saw anything out of the ordinary in a governmental edict which to all intents and purposes was discriminatory.

Along similar lines, with the same fears to guide them, the rabbis imposed yet another limitation to Samuel's law. As we have seen in the previous chapter, the 13th century marked a decline in the status of the Jews of Europe. Times had changed drastically. Whereas heretofore the kings had looked favorably upon the Jews, now their greed and ambition triggered a series of decrees, all well aimed to feed their insatiable needs at the expense of the Jews. They needed the wealth of Jews to support their nefarious schemes to bring about the downfall of all powers save their own. The focal point of power was to reside with the king. The struggles which ensued between the noblemen and the king, plus the mounting fear of Church influence over the monarchs of Europe, threatened to bring into being an increasing amount of new laws, all of which would be unfavorable to the Jews. The Jews did not want to deny the authority of the king. On the contrary, in this three-way struggle for power between the king, the nobility, and the Church, Jews had more to gain if they remained loyal to the king. They needed his protection as well as his approval to settle in his land. The earlier kings of all European countries had been much more liberal in their attitudes to Jews. Their edicts were far more favorable. The Jews were convinced that new legislation not within the spirit of already existing laws would prove harmful to them. Consequently, during the 13th century,[31] the rabbis ruled that all new legislation enacted by a king must follow the traditions of the nation. The new laws must be in keeping and in line with the mood of laws enacted by earlier monarchs, or else, they are considered illegal.[32] Here again, the rabbis pointed to the very words of Samuel's law *Dina D'Malkhuta Dina* "the law of the kingdom is the law," and they concluded *Dina D'Malka lav Dina*—"the law of the king is not the law." [33] If a king issues a new law, one which is not in the spirit of the laws issued by his ancestors, such a law is not valid.[34] These laws were required to be "known" statutes.[35] A number of authorities even required that these laws be recorded in the chronicles of the kingdom.[36] Any temporary edict issued by a king, or a fine levied on a whim, even if that fine is not to be repeated, such laws are considered royal robbery. Jews cannot consider these ordinances as valid.[37] At the time when Jews fought the edicts which were intended to rob them of their right to move about freely from place to place, the rabbis cited the above mentioned restriction to the concept of *Dina D'Malkhuta.* "And the law of the kingdom provided that no lord may appropriate a Jew's property after he had moved away from his town. This was the custom throughout Burgundy." [38] These were the words of the Tosafist, Isaac b. Samuel of Dampierre. The established laws of the kingdom could not be overruled by new edicts that a king might want to issue. In the 15th and 16th centuries, and in the Moslem countries where the monarchs had fixed laws of taxation, a new tax law that was not within the traditional concepts of taxation, would be disregarded.[39] This was not true of Christians Europe where the kings had greater leeway.[40]

The two restrictions circumscribing Samuel's law, namely, the requirement for "equality in law" and the requirement that no "new" laws may be enacted unless they are in the spirit of tradition, may quite conceivably come into conflict with each other. A law that is newly formulated by a king, one which is not in keeping with established law but is a law which is applicable equally to all subjects residing within a nation, presents the problem of whether or not such a law is valid. Are both points to be fulfilled ere a law be recognized?

Two opinions are cited. One demands only that the law be alike for all people; [41] the other opinion requires the law to be within the spirit of tradition as well.[42] The latter opinion sees in these limitations a means of curbing the powers of the king. They felt that Samuel's law provides too much authority for the monarchs. Any stipulation which was designed to limit such powers must be fulfilled ere a law was to become valid.

52

The first opinion saw these restrictions placed in order to combat discriminatory laws. Consequently, if such a threat is averted by any one of the restrictions, there is no further need to comply with both stipulations. A law which is to be binding upon everyone, even if it is an entirely new law, is not discriminatory.

The Jews feared powerful local rulers, whose greed was boundless, especially where the influence of the Church was strong. Their fear shifted from fear of the king to fear of the nobility and the Church. The emphasis now was not so much on restricting the king from issuing new laws, as it was to prevent random confiscation by individual, powerful noblemen and church officials. In consequence thereof, the rabbis ruled that only the known, established, constitutional statutes of the land were to be obeyed, but under no circumstance would Jews recognize the ravenous fleecing of Jewish property by greedy local rulers or bishops.[43] Any Jew who purchased such articles was the recipient of stolen goods.[44]

Alongside these restrictions, other guidelines were developed. "The law of the kingdom" was operative whenever the welfare of the nation was at stake. If conditions warranted it, the king had absolute power. He could deprive his subjects of their money and grant it to anyone else. It was considered theft only when the welfare of the State was not involved.[45] When the king needed taxes to improve, or erect new public projects, such as city streets, he might levy them at any time.[46] It was considered that the people made up the nation and when their welfare was at stake, the king was granted unlimited powers.[47]

Two opposing views arose as to whether or not secular law may be invoked when the case at hand does not involve the king directly, or when the matter neither concerns nor benefits the monarch. One view held that it is absolutely essential that the king be involved and/or accrue some benefit ere the concept of *Dina D'Malkhuta* becomes operative.[48] The king's law could not

53

overrule Jewish law if the situation did not directly concern him.[49] Issues which involved individual disputes and were of a private nature were not to be tampered with by the king. Only in that which had direct bearing upon the crown, did "the law of the kingdom" prevail.[50]

A wide variety of conditions were included in the definition of "concern and/or benefit" to the king. Any financial revenue for the king is considered sufficient reason to invoke *Dina D'Malkhuta*. When the king demands that a writ, which assigns property to the crown in the event it is left without heirs (*wakof*), be issued only by Gentile courts, such a decree is valid for it directly involves and benefits the king.[51] The king may insist that specific documents be issued by his court if he in turn receives a specific tax for each document so issued.[52] Should the king become part heir to property left by a deceased, that is considered a matter involving the king.[53] One opinion even considered the mention of the king by name and the year of his reign in any document as being ample grounds to consider this a matter of concern to the king.[54]

Whenever a government changed the value of its currency, or issued new coins, there resulted a problem concerning payment of debts or payment for articles purchased. When the nation's currency was devalued, the extra amount which was now required for payment might be considered the taking of interest. When the two parties involved were Jews, this might constitute a violation of Jewish law. However, since this was a problem for Jews and non-Jews alike, the question was raised whether or not "the law of the kingdom" should be invoked. Even those medieval authorities who required the involvement of the king were divided. According to some, there is nothing that can be considered of greater concern to the king than his currency. Accordingly, they ruled that even if by Jewish law the additional payment is considered interest, nevertheless, the law of the kingdom is to be applied provided the king specifically demands that payment must

54

be achieved in this manner.[55] There were others who disagreed. They stated that no king is concerned with the amount that is paid. He does not demand that a greater value be repaid. He merely insists that the new currency must be used. Consequently, any amount that is paid beyond the value of the loan or business transaction constitutes a violation of taking interest.[56] The problem was never solved. In later years, many rabbis did not know which of these views to accept.[57]

A number of medieval authorities agreed that the king may issue edicts concerning all affairs even if he is not directly involved or derives any benefit therefrom.[58]

The authorities who demanded that there be direct involvement, concern, and/or benefit to the king were also the ones faced with another difficulty which this requirement solved for them. The Talmud[59] questioned why the Mishneh[60] validates a writ transferring a gift issued by a Gentile court and witnessed by Gentiles, when this writ is used not merely as evidence of a transaction but achieves the actual transference. Two solutions were proposed. The first validated such a writ by invoking Samuel's law; [61] the second denied the application of Samuel's law and equated such a writ with a divorce which is excluded by the Mishneh.[62] Many authorities concurred with the second solution.[63] However, this seems to deny the concept of *Dina D'Malkhuta,* a position which was impossible to maintain. The later Amoraim (e.g., Rava, R. Ashi, Jannai, etc.) accepted Samuel's law without question. In addition, all of the medieval authorities accepted Samuel's law while at the same time ruling in accordance with the second solution. It must, therefore, be concluded that the second answer is not in opposition to Samuel's law. His law is only in effect when it involves the king directly and/or is beneficial to the king. Wherever the king is not involved, as in the case of a gift which involves only the donor and the recipient and is of no concern to the government, *Dina D'Malkhuta* is not operative.[64] Nonetheless, should the parties involved willingly abide by the law of the kingdom, regardless of Jewish law, they may do so. In money matters, man may act as he pleases. Jewish law may deny the validity of a writ issued by a Gentile court and the concept of *Dina D'Malkhuta* may be irrelevant, nonetheless, the acceptance of two individuals validates such writs as far as they are concerned.[65] In those nations where the kings insisted that all documents of the Gentile courts be accepted, it was considered by many authorities as the concern of the government and the law of the kingdom was to be followed.[66] All agreed that at a time when such writs served no greater purpose than to prove the transference of a gift, either because the actual title to a property was transferred by other means,[67] or else the secular courts merely issued such documents as proof,[68] then Samuel's law was in effect.

In Spain, the fear of individual lords and the Church reached great heights at the end of the 14th century. The Jews increased their confidence in a centralized government and would not recognize any other authority besides the king. City governments could not issue laws that conflicted with the laws of the nation. In Alfredo, the law demanded that a creditor could force a debtor to beg in the streets in order to repay his loan. Barfat ruled that the debtor is not required to obey such a law since neither Jewish law permits such a degrading demand, nor is it permitted by the law of the kingdom or of the king. It is only the law of the city of Alfredo, and no city can counteract the law of the nation. "The law of the kingdom is the law"; the law of the city is not the law. Only where it is to the benefit and concern of the king is Samuel's law cited.[69]

Another of the powers of the kings, which of necessity had to be held in check, was their right to confiscate property and to evict individuals from such property. If used properly, this right provided a tool for the king to maintain justice and assure the development of the land. If misused, it often proved to be a weapon that destroyed the morale and cohesion of a nation. We have cited the protest of Jewry when the threat of confiscation was utilized to deprive them of their right to move about from place to place at will. The Jews fought bitterly to retain their freedom of domicile. They refused to be restricted and frozen in one place. When monarchs confiscated their property, Jewish law called it royal robbery. They termed such confiscation an illegal act, albeit it was the king who performed it.[70]

Of course, this did not deny the right of a king, nobleman, or burgher to permit, or to exclude from settlement any Jew or group of Jews. More than this, he could appoint a Jew who was to determine all settlement privileges.[71] No Jew might request such right of selection of the burghers, and surely might not bribe a nobleman to grant him the right to say who could or could not reside in the city.[72] Only when the nobleman initiated such a situation, did the law of the kingdom apply.[73] Often these rights were in the hands of the Jewish community (*Kahal*). It was they who granted or denied permission to others to settle in a city. They enforced their decisions by means of the "ban against settlement" (*Herem Hayishub*). No secular authority could interfere in such a matter by nullifying such a vow. The power to abrogate or void an oath of another was granted only to a father when it involved a vow made by his daughter or to a husband with regard to his wife. No one else could assume such power.[74]

The right to confiscate all properties was given to a king only when said confiscation is permitted by the law of the kingdom. Only in situations which have traditionally allowed the king to take the property of others is it not considered royal robbery.[75] Any Jew who purchases such property becomes the rightful owner and does not have to return it to those from whom it was taken by the king.[76] Should a community fail to pay their taxes, the king has the right to confiscate the property of one individual of the community for his loss, who in turn may demand of the entire community that they reimburse him.[77]

No king had the right to random confiscation. When, on a whim, the king decides to seize properties, it is royal robbery.[78]

Confiscation by the king of property for failure to pay a debt was considered illegal since individual loans were of no concern to the king.[79] Despite the fact that such confiscation was illegal, nevertheless, a Jew who purchased such property became its owner, not because of the concept of *Dina D'Malkhuta*[80] but because such illegal seizures automatically caused the victims to resign themselves to their loss. (*Yiush* and *Shinui Reshut*).[81]

Restrictions were also placed upon the authority of the secular government when it came to trade competition. (*Hasogat Gevul*). No secular authority had jurisdiction over such matters and Jews were not bound to abide by their regulations.[82] However, this was only true when the king was not directly involved. When A negotiates with the king to purchase a contract to work a mine and B outbids him, the king may award the contract to B. Although this would constitute a violation of *Hasogat Gevul* when an ordinary Gentile is involved, with regard to the king himself, he is above all trade competition.[83]

The heretofore mentioned restrictions applied only during ordinary times. However, in times of stress or war, the king had the authority to commandeer all property, to quarter soldiers, to evict residents, and even to destroy buildings and homes. This falls under the principle of "the law of the kingdom is the law."[84]

The Jews, in every age, did not allow themselves to be strangled by the secular authorities and certainly not by means of their own principle. The law of the kingdom was the law, but when they found that the power thereby extended to the monarchs threatened to hurt them, they consistently and logically limited and curbed such power. Obviously their protests were not heeded, since the king's authority and force did not depend upon the approval of the Jewish community. Nevertheless, internally, the Jews applied the concept of *Dina D'Malkhuta Dina*.

CHAPTER V

Agents of the King

"The agents of the king are like the king." [1] With these words
the Talmud expands the king's powers and enlarges Samuel's
principle of *Dina D'Malkhuta Dina*. *Dina D'Malkhuta* pertains
not merely to the king, but to his agents and emissaries as well.
Among such agents are included tax collectors, individuals del-
egated by the king to look after the civic welfare of his state,
concessionaires and lessees, and other officials. In the Spanish
communities, the application of *Dina D'Malkhuta Dina* to agents
of the king was further broadened to include the acceptance of
secular and religious community leaders appointed by the king.
This latter position was not accepted by the Franco-German communities. They, too, accepted Samuel's principle and recognized
the authority of the king and his agents, but they vehemently opposed governmental interference with their internal affairs.

Dina D'Malkhuta Dina encompasses all agents of the king
provided they fulfill the aims and goals of the king. These aims
cannot be altered. However, the details in carrying out their mis-
sions are left to the discretion of the agents. If the king requires
wood for the erection of bridges, then the officials of the king may
decide by which method to requisition the lumber.[2] The detail of
whether to acquire it from all or any one of the king's subjects is
left in their hands.

The rights and privileges possessed by the king can be del-
egated by him to any agent of his choice. Samuel's law would
apply to the highest courtier as well as to a minor official. For
example, according to Jewish law, the Jews living in a bounded
area may pool their properties by means of the *Erub* and be permitted to move and transport objects on the Sabbath from house
to house throughout the city. The property of the Gentile must

59

be purchased or rented by the Jews. It cannot be pooled as can be done when the area is inhabited solely by Jews. The problem arises when a community wishes to erect an *Erub* for an entire city. There is the difficulty of approaching each non-Jewish homeowner individually, as well as the added possibility of failure by having to gain the consent of each. The king, who is considered the owner of all properties either actually or potentially, may delegate this right to any agent. The turnkey may act on his behalf and the right to set up an *Erub* (*Reshut*) may be purchased from him. Therefore, the gatekeeper (turnkey) of a city wherein Jews and non-Jews reside, a comparatively minor official, may be the one from whom *Reshut* is purchased in order to erect an *Erub Hatzerot.*[3]

Just as the king could not enact laws which were counter to the spirit of the statutory laws of the kingdom, so the agents of the king were similarly limited.[4] The agents had to be appointed by the king himself and not by any of his advisors.[5]

Concessionaires and lessees, in a way, are the agents of the king. Privileges granted by a king which may not be acquired according to Jewish law, can be validated by means of *Dina D'Malkhuta*. For example, a king bestowed a grant upon a Jew which entitled him to receive a certain share of meat each day. According to Jewish law, the recipient cannot acquire something not yet in existence. However, by authority of the king, Jewish law is set aside and the king's law prevails.[6] Although there is nothing tangible which is transferred by such transactions, since it is but a right to obtain or a license to sell certain items, nevertheless, it was equated to the *Heskat ha-Yishubim,*[7] the rights of settlement which could be purchased from any nobleman, a right which could be transferred because of *Dina D'Malkhuta*. Furthermore, these intangible rights are not different from any ordinary rental of a home.[8] All such concessions, be they the right to farm taxes, liquor traffic, etc., are valid since "the law of the kingdom is the law." [9]

In time, concessions were taken for granted. They were not questioned. The concessionaire was an agent of the king. A rented an *Aranda* from the land owner, who ordered all to purchase drink from this *Arandar*. B bootleged whiskey to the peasants and was brought to the *Bet Din* by A. Since the land owner stipulated that whiskey may only be bought from and sold by A, "the law of the kingdom is the law." The actions of B are considered to be theft. It is stealing from the tenant, A, who is the agent of the land owner.[10] The agency of the *Arandar* is not questioned. In fact, it is said that the bootlegger steals from the authorized concessionaire, because, as a tenant, the latter is the agent of the landlord.

The authority for Jewish lay and rabbinic leadership in the Middle Ages may be questioned. From whence came their authority? Was this authority derived from the secular governments or was it rooted in the Talmud and the chain of tradition going back to Moses? Did the lay leaders' powers emanate from the dictum *Dina D'Malkhuta Dina* or were they the results of community approval and community confidence bestowed upon them? Who appointed the rabbinic authorities and judges? What say had the rabbis in their appointments?

It appears that no uniform system was found in Europe of the Middle Ages. As so often was the case, differences existed between the communities of Spain and those of France and Germany.

In the Franco-German communities the authority held by *kahal* over its individual constituents goes back to a very early period when Jews first came to France. They modeled their community structure on the communities of Palestine from which they stemmed.[11] The Palestinian traditions and customs became theirs as well.[12] Their religious life was directed by their teachers. Such was the case until the 11th century. Until this time, the community life was controlled by the secular leaders and even the sages were dependent upon them. *Takkanot* that were issued required the consent of the community.[13] On the other hand, R. Tam acted independently of the community. In conjunction with others of a synod, he issued his regulations.[14] The title of Rab and Rabbi were also appended to the names of the religious leaders. Their spiritual authority was derived from an unbroken chain from Hai Gaon, who in turn derived his authority, according to tradition, from an unbroken chain directly from Moses. The sages also held authority by the fact that they were appointed to their position by the communities. This dual source of power strengthened the rabbis in their position of leadership even over the secular life of the community. *Semikah* was practiced in Palestine and later on in the Franco-German communities but not in Babylonia. Thus, in Spain, whose communities were of Babylonian origin, *Semikah* was unknown. They modeled the structure of their life after that of Babylonian Jewry. Their leaders held their position due to their appointment by the rulers of Spain. Samuel ha-Nagid had authority over the Jews because he held an important position in the government. Recognizing this basic difference in approach, we shall now show the role *Dina D'Malkhuta Dina* played in these respective countries with regard to the secular and religious leadership.

The Jewish communities of Spain governed themselves according to Jewish law, but the authority for that power rested in the temporal power of the secular government. It must be emphasized, that the rules and regulations that governed the procedures of the *Aljama* followed Jewish law. Jewish law recognized the lay and rabbinic leaders as representing the community and granted them the right to set up ordinances for the welfare of the group. "The majority of every city is to the individual what the Sanhedrin was to all Israel." [15] Furthermore, "Every community within its borders has the same prerogatives that the Geonim once possessed." [16]

They had the right to institute *takkanot*. The penalty for violating a *takkanah* was usually incorporated into the text of the *takkanah* itself. They generally consisted of fines, physical punishment, or the *herem*.[17] Although these were the powers which the leaders of the *Aljama* wielded, an avenue of appeal was left open to any individual. A clause was made part of the *takkanot* allowing anyone, without fear of excommunication, to appeal to the king or his agents.[18] It stated that the "court of last resort" was the king in whom all powers were vested and from whom all powers emanated. The *herem* could not be issued without the authority of the king. The king, however, could not misuse this power. "If a king or ruler or tax collector ordered the *Aljama* unjustly to pronounce the ban of excommunication, and it is dangerous not to comply with the request, the excommunication thus pronounced is null and void and one is not to heed it."[19] Similarly, no man is required to reveal the possessions of a fellow Jew when the king demands these funds unjustly. Even if the crown commands that an excommunication be pronounced against anyone who has in his possession money belonging to the victim, no one need pay any heed to this *herem*.[20] It merely confirms the position that the rights of a king are nullified if they are misused. In the above cited instances the king unjustly demands sums of money and tries to misuse the power vested in him. This he is not permitted to do.

The king often permitted the Jewish communities to select the officials who were to keep a close watch over the conduct of the Jews. A system of fines was enacted. The fines were to be collected by the king's officials. In Lerida, the Jewish officials were required to inform the local representative of the king of all charges they chose to investigate. These officials had the choice of refusing to investigate an alleged offense, but once they initiated such an investigation, they were required to report the charge to the king's agent so that no fines would be lost to the king.[21] Anyone swearing falsely before this board of inquiry had to pay one hundred *sueldos* to the king.[22] A Jewish official could receive a percentage of all fines he collected on behalf of a feudal lord for all robberies, theft, and murders. The lord could rule in his province in any manner he chose because "the law of the kingdom is the law." He could receive the fines and then pay a Jewish agent for his labors; else, the agent might receive his share directly from the Jewish offender. "The law of the kingdom is the law," and the right of the Jewish official to his revenue could not be challenged.[23]

In these countries, not only the lay leaders of the Jewish communities but also the spiritual leaders were appointed by the government. A rabbi, so appointed, enjoyed full authority because "the law of the kingdom is the law." Just as the Jewish spiritual and secular leaders during the Persian era ruled by the authority vested in them by the Persian kings who had conquered Judea, so did the rabbis during the Middle Ages who were appointed by the king have full authority. Their official position was not to be questioned for "the law of the kingdom is the law." [24] Two prerequisites were demanded ere such appointments were to be honored. The first required that such rabbis be acceptable to the community; secondly, they had to be well versed in Jewish law, virtuous in their conduct, and their integrity unquestioned.

Otherwise, no official appointment would be recognized.[25] Despite these demands, we find that in practice, these prerequisites were ignored. Many of the rabbis appointed by the crown were men of ignorance. Many were unable to read.[26] It was the practice of the government to ignore these deficiencies in their appointees, and to whitewash them. Their ignorance was not held against them.[27] The government insisted they were fit to hold these positions. Despite the cry of the Jewish communities and the men of stature against anyone seeking [28] such rabbinical appointment,[29] men still sought such appointments and disregarded certain *takkanot* made by the communities against appointments made without the consent of at least the majority of the community.[30] Rabbis went so far as to bribe the officers of the king, or the Gentile courts, in order to secure the appointment of *Hakam.*

These men forfeited the honor of being called *Hakam* but their decisions had to be upheld.[31] Perhaps their social status was impaired but not their official status. If a community had taken an oath not to accept a particular candidate for the position of *Hakam,* and if afterwards, he were appointed by an officer of the government, the townspeople had to abide by their oath. They could not accept the appointment. "The law of the kingdom is the law," but it cannot set aside an oath already made.[32] Furthermore, a rabbi of greater scholarship could prevent a man from becoming a rabbi but he could not remove from office a rabbi already holding a royal appointment.[33] No rabbi could oppose the authority of the royal appointee for it stemmed from the law of the kingdom.[34] If the documents issued by a Gentile court are valid because of *Dina D'Malkhuta,* then equally. the decisions of a Jew appointed by the king should have complete acceptance as long as a man is suitable.[35] Should a rabbi dare issue *takkanot* opposing the royal decrees, he is considered a rebel.[36] In 14th century Spain, no rabbi had authority without the king's support. The rabbi's greatest weapon, that of the *herem,* could not be issued unless it came by the authority of the king.[37]

The controversy of Barfat and Duran in Algiers concerning the royal appointment of Barfat as Chief Rabbi [38] of the Spanish-Jewish community in North Africa does not contradict the theory that the Spanish Jews accepted their authority from the secular authorities. When Barfat came to Algiers, he made his presence felt. His outstanding reputation as a scholar gained for him the powers to lead the Jewish community. However, as a result of antagonism and animosity towards him, his position was undermined. When Barfat put a ban on those who refused to admit refugees, the community lay leaders tried to restrict such a ban from taking effect by demanding the consent of lay leaders. As a result, the brothers Saul and David Astruc used their influence and procured a royal appointment for Barfat.[39]

This appointment aroused tremendous opposition, headed

65

by Simon b. Zemah Duran. This opposition was not based on the
same grounds as the opposition to such appointments in the
Franco-German communities. The major reason for their opposition was that the entire affair took place without the sanction or
knowledge of the community. The appointment was sought and
obtained solely by individuals. Furthermore, the appointment as
it was made, gave Barfat all-embracing powers. No one other
than he was permitted to engage in any judicial function.[40] The
penalty for disobedience was a considerable fine. Duran maintained
such appointments to be illegal. The rabbinic dictum of *Dina
D'Malkhuta* was inapplicable in this case since it was unconsti-
tutional.[41] The king had no such rights when the community was
not consulted. The exclusive power of Barfat to act as judge would
preclude anyone from adjudicating in litigations in which those
associated with Barfat were involved. Who, then, would judge
such cases? What of all the rabbis who held positions prior to
Barfat's appointment? What of cases which could only be tried
by a minimum of 3 judges? Why were no provisions framed for
these exceptions? Finally, we find that at no time was a judge
permitted to compel litigants to try their case before him if they
selected another judge. Duran insisted that governmental intervention in matters of this kind be ignored by the Jewish community. He stated that the appointment of Barfat marked a deviation from the policy of non-intervention in the internal affairs of
the Jews, a policy hitherto in practice and affirmed by the kings
of Tlemcen. Such new policies were not in accord with the principle of *Dina D'Malkhuta Dina*. In addition, this new policy, being
in effect in Algiers alone, was discriminatory in nature, and *Dina
D'Malkhuta Dina* did not apply to measures which were enacted
for one locale alone.[42]

When the exclusive powers of Barfat's appointment were
abrogated, and all rabbis, provided they received Barfat's authorization, were once again permitted to function, Duran ceased his
opposition.[43] The main grievance was removed.[44] The fact that

Duran refused to seek to obtain the office himself after Barfat's death only points to the reluctance to seek such appointments, but not that they refused it when it was made.[45]

The Jewish community, as well, derived its power from the secular authorities. Its edicts were authorized by the government, and it was by "the law of the kingdom" that they derived their power. Individual rabbis could not oppose their edicts. Should an attempt be made to do so, even by the greatest scholars, it was considered rebellion against the crown and the rabbi's life was forfeit.[46]

In the Jewish literature of Germany and France we can find no indication that the community leaders claimed powers over the people of their community on the basis that such authority had been given them by the secular government. They constantly averred that their authority stemmed from the chain of tradition going back to the talmudic scholars and even to Moses. It was the authority granted them by talmudic law and not the privileges emanating from the king. The kings merely allowed community autonomy by their non-interference. For example, they permitted them to adjudicate their problems according to Jewish law, but it was not the king who instituted their power.[47]

The Franco-German scholars had two-fold authority over the members of the community, first, by the chain of tradition that went back to Moses, and second, by election of the community. R. Gershon b. Judah, "the light of the exile," based the secular powers of the community leaders on the principle that those elected by the community have the status of a Bet-Din and that even if they are not learned they may wield the same authority as Shammai and Hillel. They possessed the right of confiscation of property based on the talmudic principle of *Hefker Bet-Din Hefker* (confiscation of private property by a court is valid).[48] The titles of the spiritual leaders, Rab and Rabbi, showed the source of their two-fold powers. Rab is a Babylonian title, Rabbi a Palestinian title. The title Rab was first given to Abba, the student of

Rabbi Judah, the prince. All his successors in Babylonia bore the same title of Rab. This title indicated position and authorization (*Semikah*). Anyone who possessed scholarship but had no position bore the title Rabbi.

To preserve the integrity of the communities, a *takkanah* was ordained that no Jew could accept a religious or secular position in a community from the government. On many occasions the German kings and Polish government tried to appoint rabbis but without success. The Jews adhered to their old tradition of retaining autonomy in the management of their social and spiritual life and they alone could choose their leaders.[49] In one instance, the majority of the members of a community wanted to engage a cantor but encountered the opposition of a few members. The duke intervened and forced his appointment. R. Meir ruled that they did wrong.[50] "In our country matters such as this are dealt with in strict measure. A similar situation arose in Cologne during the time of R. Eliezer b. Joel. A Jew, wanting to honor the newly elected cantor, intervened so that the bishop would invite the cantor to his house. The bishop removed his mitre and put it on the rabbi (cantor) and said, 'Here, take the office of cantor.' The cantor became enraged and shouted, 'Sir, our law does not permit me to accept the office to worship our Lord from your hands.' He then resigned the post which he originally had accepted. I believe he fined the Jew (Jews) who was responsible for the bishop's actions." [51]

R. Meir considered talmudic law the only law binding for Jews. The king could not interfere with religious autonomy by delegating powers to a chief rabbi. The king possessed no legal powers over the life or conduct of the Jews and therefore could not delegate powers to a chief rabbi. The position of a chief rabbi was not possible in these centers. Thus, the Franco-German Jewish communities were firm in their fight to maintain their absolute sovereignty in ministering to their religious needs. Even with the consent of the majority of the Jewish communities, no rabbi could hold office if the secular authorities intervened to influence his appointment. The communities would permit no outside interference whatsoever.

The ideology of the Franco-German communities came into conflict with the ideology of the Spanish centers in the clash between R. Meir Halevi of Vienna and Barfat. The real core of this conflict was the status of a rabbi who held his position by virtue of a royal appointment. The issue was not the reinstitution of *Semikah* by Meir Halevi as some maintained.

This controversy began after the death of the Chief-Rabbi of France, Mattithiah, when his son, Johanan, had served for five years.[52] Johanan had succeeded his father with the approval of the communities and the sanction of the secular government. Joshua (Isaiah), a student of the deceased Chief Rabbi, opposed Johanan. He did so on the basis of a *takkanah* which ruled that no Jew may accept a religious position with the sanction of the secular authorities.[53] Barfat supported Johanan, whereas Meir Halevi gave *Semikah* to Joshua and ordained that no man in France could wield any authority over religious matters without the express consent of Joshua.[54]

Barfat's support of Johanan was based upon four reasons. First, Johanan's father held the position with the consent of the Jewish communities and the approval of the secular government. As such, Johanan had claim to the office by right of descent. His father held it and according to law he should succeed him.[55] Again, Johanan had already been established in the position. It would not be proper to either expect the incumbent to resign in favor of another aspirant for the position or else remove him and appoint another in his place.[56] Third, Johanan was named Chief-Rabbi with the consent of the Jewish communities. According to law, as their rabbi, he could be removed by no one.[57] Lastly, the appointment by the secular authorities is binding upon the Jewish communities for "the law of the kingdom is the law."[58]

Barfat also investigated the practice of *Semikah* in France and Germany and came to the conclusion that this practice had no basis. The *Semikah* as was known in earlier days had been abrogated. The Franco-German *Semikah* had no validity.[59]

It has generally been accepted that the controversy centered around the acceptance of the *Semikah,* or authority, reinstituted by Meir Halevi of Vienna, and which he bestowed upon Joshua. He deputized him to supervise the spiritual affairs of the Jews of France. This, of course, was resented by Johanan and the controversy recorded in the responsa of Barfat ensued. According to this opinion,[60] it was Meir Halevi who reinstituted *Semikah* and who initiated the title of *Morenu* for those who had received *Semikah.* However, it must be pointed out that the title *Morenu* antedates Meir Halevi. For example, Meir of Rothenburg was known as *Maharam,* i.e., *Morenu ha-Rab* Rabbi Meir. There were others such as *Maharil, Maharash,* and *Maharap.* Accordingly, *Semikah* was not reinstituted by Meir Halevi, but was already in existence. Furthermore, Barfat speaks of *Semikah* in France and Germany as being in existence for a long time.[61]

In addition, other pertinent questions were posed.[62] Is it conceivable that Meir Halevi would choose an ambitious man such as Joshua,[63] bestow *Semikah* upon him, and authorize him to dethrone another rabbi who had been in office for a number of years? [64] He certainly could not have had him removed merely because he had not been sanctioned by him.[65] Third, it is incomprehensible why Johanan wrote but two letters, one to Barfat and the other to a Catalonian rabbi, wherein he utilizes magnificent phrases and masterfully denounces his opponents, but fails to mention even one source from the Talmud that could prove his point.[66] Finally, why would Johanan refrain from calling on the government, which appointed him to his office, to help maintain him as Chief-Rabbi? It appears as if Johanan was not able to ask for government aid.[67]

It is far more understandable if we take the controversy to revolve on an entirely different issue. The old *takkanah* mentioned earlier, dating to the time of R. Tam, R. Samuel b. Meir, and R. Eliezer b. Nathan, stipulated that no Jew, under threat of the *herem,* may accept a religious position in the community via appointment by the government.[68] The real issue in the conflict of Meir Halevi and Barfat was the status of a rabbi who had accepted his position by a royal appointment. Meir Halevi felt that the old *takkanah* should be observed. Johanan turned to Barfat, than whom he could find no better lawyer to defend his cause. Barfat, himself, had accepted the position of rabbi in Algiers by appointment from the king of Tlemcen.[69]

To this must be added one other, and perhaps more important reason for Barfat's strong support of Johanan. In defending the rabbinical position in France, he was "really defending the ideology of Spanish Jewry. Isaac bar Sheshet, in upholding Johanan, not only opposed Franco-German ideology, but tried to justify the ideology of Spanish Jewry, under which a rabbi appointed by the government was considered the lawful Jewish spiritual leader." [70]

Some have objected to the above mentioned theory on the following grounds: [71]

1. If it be true that the controversy revolved about the validity of a royal appointment to a rabbinical office, then most of what Barfat argues is beside the point. The greater part of his responsum deals with the meaning and scope of *Semikah* in vogue in the Franco-German communities.

   To this we must answer that the problem of *Semikah* was not beside the point. It was a vital part of the issue. As has been pointed out, *Semikah* had been in vogue in France and Germany without a break. These communities based their religious authority on this transference of power from teacher to disciple, and also upon a rabbi's election by the community. Thus, when one deals with the source of a rabbi's authority, the question of *Semikah* must enter the discussion.

Consequently, in the nations where *Semikah* existed, no other authority would or could be recognized. Hence, we find the *takkanah,* so often repeated afterwards, prohibiting the acceptance of a religious position at the hands of the secular government. In the Spanish communities such authority did not stem from the same source. There was no *Semikah.* Hence, there was no conflict at all when a rabbi was appointed by the king.

2. It was also asked: "Did Barfat know the underlying causes of the motive which prompted Meir Halevi to oppose Johanan? Did he know the arguments advanced by the other side? If he did, we cannot escape the conclusion that there was a deliberate attempt on his part to becloud the issue." Barfat clinches his arguments in favor of the incumbent with the statement that he had been confirmed in his office by the king. If the pivotal question was the right of Johanan to retain his position after having been appointed to office by the government, then Barfat cannot use that appointment as an argument to sustain his views.

3. A third objection was raised. Why did Meir Halevi wait for five years before raising his voice in protest against the royal appointment of Johanan?
This objection could be raised no matter what the issue at hand was. Furthermore, methods and speed of communication were not the same as in our day.

4. The responsum of Meir of Rothenburg which deals with the refusal of a *hazzan* to accept the position at the hands of the bishop cannot be cited as proof of the Franco-German position. It is quite different from the case at hand. The act of removing the mitre and handing it to the *hazzan* was tantamount to bestowal of office, whereas the royal appointment in the case of Johanan was but a formal recognition of the action taken by French Jewry. Furthermore, in the case of the *hazzan,* only a majority favored his appointment while

he was opposed strenuously by a minority. It was the outside influence that persuaded them to change their attitude. Johanan, on the other hand, had been appointed by the French communities, so far as we know, without a dissenting voice.

In answer, we challenge the basic premise that Johanan was merely confirmed in his office. This assumption comes as a result of differentiating between an unanimous election or election by majority. Nowhere do we find such a distinction with regard to the election of a religious office. Whether there is or is no minority opposition makes absolutely no difference. The communities elected their clergy by a majority. On the contrary, we find *takkanot* which forbade the royal appointment of rabbis in Spain unless at least a majority of the community consented to the appointment.[72]

There is no doubt that two philosophies existed with regard to the government-appointed rabbis. These philosophies were different in the Franco-German and the Spanish centers. The controversy of Meir Halevi and Barfat high-lighted their differences.

CHAPTER   VI

Taxes

No state can exist without collecting taxes. The king may
demand and legally collect taxes for all civic projects necessary
for the improvement of the nation. This includes national or city
projects, highways and streets, etc.¹ The Jews recognized the
need and the obligation of every resident to pay such taxes. This
was included in Samuel's dictum. However, to repeat, Jewish law
did not recognize the right of kings to extort taxes and to levy
exorbitant amounts.² Religious books or scrolls of the Torah could
not be taxed. The "yoke of the kingdom" does not fall upon the
Torah. "The law of the kingdom" is not valid in such matters.³
A tax farmer could only collect the amount to which the king was
legally entitled. He was also not permitted to add to the amount
for his own benefit. To some, this regulation was applicable to
Jewish or non-Jewish tax farmers alike. The legality of their
claim depended upon whether or not the amounts were padded.⁴
Others maintained that all non-Jewish tax farmers were automatically disqualified because they were never content with the legal
amount. They always added to the figures.⁵ Thus, all forms of
extortion with regard to taxes initiated by the king or by a tax
farmer were considered royal robbery.⁶ Extortion is also illegal
when it affects an entire community. If an individual who is not
required by law to pay a tax is forced by the king to do so, he
is not obliged to pay, that is, Samuel's law of *Dina D'Malkhuta*
is not invoked.⁷

When was a tax considered exorbitant? The Talmud apparently equated this with an amount that had no limit. In the
Middle Ages the rabbis concluded that it had nothing to do with
the amount itself. A tax was considered exorbitant when the
amount was "unheard of" or a preposterous amount for a specific

74

situation. It had nothing at all to do with being fixed or unlimited. If under normal circumstances and for a normal function the king required an unlimited amount for the time being, this was considered legal and Samuel's law was invoked.[8] If a king levied a specific amount but had no apparent reason or valid need for the tax, other than his personal desires and greed, this was absolute extortion despite the fact that the tax was of a limited amount.[9] The tax farmer who purchased the right to collect a fixed amount of taxes could earn a legal rate of profit for his services to the government. It did not render the collection invalid and the full amount collected by him was not considered exorbitant.[10] The tax farmer was disqualified from testifying in the courts. He was so disqualified because his testimony could not be relied upon. By the nature of his profession, he treated various people in different ways. He was lenient and obsequious to the rich, treating them with honor and respect, while condescending and harsh to the poor. Consequently, his testimony would be biased and as such was disqualified.[11]

The Talmud also disqualifies a self-appointed tax collector.[12] Any strong armed officer or feudal lord who issues new laws to collect new taxes is considered as acting beyond the law. Even if later on the king becomes aware of this act, and by his subsequent silence, appears to consent to such highhanded action, it is not considered as part of the law of the kingdom. It is royal robbery.[13] The phrase *Omed me'Elov*—"self-appointed," refers to someone who is unauthorized by the government. It does not mean someone who himself sought the position of tax collector or tax farmer. Should a Jew seek out such a position of his own accord, he may collect for the king and all his collections are legal. Were he not to assume this task, someone else would.[14]

The taxes were collected by the *Kahal*. The *Kahal* of one province was not permitted to tax someone of another province. It was the right of the king to divide his land into provinces and to grant it to various nobles. The Jews could not force payment under the above mentioned conditions even by means of the *herem*. However, they were permitted to boycott or refuse to do business unless such taxes were paid. Such sanctions were permissible to the *Kahal* because the king could refuse to allow foreigners to enter his land for the sake of transacting business unless they paid taxes. Consequently, the power of the *Kahal* to collect the taxes for the king was closely linked with the power the king himself wielded in such matters.[15]

One of the ways kings rewarded those who had found favor in their eyes was by exempting them from taxes. This was a prerogative which kings enjoyed without asking the consent of the communities.[16] However, such exemptions presented problems [17] to the communities who usually had to bear the brunt of the burden [18] created by a king's magnanimity towards an individual.[19] The Talmud makes the following distinction: an individual who seeks an exemption for himself must pay his taxes even if his attempts are successful. If, however, the exemption is granted him without his express request or else is merely the oversight of a careless collector, he reaps the fruits thereof.[20] The Geonim reinterpreted this talmudic ruling. The Talmud states that the validity of an exemption hinges upon who initiated it. If the privilege was secured, it is not valid. If it was granted, it is valid. The Geonim permitted such an allowance only if it was made prior to the time this tax was levied upon the community. If the individual had already been assessed his tax together with the rest of the community, then no special dispensation could be made for any individual whose burden must now be carried by the other residents of the city.[21] In fact, once a community negotiated its tax and agreed to pay a certain sum, those who leave or flee the town afterwards are equally obligated to pay their share. Their departure from the community does not alter or cancel their debt.[22] The focal point became the time a new tax law took effect. Prior to such a law it makes no difference who initiated the exemption since in any case no additional burden was put upon the community. However, after the law went into effect, should even the king forego collecting the tax from one taxpayer, it was considered royal robbery since the community had to make good the king's magnanimous gesture. Two points emerge from the statements of the Talmud and Geonim. The Talmud does not permit an individual's selfish scheming to benefit him at the expense of the community, whereas the Geonim look at whether or not the man once became partner to the community's responsibility of paying their taxes. If, however, the exemption was of such a nature as not to cast a burden upon the other members of the community, then it makes absolutely no difference how the dispensation was secured.

A very similar discussion is recorded in the Tosefta.[23] Should partners be relieved of their tax payment, the exemption does not apply to them individually, but is reckoned to the partnership. However, if the tax collectors on their own state that the exemption is for one of the partners, then it is valid for this partner alone.[24]

The rabbis of the Middle Ages wondered how this allowance was secured. One opinion held that if both partners requested the exemption, then the ruling of the Tosefta is obvious and thereby superfluous.[25] If the request was granted to both partners, then, of course, it is the partnership that ought to benefit. Therefore, only when one of the partners requests the exemption does the Tosefta make sense. Partnerships operate on the principle that all that is done by one of the partners is done for the good of the entire partnership. Even if one partner, through his efforts, obtains a tax dispensation, it is the partnership that derives the benefit of the fruits of his labors.[26] It is only when the tax collector on his own [27] specifically grants the exemption for one partner that he and he alone reaps the benefits.[28] An actual occurrence was related by R. Simha concerning his uncle, Kolonymus, the *Parnas,* who after the tax quota was issued by his community requested and received an exemption of the bishop but afterwards returned the money to the community. At first, the act was considered one of generosity or charity on the part of Kolonymus. However, we see that repaying the burdens of the community is more than an act of charity. It is the law.[29]

Another opinion interprets this Tosefta in a different light. The Tosefta only deals with a situation where a request was made by one of the partners. However, there is a difference as to how the grant was phrased. If a blanket dispensation was granted, then the entire partnership stands to gain.[30] If one partner was named specifically in the grant, it is he alone who gains.[31] It then follows that if a tax quota had been set and a request for a tax allowance had been specifically granted to one individual, he alone benefits thereby.[32] This, of course, is only true when the loss of revenue sustained as a result of the exemption is not to be made good by the rest of the community. If, however, the rest of the community must shoulder the burden of the entire tax quota, including the amount of the exemption, then the individual taxpayer may negotiate his own terms with the collector or overlord only if the tax quota for the community has as yet not been set. At such a moment it is the right of each lord to stipulate who shall and who shall not pay taxes.[33] This right belongs to the secular officials for "the law of the kingdom is the law." However, once the community negotiations have been concluded and a tax quota has been set, even the lord himself may not stipulate any changes which involve casting additional burdens upon others.[34] The overlord who attempts to change the law is guilty of royal robbery. It is not the law of the kingdom.[35]

The two opinions expressed with regard to the interpretation of the Tosefta cited are in essence the two points of view as expressed by the Talmud and the Geonim. There is absolutely no difference between a partnership and the community which is but a partnership on a large scale.[36]

There is yet a third opinion which denied the right of exemption to a king if that exemption caused the burden to fall upon the rest of the community. One was neither permitted to plead relief for himself under such circumstances, nor was the king granted the freedom to exempt anyone, even prior to the time that a tax was negotiated for the entire Jewish community. Such powers were not granted the king and should he deviate from the accepted ways, it was considered a breach of the "social contract" which this opinion considered the basis for Samuel's law. As a result, illegal exemptions of any kind were not the law of the kingdom but royal robbery. No community would accept such changes of their free will.[37]

These regulations came as a result of the community's desire to strengthen its unity and to negotiate as one body rather than that each individual be at the mercy of the overlord.[38] Furthermore, it was ordained to prevent individual negotiations which would benefit some at the expense of casting an added burden upon the communities. As a consequence, an additional stipulation was made; namely, no individual may separately negotiate his tax assessment with the overlord without the express consent and permission of the *Kahal*.[39]

It was resolved by the community of Saragossa that no one be exempt from royal taxes to which they were liable according to the quota fixed by the *Mukdamim*. Were anyone to seek exemption, or even seek aid of non-Jews to this end, or protest against a duly levied assessment, he should be placed under the ban of excommunication.[40] In Valladolid in 1432 the Jews strengthened their efforts against private exemption . . . "In general no one shall take advantage of any letter obtained . . . to free himself from taxes, imposts, loans, or any other demands which our lord, the king, may make on the communities." If a community, because of fear of the authorities, made an agreement with a resident to reduce his taxes, such an agreement was void.[41] Any person involved in the violation of the above regulations was to be declared anathema and excommunicated.[42] Any change in these matters constituted royal robbery.[43] However, the king, on

79

his own accord, may free any individual even without the approval of the *Kahal*.[44] Furthermore, if a man does no business in the community, he may be freed of all taxes, regardless upon whom the burden falls. This is true whether the man is a pauper or wealthy.[45]

Everyone agreed, however, that if an individual residing in one nation had received directly or through his ancestors an exemption from a king of another nation and by a turn of fate that king now rules the nation in which he resides, such an individual should automatically be freed of all taxes.[46]

It is to be clearly understood that matters of tax negotiations varied with the times and with the place. What might be true for one generation could be altered when circumstances were changed. Consequently, the opinions of the Talmud, the Geonim, or of the rabbis of the 13th century, were valid for their day when comparatively few Jews lived in small towns. If one Jew was exempt, the burden fell upon his coreligionists residing in the same town. However, in other days, the custom varied.[47] For example, in 16th century Salonika there were many who were not required to pay taxes but no one of the community was affected by it.[48] In the same city a century later, a Jew bought the tax farming rights to cattle. The custom was that tax farmers were themselves free of all taxes, not only of the ones they bought. Since such was the law of the kingdom, Samuel's law freed this Jew from having to share the tax burdens of the community. Of interest is the reasoning employed in addition to *Dina D'Malkhuta;* namely, that in such matters we may learn from Gentile law which exempts the privileged individuals.[49]

By and large, the gamut of Jewish history in the diaspora shows that the taxes levied upon Jews were enormous. One could hardly blame the Jew if he tried to evade payment. The burden was so great. Nonetheless, the rabbis specifically forbade the evasion of tax payments. No Jew might attempt to escape paying a legally instituted tax by means of swearing falsely or by any

other method. Doing so was considered outright robbery.[50] Even
when there existed no debtors' prison, the community was able to
jail the Jew who evaded paying taxes.[51] Unless the king levied an
unauthorized tax, no legal loophole (*Aramah*), such as an oath
or a vow was permitted in order to release oneself of the burden
of paying his tax.[52] If the tax was legal, such methods were not
permitted should the king even use force to implement his regulation.[53] When someone was caught and was to be fined for tax-
evasion, even though this fine was without limit, it was not permissible to utilize the ruse of an oath in order to escape payment
of the fine. Such leniency with regard to an oath was sure to lead
to mistrust and would minimize in the eyes of the public the
importance of one's word.[54]

Not even mental reservations were permitted while uttering
an oath in order to invalidate it. When an oath was administered
as a result of a legal procedure, the mishnaic ruling was not applicable. Only with regard to extortionists whose demands were
unlawful were such evasions permitted. Were Jews to be permitted
to disregard their oaths, the resulting consequence would be the
firm distrust of any Jew's word. No Gentile would ever again believe the statements of Jews.[55] However, in 14th century Spain,
when special taxes or fines were levied upon Marranos who desired to leave their cities in order to reside in places where they
could openly embrace their faith once again, the rabbis protested.
Equally loud was their protest when laws were enacted to confiscate their land for failure of payment. Under these circumstances,
all means available to the Jew to protect his property, even to the
extent of uttering a false vow, were permitted him. "The law of
the kingdom is the law" did not apply.[56]

We have already mentioned that a tax farmer or tax collector, who is extortionate in his demands, has no legal rights. In
16th century Turkey, the question was raised whether a tax farmer who pads his demands and whose requests are limitless loses
his entire status so that anyone may evade the entire amount de-

manded, or else, does one have to pay the part for which the collector has legal claim?

Two opinions arose. One claimed that the duty to pay taxes stems from the concept of *Dina D'Malkhuta Dina*. However, a Jewish tax collector who increases the tax rate of his own accord is established as a robber,[57] as one who defies the law of the kingdom. Consequently, *Dina D'Malkhuta* does not apply to him and his entire demand is no more than extortion.[58] Another opinion stated that two wrongs do not make a right. Although the collector attempted to steal by increasing the king's rates it does not give anyone the right to steal from the collector. As a result, the part to which he has legal claim must be paid to him.[59]

Evasion of governmental law was denounced by Jewish law whether it involved taxes or any other civil or criminal edict. The shaving or clipping of coins was considered a violation for which the perpetrators were to be flogged. It was a crime comparable to robbery or theft. Once when Jews were caught clipping coins and an oath was administered on the scroll of the Torah that they would not shave coins again, their mental reservations with regard to the oath did not void their actual utterances. The law of the kingdom made it illegal to shave coins and mental reservations did not permit them to break their solemn oath to their burghers. With regard to the royal currency, it is legal and quite proper for a monarch or his delegates to prohibit the shaving of coins. Such acts presented a serious matter. They endangered not only the people involved in the actual crime, but also caused harm to other Jews, the innocent recipients, who would unknowingly pass these defective coins and who might be accused of the crime itself.[60]

Whether or not it was permissible for a Jew to take a country's currency out of its borders, was another problem discussed. The Talmud records the following dispute with regard to currency which was voided by the king. Rab states that debtors[61] must make good their debts by paying the currency in use at the time of payment.[62] Samuel rules that as long as currency has value anywhere at all, even if they are valueless in this nation, the debtor may still repay with such coinage.[63] R. Nahman, however, stipulates that the creditor must have the opportunity to go to wherever the coins have value or else the decision of Samuel is meaningless.[64] Some have questioned Samuel's law. If "the law of the kingdom is the law," how can Samuel rule that the debtor may force the creditor to violate the command of the king, who forbids taking currency out of the land? How can Jewish law demand he cash his coins out of the country?[65] In answer it was said that when the king disapproves of the nation's currency being exported from his borders, then it is as if the creditor is unable to reach the place where the coins have value, a stipulation which renders Samuel's law invalid.

Actually, Samuel's law, as well as R. Nahman's addition, have been misunderstood and this led to a number of problems. Samuel and R. Nahman merely require potential value for the coins and the potential capability of the creditor to cash his coins. Neither requires the creditor to actually do so. He must be capable of taking the currency out of the country to a place where this currency has value.[66] Rab demanded that currency must have actual value in the nation in question for it to be considered legal tender. However, neither Samuel nor R. Nahman order the creditor to violate the law of the kingdom. The creditor is not required to leave the land. He must only be capable of doing so.[67]

In all matters dealing with currency changes, "the law of the kingdom is the law" regardless of Jewish law. In a particular case, a change of currency was ordered to take place by the first of the year. However, because of the impending change, the present currency immediately began to decrease in value. Jewish law would charge the loss to the creditor, if payment is made prior to the first of the year and with old currency, and to the debtor if payment is made after the first of the year and with the new currency. However, if the law of the kingdom demands that payment be made with the currency in use at the time a note is due, regardless of when the debt was actually discharged, the law of the kingdom must be obeyed.[68]

In any religious or civil transaction wherein Jewish law requires currency to be "acceptable to everyone" (*over la'soher*), it is not only silver coins that are good. "Acceptable to everyone" means to everyone who deals in or with a nation. A country's paper money, or banknotes are valid as long as they are acceptable to everyone in the meaning described.[69]

The instability of currency at times involved a conflict with the laws against usury and interest. A person in need of ready cash might be anxious to borrow money from his fellow Jew and be tempted to repay that loan with currency of a more valuable mintage. Amounts which are in excess of the loan and that came as a result of such a transaction were stamped usurious and Jewish law forbade such an agreement to be fulfilled.[70] Nevertheless, the law of the kingdom may demand the use of the new and superior currency. This is not considered usury.[71] The law of the kingdom, in this instance, does not really overrule the Jewish law prohibiting usury. The rabbis ruled that a violation of the prohibition against usury only occurs when there is intent to violate by the parties involved. In the case at hand, neither party had any intention of giving or collecting interest.[72] They merely tried to fulfill the wishes of the government.

There were many objections raised by the rabbis, but in actual practice, we find that the public paid no heed to these objections. The people justified their practices partly because the "oppressive taxes of the kings and noblemen allow them barely enough to sustain their lives," [73] and partly also because "living among the nations we come in constant contact with them in our business dealings for we cannot earn a livelihood unless we deal with them." It is evident that the usual reason given for the prohibition against taking usury from Gentiles, namely, in order to prevent intercourse with them, no longer applied. It had no greater meaning with regard to money lending than it had to any other kind of business.[74] Theoretically, the taking of interest or usury violated principles professed by the Church. However, the circulation of monies became an essential requisite towards developing commercial empires. Without ready money available it would not have been possible for the kings to build up great armies and Europe would have been doomed to stagnation under feudalism.[75]

In as much as Jews were considered to be outside the pale of the Church, the ban on interest did not apply to them. The Jew was to play the role of the moneylender which allowed him to function as a partial architect in the economic structure of Europe, but which also left him vulnerable to the inevitable antipathy which this function brought about.

Let it equally be said that the profession of moneylending was practiced by both sides. The biblical prohibition [76] against usury was also interpreted to be binding on Jewish coreligionists only. Thus, loans with interest were usually transacted between people of different faiths.[77]

Should a royal edict forbid all loans on interest, then "the law of the kingdom is the law." [78] However, let it be understood that such laws were rare and when they occurred were usually aimed at Jews alone and were considered an attempt at royal theft.[79] Such laws, being discriminatory in nature, were not binding.[80]

CHAPTER VII

Courts and Judges

Throughout the centuries of Jewish life in the diaspora, the Jews were able to maintain the way of life which they had inherited from their ancestors as the basis for their system of jurisprudence and were able to keep the Jewish courts as the tribunals that administered justice. In matters of religion and in their internal legal problems, the Jews applied Jewish law within their own courts.

The Jews developed an aversion towards frequenting non-Jewish courts. In fact, according to the principles of medieval Jewish law, the jurisdiction of the Bet Din was exclusive. Based upon the interpretation of a Pentateuchal verse,[1] R. Tarfon forbade the Jew from seeking judgments of a non-Jewish court,[2] even if the decisions of that court coincided with Jewish law. Continuing in the tannaitic spirit, the Geonim, too, eschewed any attempt on the part of Jews to bring their disputes before non-Jewish courts.[3] They objected because of the corruption which was rampant there. Wherever the courts were known to be honest and fair, the Geonim recognized their decisions.[4] Witness the testimony of one Gaon: "Because in the city in which we live, (Bagdad) the courts accept as witnesses only such persons as are trustworthy and reliable, those who are of outstanding prominence in the community by reason of their wealth or culture, and those who have never been suspected of robbery or falsehood, who are faithful followers of their religion . . . The same is true of nearly all Babylonia; and for that reason, it is a daily occurrence with us to accept their validity . . ."[5] The Geonim also granted permission to a plaintiff to seek justice in a secular tribunal if the defendant refused to appear before the Bet Din and the court feared tangling with the power of this defendant.[6]

86

This jurisdictional status prevailed in Europe throughout the Middle Ages. The Jewish court was by far the most distinctive and characteristic institution of Jewish self-government in the Middle Ages. It was the purpose of the medieval rabbis to keep litigations between Jewish parties before Jewish tribunals in order to strengthen Jewish judicial power and maintain their autonomy. Their fear of unjust treatment by the non-Jewish courts, which so often was well founded, served as an additional deterrent. We may trace the gamut of Jewish history of the medieval Jewish communities from Palestine to Spain, and from the Barbary Coast to Poland, and in almost every century we find at least some rabbinic affirmation of this aversion to allowing disputes between Jewish litigants to be heard in a Gentile court.

In the 12th Century, R. Tam initiated the following *takkanah*: "We have voted, decreed, ordained, and declared under the *herem,* that no man or woman may bring a fellow Jew before Gentile courts or exert compulsion on him through Gentiles, whether by prince or a common man, a ruler or an inferior official, except by mutual agreement made in the presence of proper witnesses." [7] Herein, R. Tam reiterated the prohibition against taking Jewish disputes to non-Jewish courts. There is, however, one additional and very pertinent ruling mentioned in this *takkanah*; namely, if both parties agree to submit their litigation to a non-Jewish court, then permission is granted them.[8] No such exception was ever made by talmudic law. However, the Talmud did recognize a principle which went beyond the law; namely, that in all civil matters, a person may do with his money as he chooses. R. Tam, in the above mentioned *takkanah,* applied this principle and permitted litigants to accept the decision of a Gentile court, provided both parties agree to this procedure. It was the prerogative of the litigants to submit their dispute to any court they desired, since in money matters, people may do as they please.[9]

The communities were very strict and dealt severely with

those who violated this *takkanah*. In the 13th century, in Germany, anyone who summoned his fellow Jew to a Gentile court was to be publicly flogged [10] unless he had received express permission of the Bet Din or the *Kahal* to do so.[11] Once such permission was received, the plaintiff could not be accused of betraying the autonomous rule of the Jewish communities. Even the threat to appeal the decisions of a Bet Din to a non-Jewish tribunal subjected the offender and his accessories, advisors, and supporters to the ban of excommunication.[12] So jealous were the Jews of that era and of that locale of their religious and judicial autonomy, that should a Jew even wish to enforce a decision rendered by a Bet Din, or force the appearance of a defendant before a Bet Din by bringing a complaint to a Gentile court, he was deemed an "informer." One authority stated that in order to prevent such an offender from fulfilling his evil designs, he may be maimed or even killed [13] while on his way to the Gentile court.

If witnesses testified to the effect that A threatened to denounce B to the Gentiles, and subsequently B suffers at the hand of the Gentiles, it may be assumed that A carried out his threat. On the basis of such circumstancial evidence, A is to be held liable for all damages incurred by B.[14] Furthermore, it was not even justified to inform against an informer. Should B, the intimidated party, attempt to revenge himself by denouncing A to the Gentiles, the second informer, too, was to pay all damages to the man who suffered through denunciation.[15] In general, indignation or revenge for any sort of wrong done did not justify resorting to the Gentile court. Once, a son saw his father bleed because of a blow given him by another. While enraged, the son denounced the attacker to the authorities. The son was required to indemnify the assailant for any loss he might have sustained. He had no right to inform against the attacker regardless of what had been done to his father.[16]

How different was the situation when the *Kahal* itself was involved. In a dispute between the *Kahal* and a minority group, the *Kahal* or its duly authorized officers could coerce the minority to abide by its decisions. Compliance with any decision of the *Kahal* may be enforced by a court order, be that an order of the Bet Din or a Gentile court.[17] If this power was granted to the *Kahal* when opposed by a group of people, then it certainly possessed the same rights with regard to the opposition of an individual. How ironic it appears that the *Kahal,* in order to preserve its power, utilized the very means that threatened its autonomy, namely, the Gentile tribunal.[18]

A noteworthy phenomenon of Jewish history must be mentioned. It appears as if neither the *Kahal,* nor individul Jews ever availed themselves of the powers of the German secular courts. No record at all is handed down of cases where both parties to a dispute were Jews. The records of literally thousands of cases handed down by the *Oberhof* of Magdeburg, Germany, contain not a single instance of a Jew bringing suit against a fellow Jew, although there are a number of cases involving a Jew and a Gentile. We even find that Jews engaged attorneys to represent them in the Jewish and secular courts.[19] There are no records even of cases where the Jew could have obtained the sanction of Jewish law to seek recourse in a Gentile court. This was true from the 13th to the end of the 16th centuries.[20] The jurisdiction of the Jewish courts was exclusively established, so that even in cases of physical violence and the resultant damage suits which, in their day, were no longer under the jurisdiction of the Bet Din, Jews were not permitted to hail their coreligionists before the secular courts of law.[21]

In fact, German influence was felt in other lands as well. R. Baruch b. Isaac of Worms,[22] on his way to the Holy Land, stopped off in Crete. The Jewish population of this island was not of a scholarly nature and they were lax in many observances. The German rigorist was appalled by what he beheld. For example, no member of the German communities would work on Friday towards sunset, thereby possibly violating the Sabbath. However, this was common practice in Crete. Perhaps a mid-day quitting hour for the eves of the Sabbath and holidays was too difficult for the Jews of Crete, many of whom were employed by Gentiles who refused to release them so early.[23] The Jewish islanders saw no harm in conducting their litigations as well on Friday or on the eves of holidays. Under the influence of Baruch b. Isaac, regulations were drafted which at least restricted the Jew from presenting their disputes before Gentile courts on such days, although they still continued doing so on other days of the week. In fact, this *takkanah* has little, if anything, to do with the prohibition to go before Gentile courts. The *takkanah* was promulgated because the communities were fearful that a Jewish defendant might be "prevented from enjoying the festival," and so forbade anyone from hailing his fellow Jew before a court, Jewish or Gentile alike, so that "he may also prepare the needs of the Sabbath for the Lord, and that the community of the Lord may not be like sheep which have no Shepherd." [24]

Apparently this all exclusive power of the German Jewish tribunals of the Middle Ages was challenged in the 17th century. The Jews had suffered immensely at the hands of offenders who refused to obey Jewish law and compelled litigants to present themselves before Gentile courts. The community finally passed a severe *takkanah* in the hope of rectifying some of the ills of their day. The offender was not permitted to marry, to be called to the Torah, and in general was to be separated from the community. Even should the Gentile court decide in his favor, the plaintiff must release the defendant of all charges against him. If the defendant incurred any expenditures, the plaintiff must make good the expense.[25]

If the transgressor of this *takkanah* was a rabbi, then his title was forfeit. Anyone who afterwards granted him that honor was also punished. Secular leaders of a community, teachers, or those holding any other community office were to be removed if they violated this *takkanah*.[26]

90

So strong were the communities set against this offense, that they even set up central district courts to have their seats in Frankfort, Worms, Fulda, Friedburg, and Ginzburg. These courts would handle all cases in which the local courts feared to intervene because powerful individuals rendered the local courts ineffective.[27]

We may then conclude that the medieval German Jews recognized only Jewish law and Jewish law courts. Just as they would not tolerate any outside interference with regard to the appointment of rabbis, so they gave their full support to all ordinances aimed at making the jurisdiction of the rabbinic tribunals all encompassing. Obviously, such support provided the communities with the autonomy they so jealously guarded.

Such unanimity did not exist in medieval Spain. The Jewish courts did not receive the same support for exclusive jurisdiction as did their counterparts in Germany. Jews often had recourse to the secular tribunals. Jewish litigants in Spain did not practice the same uncompromising fidelity nor feel the strong necessity to bring their disputes before Jewish tribunals as did their German brethren. This attitude developed despite the continued teaching of the Spanish sages that Jewish law prohibited Jews from bringing their suits before Gentile courts of law. In fact, it is precisely the continued repetition and reaffirmation of ordinances and *takkanot* prohibiting the use of Gentile courts which leads to the conclusion that these regulations were not successful or else there would have been no need for the constant repetition. Let the overwhelming evidence speak for itself.

On the basis of the talmudic text mentioned above and the ordinances of the Geonim, we find that the Spanish Jewish authorities as early as the 11th century subjected an offender to the ban of excommunication.[28] It was forbidden to frequent Gentile courts even when their law coincided with Jewish law.[29] In the 12th century, one codifier labels the offender as a "wicked one who blasphemes and rebels against the Torah of Moses, our teacher." [30] Should the decisions of the Gentile court coincide with Jewish law and the defendant be a powerful individual who refuses to subject himself to the Bet Din, the plaintiff may bring suit against him in a non-Jewish court of law.[31] Permission of the Bet Din was required before such action might be undertaken.[32]

Again, the 13th century sages were vehement in their denunciation against such violations. *Dina D'Malkhuta Dina* is not operative with regard to taking a dispute to a Gentile court. Only in matters involving the statutory laws of the kingdom may Samuel's law be invoked. In one situation involving the property of a woman who died without leaving any children, the sages ruled that such property became the estate of her father. The Jewish laws of inheritance, even though in conflict with secular law, must prevail. Were the litigants to institute suit in a Gentile court, they would transgress the talmudic admonition against such a practice.[33] "The law of the kingdom is the law" does not apply or else Jewish laws of inheritance would disappear. Daughters would be required to inherit equally with sons; the law of primogeniture would be voided, etc. Anyone permitting this is not only in error but is guilty of robbery.[34] However, not only where Jewish and secular law conflicted were Jews prohibited from frequenting these secular courts, but even where secular law was identical with the law of the Torah, was it forbidden.[35]

One authority of this century bitterly bemoans any attempt at such legal suicide. He warns: "In general under such a provision, all the laws of the Torah would be uprooted. What need would we have of all our holy writings such as were composed by Judah, the prince, and by Rabina and R. Ashi after him? We might just as well teach our children the laws of the Gentiles and build our "high places" in the sanctuaries of the non-Jews. May God forfend that such come to pass in Israel; may God forbid that we cause the Torah to be girt in sackcloth."[36]

And again he writes:

92

"Among all the nations there are certain fundamental rights and privileges which belong to a sovereign. Within this scope, the commands of the king are law. This does not hold true of the judgments rendered in their courts. The laws which the courts apply are not part of the essence of royalty. Rather they are based upon legal precedent found in the writings handed down by the courts. You cannot dispute this distinction, for otherwise you would void, God forbid, the laws of the Jews." [37]

Another sage stated: "God forbid that the holy people shall walk in the ways of the Gentiles and according to their statutes."[38]

Here we find the opinion that "the law of the kingdom is the law" did not apply to the decisions of the Gentile court, since they are not based upon the statutory laws of the kingdom. They are but the innovations or interpretations of law made by individual judges. The decision rendered by one judge may be modified or even altered by another justice of another time. The sovereign is not affected nor concerned by such decisions unless they involve the known statutes of the kingdom. Concerning such laws, the courts have no choice in the matter. They must follow them.[39]

The Spanish sages, as did the authorities of earlier generations, also granted permission to a plaintiff to seek justice in a Gentile court if a powerful defendant refused to appear before a Jewish court and the Bet Din hesitated to interfere.[40] However, they would not allow anyone to seek intercession of the Gentile courts to force a defendant to appear in a Bet Din.[41] Even so, when the parties involved in a dispute agreed to submit to the jurisdiction of a secular tribunal, they might do so. In civil matters, any defendant may decide what to do with his money. It is only his concern if he chooses to pay without being legally obligated to do so according to Jewish law.[42] Such an agreement was valid only as long as both litigants chose to remain under the jurisdiction of the Gentile court. Whenever they changed their minds and resubmitted their dispute before a Bet Din, it was the

93

Jewish court which now had full jurisdiction. For example, if at first two individuals agreed to abide by the stipulations of a Gentile court with regard to a document issued by that tribunal, and later they choose to submit to a Jewish court, the Bet Din is to try the case on the merits of Jewish law even if such law contradicts their agreement previously made before the Gentile court.[43]

The attitude of the Spanish legalists concurred with that of the German rabbis. They, too, branded an individual as an informer who aired his grievances or sought redress from the secular courts rather than the Bet Din.[44] The offender desecrates the Name of Heaven even where the decisions of the secular courts are not different from those of the Bet Din.[45] Concern was expressed for those living in areas where learned men were not available. What were they to do with their disputes? If no solutions were found for them, it would surely cause them to submit their cases to the Gentile courts.[46] Such a state of affairs would only lead to extortion and robbery.[47] No defendant was permitted to suggest a change of venue to a Gentile court of law while the case was being heard by a Bet Din. The Jewish court could prevent the plaintiff from instituting such a change. The effrontery of such litigants could be punished by placing them under the ban of excommunication.[48]

Not only the decisions of the sages but also communal ordinances stressed the quarantine of the Gentile courts and the consequence of any breach. "He who brings suit against his neighbor before the Gentile courts and thereby causes him to suffer financial losses shall be excommunicated and remain in this state until he shall render full compensation for the loss sustained."[49]

The sages of the 14th century reiterated and reaffirmed similar sentiments. Excommunication was the weapon used to insure obedience.[50] Neither was there silence in this matter in the 15th century. A *takkanah* enacted in Valladolid at the Synod of 1432 stated: "No Jew or Jewess shall bring his or her neighbor whether a Jew or Jewess before any judge, ecclesiastic or secular, who is not of our faith, although such a judge should decide in accordance with the law of Israel, unless it be a matter of payment of taxes or imposts or coinage or other rights of our lord, the King, or of our lady, the Queen, or the money or rights of the Church or of a lord or lady of a place. Whoever transgresses this law is to be declared anathema and excommunicated, and no one shall have any dealings with him; he shall not be buried among Jews, his bread shall be like that of libations to the idols. For each transgression he shall pay one thousand *maravedis* to the Jew who suffered by the defamation or to whomever the Rabbi of the Court will order that it should be paid. But if any Jew refuses to come to a Jewish court after being summoned three times, the rabbi and the judges of the community may give the plaintiff permission to apply for redress to the Gentile courts."[51]

Furthermore, in all disputes the Bet Din was obligated to institute a temporary truce. Both parties were obliged to abide by this truce. Whoever broke this agreement would be subject to a suit. However, should the Bet Din refuse to interfere in such a matter, the petitioner had the right to proceed before a Gentile court.[52]

The evidence shown displays the abhorrence felt by the religious and lay leadership towards bringing litigation to the outside courts. By communal ordinances as well as by religious teachings the ancient doctrine was well expressed that forsaking the Jewish courts in favor of the more expeditious outer judiciary was tantamount to perfidy.

However, the Jewish authorities of Spain were not successful. As so often happens, the pressures and forces of everyday life exerted greater influence than the teachings of the sages or the desire to preserve self-rule. Expediency often won out. The Gentile courts were far more effective and often Jews resorted to the courts especially when physical constraint was required.[53] The secular authorities could even force Jews to stand trial before the Bet Din as long as they did not interfere with the due process of law.[54] The Jews of Spain were prone to bring their suits to the non-Jewish tribunals. Such was especially the case when belligerent Jewish litigants, in defiance of the Bet Din, reinstituted suit in the secular courts after a decision of the Bet Din went against them. At times, such adverse decisions and the resultant spite suits, brought violence and danger to the Jewish community and certainly always threatened the foundation of the Bet Din.[55]

The kings often interfered with the procedure of the courts. In a number of instances, especially when litigation continued for a long time, the monarchs personally communicated with the Jewish authorities urging them to settle the matter in accordance with the demands of truth and justice.[56] At times the kings ordered the secular judges to adjudicate according to Jewish law when the opposing litigants were Jews.[57] Their decisions were valid because of *Dina D'Malkhuta* but should the judges on their own accord adjudicate by law other than Jewish, their decisions were not accepted.[58]

So prevalent was this practice among the Spanish Jews, that they found it necessary to engage attorneys to direct and process their disputes in the Jewish or in the secular courts.[59]

In fact, that the Jewish courts of Spain were not the exclusive bodies to solve the disputes of Spanish Jewry may be attributed to the legal situation existing in Spain. Although the Jewish courts received recognition from the secular authorities, royal policy did not permit them entirely to negate the right of jurisdiction of the crown. As a result, confusion existed since the areas of jurisdiction were not clearly spelled out. At times these areas overlapped and invariably the Jewish courts were forced to relinquish their prerogatives. Such rival jurisdiction weakened the authority of the Jewish courts and the trust of Jewish litigants.[60]

On the other hand, medieval German law strictly recognized the Jewish courts.[61] They gave support to these seats of justice and helped make their jurisdiction exclusive. The policy of non-interference in such matters was strongly in favor of Jewish communal autonomy. No confusion with regard to jurisdiction existed. The Jews were permitted to operate within their own legal system. Without any outside intervention, the Jewish courts ruled supreme.

Italy presents a dual picture. Prior to the end of the 15th century, when Italy was under the influence of the German rabbis, we find a rigorous attitude with regard to frequenting a Gentile court. Even the appeal of a Jewish plaintiff that the Gentile court, with its superior power, coerce a reluctant defendant to stand trial before a Bet Din, was forbidden.[62] The offender was to be placed under the ban [63] since he was considered an informer.[64] Nonetheless, the continued refusal on the part of the defendant exempted the plaintiff of any guilt and he was permitted to seek redress in the Gentile courts.[65]

However, towards the end of the century, as the status of the Jews of Italy gradually began to decline, and with the influx of Spanish Jews, we find a different attitude developed.

On August 3, 1484 the community of Pesaro elected to put a stop to bringing religious articles such as *tephilin,* or one of the books of Scripture before a Gentile court whenever an oath was to be administered. They felt that since the Gentiles do not realize the holiness which is attached to the *tephilin* and look upon them with contempt and consider the straps of the *tephilin* as they do shoelaces, the Name of God is profaned. As a result, the community of Pesaro ordained that such practices be no longer followed but that any future oath be taken over the "pen." Should the plaintiff be dissatisfied with such an oath, the parties ought to come before a Jewish judge for the administration of the oath.[66]

Here the community of Pesaro expressed no criticism of litigants going to a Gentile tribunal. The concern was the desecration of holy objects. Their cry was against the desecration of the Name that cheapened the importance of *tephilin* by bringing them before a Gentile court where they were held up to ridicule. There appears no objection to the litigation itself which was submitted to a Gentile court.

97

Seventy years later a similarly mild *takkanah* was enacted in Ferrara. The ordinance was declared on Thursday, June 1, 1554. It prevented any person who compelled his neighbor to defend himself before a secular court without the permission of the *Kahal* or the rabbi of his city, from hereafter bringing the matter to a Jewish court.[67]

By mid-sixteenth century the authority of the Jewish communities had so far deteriorated, that perhaps they were no longer capable of prohibiting Jews from appealing to the Gentile courts. The *takkanah* of Ferrara had none of the sanctions previously attached to such enactments. They now resorted to this rather mild refusal to hear any case after it had been considered by a Gentile court. The form of earlier *takkanot* was still observed, but the severity with regard to dealing with any breach was no longer feasible.

In North Africa, the ordinance of R. Tam apparently was not in effect. Cases wherein Jewish litigants availed themselves of non-Jewish courts were a daily occurrence. In Majorca, the Jewish courts did not function since the crown did not permit them to adjudicate their disputes.[68] Only by special requests submitted by the litigants could a court be convened.[69] However, at the end of the 14th, beginning of the 15th century, action was taken to place under the ban all litigants who sought the secular tribunals to settle their internal disputes.[70] Some authorities thought that to frequent a non-Jewish court was tantamount to "following in their ways," a practice which was prohibited by Jewish law.[71] However, it was forbidden to do so even where Jewish law and the law of the non-Jewish courts were identical. "Let such a thing not occur in Israel . . . for did not our Torah demand that our disputes be placed exclusively before Jewish courts?'[72]

The situation in the Middle East during the 15th-17th centuries was somewhat similar to the conditions prevalent in Spain during the earlier centuries. This should not be at all surprising since the Jewish inhabitants of this area during these centuries were predominantly the exiles from Spain and Portugal or their descendants. Here, too, we find a discrepancy between daily life and the wishes of the spiritual and lay leaders of the communities. Perhaps here too the constant protest of the religious authorities against Jews taking their disputes to Moslem courts are in themselves evidence of the prevalence of such acts in the daily life of the communities.

At the end of the 15th, beginning of the 16th century, the religious authorities curbed the extent of Samuel's precept. "The law of the kingdom is the law," but not the law as formulated or initiated by the Moslem courts. These authorities reiterated the stand expressed centuries earlier by one of the well known Spanish authorities. No Moslem court could overrule Jewish law for this would mark the destruction or end of the Jewish system of jurisprudence.[73] One figure, who dominated the life of 16th century Jewry of Salonika, looked with great disfavor and alarm at this breach of Jewish solidarity. "Is there no Law (Torah) in Israel," [74] he cried, that Jews must seek justice elsewhere? The Moslem courts were not in power to do away with the religious laws of any other group, be they Jews or Christians.[75] In fact, *Dina D'Malkhuta* is only applied to those laws of the kingdom that have no basis in the religious system of those who are in power. The religious laws of the Moslems are not binding upon Jews.[76]

These decisions had little effect upon the Jews of that day. The rich of Cannea wanted the estates left to them in wills as well as dowries (*Ketubot*) to be adjudged by Turkish law and in secular tribunals rather than by a Bet Din. Apparently the processing of wills and documents dealing with dowries in the secular courts was a common practice. To stem the tide, the Jewish community leaders on Wednesday, Tebet 9, 1557-8, gathered in the synagogue of the Catalonians in Salonika and passed a resolution forbidding such practices. "Therefore we have resolved that no Jewish man or woman may process a will or *Ketuba* in a non-Jewish court. Anyone who violates this *haskama* shall be deemed

99

an informer . . . and shall be separated from the community. This *haskama* shall be proclaimed in every synagogue on each Sabbath preceding the festival of the New Moon as in the case with the *herem* against informers."[77]

The rich of Cannea were not to be stopped by this *haskama* and a few individuals informed the secular authorities that Jacob b. Samuel Samut, their spiritual leader, forbade them to frequent the secular tribunals. They reported that he did not recognize the courts of law of the land.[78] Samut was in danger of his life and his enemies forced an oath upon him forbidding him to enter Cannea for a period of ten years.[79] Samut, for safety's sake, assumed a smaller position in Calabria.

Thus, despite the efforts of the religious community leaders, the economic forces won out. Nonetheless the religious authorities ruled that the decisions of a non-Jewish court had no validity for Jews.[80] *Dina D'Malkhuta Dina* is operative only where legal procedures are followed. Thus, a king only has the right to collect such taxes to which he is legally entitled. A Jew who hails his fellow Jew to a non-Jewish court follows illegal procedures and to him, just as to a king who attempts to collect an illegal tax, Samuel's law is not applicable.[81] More than that, the offender is to be placed under the ban of excommunication.[82] The defendant who was coerced to appear before a non-Jewish tribunal may even swear falsely to protect himself, especially if there is the threat of bodily harm.[83]

Again we find that towards the last quarter of the 16th century, the offenses got out of hand in the city of Constantinople and in 1576-7 that community passed a resolution in the hope of stopping these transgressions.

From the time when Jews settled in Turkey, it had been recognized that no Jew might trespass or ignore the rights of "possession" (*hazakah*) with regard to the home, property, or business of another Jew.[84] However, the avaricious tendencies of some brought about countless disputes,[85] to the point where the secular

100

authorities severely criticized and complained with regard to such property rights.[86] Obviously, the authorities became aware of these disputes because the Jews hailed their coreligionists to the non-Jewish tribunals. In the year 1576-7, the communal leaders agreed to set up their own agency of duly appointed members who would hear and decide these litigations.[87] A system of rules and regulations were to govern such altercations. To prevent interference by the secular authorities, they declared: "No Jew may seek aid of the secular authorities or even have them interfere with the tax of the duly appointed of the community (*Memunim*-Overseers). Nor may any one reveal that these *Memunim* are engaged in settling property disputes in order that no resentment of these secular authorities directly or through informers be invoked. Offenders of any portion of this *haskama* shall be excommunicated and thereby lose all their rights."[88]

Indeed the situation in the Turkish centers appeared to have been similar to that found in the earlier Spanish centers. This conflict of the spiritual leaders and the daily practice of the general populace also existed in Palestine of the 15th and 16th centuries.

When Obadiah Bertinoro arrived in Jerusalem he found chaotic conditons in existence. He introduced a series of *takkanot* which were engraved on a tablet in a synagogue. Among them was one which stated: "No man may hail his coreligionists to a secular tribunal unless the defendants had been summoned three times and refused to appear before the Bet Din."[89] The clause which demanded that at least three refusals be required before further action may be instituted shows how chaotic indeed were the conditions of the Jewish community, and it indicates the lack of authority of the Bet Din of that time. The Jews of that era obviously did not have the same autonomy that the Jews of Germany or even Spain enjoyed.

In 16th century Safed as well, we find the religious authorities opposed to Jews frequenting the non-Jewish courts. The decisions of a Moslem court were considered valid only if the king specifically demanded their use by everyone. It is then that "the law of the kingdom is the law."[90] A litigant who takes his dispute over property to a Gentile court is to be excommunicated and remain under the ban until he restores the situation to the status it had prior to his illegal suit in the Gentile courts and is ready to submit to the Bet Din.[91]

However, one legal authority of Safed complained of the prevalent violations. He referred to this practice as "the evil custom that voids Jewish laws. In all their disputes, Jews are obligated to settle them in accordance with Jewish law and before Jewish tribunals." [92] It had become "the evil custom" for Jews to submit to outside authorities even though it was in defiance of the sentiments of their own religious authorities.

On the other hand, the religious authorities, too, recognized the right of a Gentile to summon a Jew to the secular tribunals. All decisions handed down by these courts for such disputes, as long as they are within the laws of the kingdom, are binding. *Dina D'Malkhuta* is applicable to all judgments be they even contrary to Jewish law. If a Jew purchases a property held by a Gentile as a result of such litigation, the original owner has no claim upon the property at all.[93]

In general, quite another story presented itself with regard to testimony in litigations involving a Jew and a non-Jew before a Gentile tribunal. Testimony rendered in favor of a Gentile and against a fellow Jew was permissible provided such testimony did not aid in arriving at a judgement which contradicted Jewish law. The Talmud ruled: "A Jew who testifies that his coreligionist owes money to a non-Jew is to be placed under the ban of excommunication." [94] In civil matters the testimony of one witness was not recognized by Jewish law as valid. If a deed or a note was presented with one witness, it was not valid.[95] The Jew, therefore, was not permitted to testify since the Gentile courts, in this instance, contradict Jewish law. However, two Jews may testify in favor of a Gentile since Jewish law as well would accept their testimony.[96] In the Middle Ages, R. Tam extended this talmudic decision to include the testimony of one witness in favor of a Gentile, when such testimony substantiates the claim of the Gentile that he does not owe anything to the Jew. Jewish law as well would demand that the burden of proof fall upon the alleged creditor. [97] Such testimony is permitted only when a Jew-Gentile litigation is involved. However, when the disputants are Jews, no one may testify in their behalf. It is considered aiding and abetting offenders in their transgressions.[98]

As time passed and Jews mingled far more freely with the non-Jewish world, the power of the Bet Din waned. Today, very few Jews would institute suit in a Jewish tribunal if, indeed, they are aware that such tribunals still exist. A once powerful and significant institution in Jewish life has all but disappeared except in areas dealing solely with religious law. How have the mighty fallen!

CHAPTER VIII

Documents of a Gentile Court

"All documents drawn up in a Gentile court, even if witnessed by Gentiles, are valid except for divorces and bills of manumission releasing a slave from his servitude." So reads a tannaitic ruling.[1] The Talmud distinguishes between documents that serve merely to substantiate a transaction, such as bills of sale and notes of indebtedness, etc., (where it may be understood why they are valid even if issued by a secular court), and documents that actually effect a transfer, such as deeds for a gift (which should not be recognized under such conditions.) [2] Two conclusions are mentioned in the Talmud. The first, by making use of Samuel's law, validates all such documents except those specifically excluded by the Tannaim.[3] The second recognizes the distinction previously made by the Talmud and emends the text of the Mishneh to exclude all documents that in themselves effect a change of condition.[4]

The Geonim, as we have seen,[5] ruled strictly according to the second conclusion. Just as they limited *Dina D'Malkhuta Dina* in general, so they limited the type and number of documents to be recognized when issued by a Gentile court. The early Spanish sages continued in the path trodden by the Geonim. They, too, ruled according to the second conclusion.[6]

The first change and innovation came during the 12th century when one codifier dissented from the opinion of his teachers and recognized, albeit with some reservation, the notes of indebtedness issued by a secular tribunal.[7] This presented the first deviation from the prevailing attitude and was not permitted to pass unchallenged. The traditional view was defended.[8] At this time, the approach to the talmudic passage still was the same as in earlier days; the first and second conclusions conflicted with each other. The first conclusion ruled in accordance with Samuel's law and validated all civil documents of the non-Jewish courts; the second conclusion accepted only such affidavits that served no greater purpose than as proof of a previous transaction.

A problem arose with regard to those authorities who ruled according to the second conclusion. On the one hand, they fully endorsed the acceptance of Samuel's dictum whereas at the same time, by denying the validity of all civil documents issued by the Gentile courts, they ruled against conclusion number one, which accepted *Dina D'Malkhuta Dina*. From the first conclusion it would appear that if *Dina D'Malkhuta* is operative, then no document could be excluded and no legal instrument of the secular courts could be challenged. How could the sages of Spain accept both simultaneously? Of course, the same may be asked of those concurring with the second conclusion in the Talmud. After all, Samuel's law was unquestionably accepted in talmudic times. How could conclusion number two deny this accepted precept?

It becomes obvious that the dispute of the two views concerns not the basic law of Samuel. Both opinions adopted his law. The dispute revolved about the limitation to Samuel's law. Was it to include all or only some documents? It was to this question that the Geonim and the early Spanish authorities addressed themselves. They saw *Dina D'Malkhuta Dina* in a limited light and would validate only bills of sale.

It was not until the next century that an entirely different approach developed. As commerce developed and relations between Jews and Gentiles became more intertwined, a new approach to the notary documents of the Gentile courts was necessary. The two opinions of the Talmud were re-evaluated. They no longer were considered as conflicting views. They were but two phases of one idea. When a specific decree of the king demanded the use of Gentile courts for all civil documents, then they were to be recognized as valid. "The law of the kingdom is the law." However, even when no such decree existed, some documents, such as bills of sale and promissory notes, were acceptable.[9] In accordance with this new approach, these authorities vested documents such as those transferring a gift or those that formally acknowledged an obligation (*Hoda'ah*), and those that released a debtor from payment (*Mehila*) with juridic status and binding powers. Even oral business transactions made by a Gentile court were binding.[10]

What caused this change with regard to the documents issued by the Gentile courts? Why did the religious authorities of Spain from the 13th century on accept the validity of all such documents heretofore rejected by their predecessors? An expanded system of commerce cannot be the reason since bills of sale had been acceptable for centuries and even promissory notes became valid by the 12th century. What, then, caused this change?

It appears that in the 13th century, Jews and non-Jews of Spain alike began to look upon all notary documents in a different light. Heretofore, some documents were the ones to actually effect a transference of property or right. As a result, such instruments were likened to divorces which were excluded by tannaitic rule. In this century, the Jewish and secular tribunals no longer vested these documents with such power. Acquisition required means other than the document itself. The document was relegated to serve merely as proof that a transaction had occurred. In other words, all documents now had the same status as bills of sale. As a result, *Dina D'Malkhuta* now included all civil documents issued by a Gentile court with only those excluded by the Mishneh left out.[11] Thus, deeds for a gift, wills,[12] and documents that admit to a loan or release a debtor from payment,[13] were recognized as legal no matter which court, Jewish or Gentile, issued them.

Documents issued by a Gentile court had equal validity with the ones issued by a Bet Din. They were equally binding and were vested with equal power. A bill of indebtedness that was lost and

106

was ordered re-written by a Gentile judge was sufficient to collect a loan.[14] Such documents placed a lien on the property of a defendant even if said property was no longer in his possession but had been sold subsequent to the loan.[15] However, if a flaw is detected in a document which would invalidate it before a Jewish court, even if it has the full support and recognition of the Gentile courts, the document is rendered valueless. The issue at hand would have to be settled as if it had been an oral transaction.[16] The documents of a Gentile court are equal to those issued by a Bet Din but they are not better nor have they greater power than those issued by the Jewish tribunals.[17] The documents must meet all conditions required by Jewish law as if they were actually issued by a Bet Din. For example, if the Gentile court issued a document for the sale of something not yet in existence (which presented no obstacle to the Gentile courts but which would be sufficient cause to invalidate the sale according to Jewish law), such a document is void. If such a bill of sale had been issued by a Bet Din, it would be no more than a meaningless piece of paper. Accordingly, the same document issued by a Gentile court under the same conditions can have no greater power or validity.[18] No king is concerned with the details concerning deeds and documents. A monarch may demand recognition of documents issued by his courts. *Dina D'Malkhuta Dina* applies to the courts and their right to issue such documents which must be accepted by Jews. Samuel's law is not to be applied to the specific forms and the details of these instruments.[19]

Jewish law governing the validity of such documents also came into conflict with regard to regulations involving interest. A responsum relates the following incidents: "For the sum of one hundred *sueldos* A "sold" B an annual tax of one *maravedi*, which became a lien on his land. In effect, B then held title to the land—it was so recognized by Spanish law which imposed the feudal transfer tax, known as *luismo*, on the lien. B continued in the possession of the field and the produce as long as

107

he met the annual tax. The "sale" was revocable, however, and A had the right to free himself from the tax and to regain free title to his property by refunding the original sum to B."[20]

Spanish law recognized such a document and considered the transaction as a legitimate "sale." Jewish law refused to recognize the transaction as anything more than a disguised interest bearing loan. *Dina D'Malkhuta Dina* could not alter the situation and could not invest the document with greater power than had it been issued by a Bet Din. In that case, too, it would not be recognized as a sale.[21]

The reverse situation was also true. A document issued by a Gentile court which contained a flaw according to the standards of the secular law, was not acceptable even if according to Jewish law the document was valid. In other words, Jewish law would not accept a document which was not acceptable according to the law of the kingdom. Jewish law will not go beyond the secular law.[22]

The 15th and 16th centuries brought no change in this basic attitude. The communities of North Africa or the Middle East recognized the documents of the Gentile courts when the king specifically demanded their acceptance,[23] but granted them only equal but not higher status. The details governing a transfer of ownership had to meet the strict requirements of Jewish law or else the document was ignored.[24] *Dina D'Malkhuta Dina* granted recognition to these documents as long as they recorded methods of transfer considered legal by Jewish law.[25]

In Italy, a difference of opinion arose with regard to the witnesses who signed such documents. On the basis of the above mentioned principle, namely, that the documents of a Gentile court had to conform with Jewish law in all details and could not exceed the authority of those documents issued by a Bet Din, it was stipulated that witnesses to such documents could not be related to each other or to either of the litigants involved. Thus, a receipt for payment of a debt (*Shober*) issued by a Gentile court which had signatories who were related to each other was not recognized by three of the sages.[26] One dissenting opinion is recorded. This stated, since Gentile witnesses, normally disqualified by Jewish law, are recognized when signing documents drawn up in a Gentile court because of *Dina D'Malkhuta Dina,* the Jewish law disqualifying relatives' testimony is similarly waived. Once a distinction has been made between witnesses acceptable in a Jewish court and in a Gentile court, a witness cannot be disqualified because of his inacceptability to a Jewish court. We rely on the Gentile court and the secular judge to determine the truth. *Dina D'Malkhuta Dina* granted Gentile judges this authority. The veracity of a document which passed the scrutiny of a Gentile court cannot be challenged on these grounds.[27]

The rabbis of Poland [28] also accepted such documents. However, they, too, stipulated that in order to accept such documents, a specific demand on the part of the king was required, or else *Dina D'Malkhuta Dina* was not operative. Poland of that era had no such decree. As a consequence, only bills of sale or promissory notes issued by the secular tribunals were acceptable, provided they did not counter Jewish law.[29] In areas which were only sparsely populated by Jews and where Jewish courts or scribes could not be readily found, Jews were permitted to avail themselves of the Gentile courts and utilize their services with regard to all documents. Such a situation is comparable to a requirement made by the State that the royal courts be accepted since no other courts were accessible.[30] Of course, here, too, the rabbis demanded that the documents of a Gentile court were not to exceed in authority those issued by the Bet Din.[31] In the 17th century in Holland it was agreed that although Jewish law allowed the creditor to release a debt even after he sold the note he was holding,[32] it could not be done with a note issued by a Gentile court. *Dina D'Malkhuta Dina* does not recognize such manipulations, and as a result, the documents cannot be set aside.[33]

A century later still another question was raised with regard to documents not valid according to the law of the kingdom. Do such documents maintain their validity according to Jewish law? Does the law of the kingdom destroy their validity completely?

Jewish law believed the debtor who claimed to have paid his personal note even if he did not reclaim his I.O.U.,[34] a view not shared by the secular law of 18th century Hungary. Governmental law recognized no such claim against a creditor who held a valid I.O.U. The practice of that day was to write such promissory notes in the manner prescribed by the secular law (*Wechsel*). *Dina D'Malkhuta Dina* validated this practice even though Jewish law itself would have disallowed the creditor's claims in the event the debtor claimed prior payment. This held true as long as the I.O.U. was a valid one, fulfilling all the requirements made by secular law. If all conditions were not met, the perpetrator could be fined by the court. A creditor who accepted a post-dated promissory note, could not present the I.O.U. before a Gentile court, lest he be fined. When he presented the note to the Bet Din, one authority ruled that since *Dina D'Malkhuta Dina* would not be operative, the note should now be adjudged according to Jewish law. The claim made by the debtor that he had paid the note would then be honored.[35] The respondent who was asked to examine the above mentioned ruling came to the same conclusion; namely, that the note was valueless.[36] However, he arrived at this ruling by another method of reasoning. He concluded that this note was but a scrap of paper because "the law of the kingdom is the law" and secular law completely invalidated a post-dated promissory note. Jewish law could not invest this note with new powers.[37]

The will and the *Ketubah* stand out in rabbinic literature as the two documents which Jews most often submitted to the Gentile courts. To be sure, the Geonim, Alfasi, Maimonides, Ibn Daud of Posquieres, and Meir b. Todros Halevy Abulafia considered wills on a par with the other documents that were disqualified when issued by a Gentile court.[38] However, in the 13th

110

century, wills were included among such documents that were
recognized even when issued by a Gentile court.[39] Of course, not
everyone recognized this lenient point of view. Some authorities
strenuously protested any such recognition. *Dina D'Malkhuta
Dina* had no place with regard to inheritance laws lest the laws
of the Torah be nullified.[40] In the 14th century, the question was
still open and one authority cited Maimonides as also permitting
wills to be issued by Gentile courts. They argued that the transference of the property to be inherited took place by word of
mouth and that the document of the will merely served as proof.
This would make the will similar to the deed of sale which is to
be recognized even when issued by a Gentile court.[41] Despite this
change in attitude a *haskama* was issued in the 16th century involving the communities of Salonika, Safed, and Constantinople
forbidding anyone to subject an inheritance or a *Ketuba* to a
Gentile court.[42]

The *Ketuba* at times consisted of two parts, the basic requirements necessary for every marriage, and the *Tosafot Ketuba,*
the voluntary additions to the *Ketuba* which were determined by
the wishes of each husband and the customs of each community.
In 13th century Spain, it was recognized that the voluntary aspect of the dowry may be determined by the custom and law of
the land. Thus, *Dina D'Malkhuta Dina* determined the law for
these additions to the *Ketuba*.[43] In later days, when checks came
into use, the additional parts of the *Ketuba* could be paid by
means of a check which was validated by "the law of the kingdom."[44]

The *Ketuba* itself, when written by a Gentile court, even if
written in a foreign language,[45] has validity and is similar to any
other promissory note.[46] It is valid even if the secular tribunals
insert conditions not acceptable to Jewish law, e.g., that the
wife inherit half her husband's property after his demise,[47] or
that the wife's children inherit the property.[48] Even when a marriage was performed by a secular court, although it was not rec-

ognized by Jewish law, nevertheless the *Ketuba* issued by the court was a valid document.[49] In any case, the prevailing secular customs regarding dowries were binding upon Jewish husbands as well, whether or not they specifically incorporated these conditions into the *Ketuba* they offered their wives. It was the accepted practice that all marriages were consummated upon the basis of contemporary custom. The *Ketuba* and its clauses, recorded or not, were thus affected by secular practices. "The law of the kingdom is the law" had bearing upon all such matters.[50]

In North Africa, the Jews adopted another instrument that was in use in addition to the *Ketuba*. The *sadak* was a document issued by the Moslem court granting a wife a marriage settlement. The purpose was to grant the wife additional means to collect her due allotment. The *sadak* could be collected in a secular tribunal. It was also payable during the husband's lifetime, whereas the *Ketuba* came due only upon her husband's death or in case a divorce was issued. However, the amount collected by means of the *sadak* was to be deducted from her *Ketuba*.[51] If she collected her *Ketuba,* she had to at the same time surrender the *sadak*.[52]

Whenever the Jew was granted permission to make use of the Gentile courts, be it for litigation, or for the use of documents issued, it was only when such courts did not accept bribes. Bribes were common and were even included in the total expenses of a litigation.[53]

Some authorities demanded direct testimony to prove a specific Gentile court immune to bribery. Only when there was direct evidence that this court never accepted bribery might it be endorsed.[54] If this opinion were to be followed, it would completely eliminate the use of Gentile courts as a force in Jewish life. No court could ever be cleared in so definite a manner, no matter how honest it be. No witness could testify that a court *never* took bribes.[55] Other authorities concluded that the average Gentile court does not take bribes,[56] and their judges do not lie.[57] A Gentile court is disqualified only when there is evidence or testimony of its having accepted bribes.[58] Direct evidence was necessary to disqualify a court. Rumor of bribes alone was not sufficient.[59]

Interesting is a third view found in the 15th century in North Africa. This view reached a conclusion worth noting. The average non-Jew is ready to accept bribes at all times. "Their mouths speak falsehood [60] and their right hands are filled with bribes." [61] Even so, their courts are to be recognized and their legal instruments accepted because "the law of the kingdom is the law" and the law demands that these courts be accepted, albeit their decisions are influenced by the bribes that are offered them.[62]

Judges who were paid well and who had much to lose by chancing bribery were accepted as honest. The stakes were too great for them to risk their positions for the sake of a quick, illegal profit. Nonetheless, the practice in 16th century Palestine was to test the honesty of these judges by purposely offering them bribes to see their reactions.[63]

The same prerequisites were required of Gentile scribes. Although the Talmud excluded a group of Gentile laymen who set themselves up as arbitrators from exercising any legal or juridic powers,[64] nonetheless, the scribes who stood near the outskirts of the cities or those who wandered through the streets were recognized to the extent that their documents were valid if they were granted permission to act as scribes by the king and if they were known to resist bribes.[65] Certainly, if one was appointed to a city as the official scribe, he would not allow false documents to be issued. In all civil matters, we follow the ways of the country and its customs.[66] A notary public, that is, a scribe appointed by the king, may issue a document even if it contains the signature of only one witness. This document is to be honored. "The law of the kingdom is the law" and the king insists that these notaries be honest in their tasks.[67] It appears that a more careful selection of the calibre of men was made when they were appointed by the king to the post of notary public. Only trusted men were accepted and only their decisions were to be considered binding. They stood on an equal plane with the secular courts. However, those scribes who were appointed by the courts and not by the king were not as well screened. As a consequence, such scribes were accorded status equal to that of the secular courts only when they performed their duties before such a court. They merited no endorsement of their own. Their work had to be corroborated by a court.[68] In conclusion, we may say that the religious jurists, while often showing a tendency to be hesitant in recognizing Gentile legal instruments, continually accepted more and more of these documents as the situation demanded. They soon recognized the full validity of most documents issued by Christian courts or notaries. Sometimes when it was noticed that a particular notarial practice was worthwhile, the Jewish community accepted and emulated the practice found in the Gentile courts.[69] Thus, necessity and business expediency paved the way to greater acceptance of all Gentile legal instruments. Today, with the exception of religious documents, the instruments of the secular courts are fully accepted.

CHAPTER IX

Kings Over Israel

As the years went by and Jewish history unfolded, the land of Israel and the people became one. History records many exiles, many conquests of the land, but the Jewish people never relinquished its special feeling for the land and never considered the land outside its possession. The rabbis of the Talmud considered the land to be in Israel's possession even prior to their entrance to its borders.[1]

During times when the Land of Israel or Judea was conquered by foreign powers, the laws of the conquerors were obeyed. The conquered Jews obeyed Rome but would never admit to the legitimacy of Roman rights to the Holy Land. They certainly did not consider establishing a principle that "the law of the kingdom is the law" as was later set forth by the Amora, Samuel. This maxim is never mentioned in the tannaitic sources nor in the Palestinian Talmud.[2] Samuel's law could only see the light of day in the diaspora. In Judea, Jews would never willingly acknowledge foreign rule.

Some modern day scholars, although in agreement that *Dina D'Malkhuta Dina* was not known in the Land of Israel, are equally convinced that the rabbis of the Babylonian Talmud extended Samuel's law to include Israel as well.[3] Their arguments reduce themselves to the following three.

First, the Talmud [4] finds a contradiction between Samuel's precept that "the law of the kingdom is the law," and R. Akiba's ruling [5] that evasion of the taxes demanded by the Romans was permissible. If *Dina D'Malkhuta Dina,* why should such evasions be permitted? The scholars concluded that *Dina D'Malkhuta Dina* included Judea as well as the diaspora, or else the Talmud could have solved the contradiction by stating that R. Akiba's permis-

115

sion to evade taxation involved Judea, which was not affected by Samuel's law. Since the Talmud did not make such a distinction, it is evident that the Babylonian Amoraim considered *Dina D'Malkhuta Dina* also binding in Judea.[6]

Secondly, another Mishneh[7] is explained by the Talmud on the basis of Samuel's law. The Mishneh originated in Judea, yet the Talmud makes no distinction between the application of Samuel's law in the diaspora or in Judea. Again the conclusion was reached that the Babylonian Amoraim extended the jurisdiction of *Dina D'Malkhuta Dina* to Judea as well.

Finally, the following passage recorded in the Palestinian Talmud in the name of R. Yohanan was cited:[8] "Ere the Romans came, it was permissible to bribe the officer in charge of quartering soldiers so that he would settle them in the homes of others. However, the same practice was forbidden after the advent of the Romans." [9] It is the opinion of these scholars that here we find evidence that *Dina D'Malkhuta Dina* was valid even in Israel. What other reason would there be for forbidding the act, except that it be against the law of the kingdom?

We shall now examine these arguments *seriatim*. Regarding R. Akiba's permission to evade government taxes, it is obvious why he ruled so. Akiba lived during the time of the Bar Kokhba revolt and was a staunch supporter of the rebellion. It is hardly likely that such a man would urge the Jews to pay their taxes and support the very conquerors whom he and the other patriots were attempting to drive out from their borders. It is inconceivable that at such distressing times, *Dina D'Malkhuta Dina* should be invoked. The Talmud did not question Akiba's stand with regard to tax evasion, a stand which needed no justification. The problem facing the Talmud is how to justify Samuel's law which apparently is in opposition to Akiba's ruling. Even if the Babylonian Amoraim interpreted *Dina D'Malkhuta Dina* to include Judea of their day, as these modern scholars claim, it would not affect Akiba's position. He, living earlier than they, had no knowledge

of *Dina D'Malkhuta Dina.* The concept had not yet been established. Let us then assume that the Babylonian Amoraim did
understand *Dina D'Malkhuta Dina* to include Judea. The Talmud
still could have made the distinction that R. Akiba's permission
does not contradict Samuel, since R. Akiba himself did not accept
Dina D'Malkhuta Dina in Judea, whereas, he would certainly
not have granted equal permission in the diaspora, where *Dina
D'Malkhuta Dina* was operative. Nothing may be proven from this
talmudic passage. The problem facing the Talmud, as we have
stated before, is to justify Samuel's law which cannot oppose the
views of the Tannaim.

Similarly, we cannot conclude that the Mishneh[10] was based
upon Samuel's law simply because it was explained by means of
his law. On the contrary, we see that another opinion emended
the text.[11] Furthermore, it was not the Mishneh which needed
justification, it was Samuel's law which cannot be in contradiction to a Mishneh.

There were some who were of the opinion that the principle
"the law of the kingdom is the law" originated prior to Samuel.[12]
They argued that there is ample proof that the law long antedated
Samuel who merely re-affirmed it and gave it its legal formula-
tion.[13] The same mishnaic texts are cited to substantiate their
position.[14] They argued: "How can the Amoraim attempt to explain these laws of the Mishneh established so many years before
Samuel by means of a principle he originated? It must be that this
principle was not new."

Again it must be said that the question of the Talmud is not
how is the Mishneh understood. The Mishneh requires no justification. If there is a contradiction, then it is Samuel's law which cannot be allowed to contradict the mishnaic precepts. Also, since
in one instance the Talmud proposes two different explanations
for the Mishneh, we may conclude that the original reasoning and
basis for this mishnaic law was no longer known.

Lastly, the passage of the Palestinian Talmud has nothing

117

whatever to do with *Dina D'Malkhuta Dina.* The ruling that prohibits or permits the bribing of an officer concerns itself with the communal burdens that must be shared by everyone within a city's borders and the prohibition against any attempt on the part of an individual to shirk his responsibilities. When there is no specific obligation that a community has, it is permissible for an individual to anticipate such demands to his own benefit. He can not do so *post facto;* that is, he cannot exclude himself from a communal burden once that burden has become a fact for the entire community and all its residents, including himself.[15]

We conclude that during the tannaitic and amoraic periods, not only the rabbis of the Palestinian Talmud but also those of the Babylonian Talmud considered Samuel's law not binding for Judea. It was operative for diaspora Jewry alone. Furthermore, the Geonim, as well, excluded Israel from Samuel's precept.[16]

The twelfth and thirteenth centuries brought a change of attitude. Differences of opinion arose with regard to this matter. The discussion, largely academic, continued for centuries. It may be divided into three parts, each of which will be discussed separately. (1) Did *Dina D'Malkhuta Dina* apply to Gentile kings or foreign powers who successfully invaded and conquered the Land of Israel? (2) Did Samuel's law affect a Jewish king or the government in the Land of Israel? (3) Finally, did a Jewish king or official enjoy the powers granted by Samuel's law if he ruled outside of the Land of Promise?

The first explicit[17] statement concerning any of these questions was made by the Tosafists.[18] As we have seen, they contended that "the law of the kingdom is the law," but only when it concerned non-Jewish kings. They owned the land. They could at will expel anyone who disobeyed their decrees. The Tosafists maintained that *no* Jewish king in Israel had that right. The Land of Israel is owned cooperatively by all Jews. As a consequence, no Jewish king in Israel could legislate in accordance with his own understanding. He could not contradict Jewish law.

The exclusion of a Jewish king from enjoying the benefits of Samuel's law holds true in the Land of Israel only. Israel is the land which all Jews own in partnership. The rights to the land are an inheritance bequeathed to all, the common Jew and the Jewish king alike.[19] This is not so when a Jewish king or officer reigns in the diaspora. In this instance, the Jewish and Gentile kings enjoy equal status.[20] In the diaspora, it is the ruler who owns the land and enjoys the power to expel anyone who does not live up to his ordinances.

This dichotomy between a Jewish king ruling in or outside of Israel is possible only when *Dina D'Malkhuta Dina* is viewed in the light of the Tosafist opinion. The two central features, according to this view, are the exclusive ownership by the king of all the land within the borders of his nation, and the power of expulsion and deportation held by the sovereign. Neither of these rights are part of the powers granted a Jewish king in Israel. However, no such distinction can be made if the opinion of R. Samuel b. Meir regarding *Dina D'Malkhuta Dina* is accepted.[21] This opinion focuses its attention upon the "free will acceptance of a monarch" by the subjects of a country. Hence, it would appear that the location of the kingdom, be it the Land of Israel, or elsewhere, has no bearing upon the situation. *Dina D'Malkhuta Dina* is a law which applies to all kings if they are freely accepted by their subjects.

The opposite becomes evident when we deal with a Gentile king who conquered the Holy Land. The Tosafists would recognize *Dina D'Malkhuta Dina* as operative in the Land of Israel since the right of deportation is his, signifying his ownership of the land. Samuel b. Meir would disagree. No foreign king was ever really accepted by the conquered people of the Land of Israel. No foreign king could claim *Dina D'Malkhuta Dina* under such conditions.[22]

One other pertinent fact must be mentioned which has bearing upon this discussion. The powers of a Jewish king were delineated in the book of Samuel of the Bible.[23] Nonetheless, in tannaitic days, it was not clear to the rabbis whether the Bible, by enumerating the various powers of a king in this passage, granted these as the inherent rights of all kings,[24] or whether the listing of such powers was merely a method of discouraging the people of Israel from choosing a king.[25] The prophet cited all the burdens that would be cast upon their shoulders if a king assumed the leadership instead of the judges who had been in power. Most of the authorities of the Middle Ages decided in favor of the former opinion.[26] They equated the tannaitic and amoraic decision which granted a Jewish king the powers enumerated by the Bible to the concept of *Dina D'Malkhuta Dina* applicable to a Gentile king. The two were identical.[27] If the king has rights, and we see that he has, then it is because *Dina D'Malkhuta Dina* applies to Jewish kings in the Land of Israel as well. In fact, some authorities looked upon *Dina D'Malkhuta Dina* as applied to a Gentile king as an extension and corollary of the primary law, namely, the rights granted a Jewish king.[28]

The dissenting minority opinion had a number of difficulties to contend with. First, according to the accepted rules of the Talmud, in a dispute between the rabbis here involved, the decision should go in favor of granting these rights to Jewish kings.[29] Second, some of the authorities appeared to waver in their decisions.[30] At times they ruled one way and at other times they ruled in opposition to their own views.[31]

By the 15th and 16th centuries, distinctions were no longer made between the kings of Israel, the land of Israel, or the diaspora. A number of rabbis stated that the kings of ancient Judea, when the state was under foreign domination, ruled the land by means of the concept that "the law of the kingdom is the law." The Persians, the Syrians, the Romans, and others, appointed some kings of Judea, who ruled Judea by the powers vested in them by the conquerors of the kingdom.[32]

Even the Palestinian sages of these centuries held that *Dina*

D'Malkhuta Dina was applicable to Palestine as well. The question was posed concerning the Jewish refugees of Tiberias. They had fled Tiberias because of the dangers threatening them and remained in exile in the city of Sepporis for over a year. The native residents of Sepporis demanded that the refugees share their tax burdens. Any individual who resided in a city over one year must pay taxes to this city. The exiles refused to allow themselves to be taxed twice. They claimed that their responsibilities to the king were fulfilled when they remitted their taxes to the people of their home town, Tiberias.

A recognized authority of Safed, as well as another authority of Salonika, ruled that "the law of the kingdom is the law," and that law demands that they fulfill their tax duty in Tiberias. No man must pay double his taxes and neither must these exiles pay again in their city of refuge.[33] In addition, should the king demand double his amount, that is, payment from two residences, it is considered royal robbery.[34] Thus *Dina D'Malkhuta Dina* was applicable in Palestine not only to force a positive act of tax payment, but also to justify the evasion of an unjust, extortionate tax.

In another responsum we also find that *Dina D'Malkhuta Dina* was operative in Palestine. Many of the Jewish authorities of the sixteenth century Turkish Empire agreed that Jews were obligated to accept and abide by the Turkish law forbidding them to purchase and own slaves.[35] It was the law of the kingdom and because of Samuel's maxim must not be violated.[36] Others disagreed with the ruling. They felt that the law restricting Jews from owning slaves was discriminatory and *Dina D'Malkhuta Dina* is only valid when it applies equally to all people of the kingdom.[37] Furthermore, slave trade is not of direct concern to the monarch but is a private matter involving individual Jews.[38] Which opinion we choose is not relevant to our discussion. Suffice it to say, that none excluded *Dina D'Malkhuta Dina* because the situation occurred in the Holy Land. They accepted the premise that *Dina D'Malkhuta Dina* applies to Palestine as well.[39]

The talmudic concept of "rebellion against the king" (*Mored be'Malkhut*) must be discussed at this point. How is this concept different from Samuel's law of *Dina D'Malkhuta Dina?* If we should reach the conclusion that these are but two technical terms for the same principle, then we must again conclude, that *Dina D'Malkhuta Dina* was operative with Jewish kings in the Land of Israel.

First, a word about the concept of *Mored be'Malkhut.* The Talmud [40] arrives at this concept by citing the biblical verse: "Whosoever that doth rebel against thy commandment, and will not hearken unto thy words in all that thou commandest him, he shall be put to death." [41] Herein they affirm the power of a king to bid his subjects according to his will. He may tell anyone what to do and what not to do and disobedience could be punished by death.

The Talmud [42] and the later day scholars [43] limit this power so that a king may exercise this right only as long as he does not expect the subject to violate Jewish law in fulfilling the king's commands. It appears as if at first no difference was made between the two concepts. They were freely interchanged.[44] However, in the nineteenth century a clear distinction was made based upon the above mentioned limitation. In all decrees that do not involve Jewish law, that is, where Jewish law is silent, then the subject must obey his king or else be considered a "rebel" (*Mored be'-Malkhut*).[45] The concept of *Dina D'Malkhuta Dina* is required only when the edict countermands Jewish law. Of course, no Jewish king was permitted to do so. *Dina D'Malkhuta Dina* could apply only to Gentile kings.[46]

In conclusion, we may summarize our findings as follows: Samuel's law of *Dina D'Malkhuta Dina* did not include the monarchs of Judea. From the amoraic times to the fifteenth century, no one explicitly states that *Dina D'Malkhuta Dina* includes the Holy Land. This was true for Jewish kings and certainly was the case for non-Jewish kings. The Jews of Palestine or of the diaspora would not recognize any foreign power. However, from the fifteenth century on, no distinction was made. The rabbis looked back into history and saw that the power of Ezra and the kings of Judea rested upon the authority vested in them by the foreign conquerors.

As far as Jewish kings were concerned, by and large the rabbinic literature agrees that *Dina D'Malkhuta Dina* has no meaning for such a king. The land is not his alone and he, too, must abide by the laws of the Torah. However, in the diaspora, quite a number of scholars granted a Jewish king equal status with any other monarch. He, as any other king, was the secular head and his word was law.

It is worthy of comment, that the very principle which provided the *modus vivendi* for the Jew to live outside the Land of Israel also helped preserve his attachment to the land to which he refused to give up his title. "The law of the kingdom" presupposed legal title; i.e., the prevailing authorities must first be recognized as the legal rulers of the land. By not allowing *Dina D'Malkhuta* to be operative with regard to the conquerors of Palestine, the Jews silently proclaimed that legally this land might never be taken from them.[47]

CHAPTER X

Civil and Religious Law

The students of rabbinic literature, as well as modern scholars, have concluded that Samuel's precept, "the law of the kingdom is the law," was, and could only be invoked in connection with civil law.[1] Such a conclusion seems quite evident from the talmudic sources that cite *Dina D'Malkhuta Dina*. The Talmud mentions this concept only in connection with civil matters. It is invoked in the question of the validity of Gentile instruments prepared, signed, and issued by non-Jewish tribunals.[2] It is also cited with regard to the sale and purchase of real-estate,[3] the collection and payment of taxes,[4] and a number of other civil matters.[5] Nowhere in the Talmud may this principle be found in connection with religious law. Of course, an argument of silence is not a sufficient argument and the fact that it was not applied to religious law is not conclusive evidence that such application is ruled out.

The Geonim specifically approve the right of kings to demand obedience to their edicts. Just as the Divine Being rules over the entire universe, so do kings govern the subjects of their land. However, such power is granted to the crown in civil matters only, and is not to be extended to religious law.[6]

The rabbis of France and Germany and the sages of Spain agreed that only in civil matters may *Dina D'Malkhuta Dina* be cited. In the 11th century, Rashi declared: "the law of the kingdom is the law even if those involved are Jews, with the exception of divorces, because Gentiles are excluded therefrom by Jewish law but are commanded to establish all civil laws." [7] Rashi's grandsons continued in the same tone. The elder, Samuel b. Meir, averred that *Dina D'Malkhuta Dina* applies to "the payment of regular and special taxes and to all decrees promulgated by the government. No one may consider property or money held by another Jew as stolen goods when such holding is permitted by the law of the kingdom." [8] The entire discussion dealt only with cases involving civil law. The younger grandson, Jacob b. Meir Tam, who based the entire principle as formulated by the Amora, Samuel, upon the general talmudic power granted to the Bet Din to declare private property as *res nullius,* certainly limited *Dina D'Malkhuta Dina* to civil law, for only in civil matters does the Bet Din enjoy such powers. [9]

In Spain, during the same century, Maimonides came to the very same decision. "In all civil matters, we act in accordance with the laws of the king." [10] Similarly, a century later, Ibn Adret concurred with the above mentioned conception of *Dina D'Malkhuta Dina.* "The basic principle is that in all economic matters we follow the decisions of the kingdom and its customs." [11] Adret ruled that *Dina D'Malkhuta Dina* was binding in civil law even if such law contradicted the decisions of Jewish law. [12]

The general rule may be stated that *Dina D'Malkhuta Dina* is only operative in civil matters and is never to be invoked when religious law is at stake. No king, no officer, and no government was given the power to legislate when such ordinances nullified Jewish religious law.

There appear to be numerous exceptions to this general statement. Quite a number of responsa and other rabbinic sources of the Middle Ages and of modern times, at first glance, seem to expand Samuel's law to include religious law as well. Sources of Franco-German and Spanish origin will be cited which apparently breached the fences that contained Samuel's maxim within the confines of civil jurisprudence and although misinterpreted, nonetheless served as supports and sources of quotations for later-day Reform Judaism.

Let us examine these sources collectively and individually. It must be recognized that in Jewish jurisprudence purely civil matters are non-existent. All matters of economics are intertwined and interwoven with religious law. Intentional misappropriation of funds or property, or other devious business methods leave the culprit guilty not only of civil violations that may be punished by nullification of the particular transaction and by payment of losses as well as fines, but also guilty of violating the religious command, "Thou shalt not steal." It is a crime and a sin. Despite such indirect involvement of religious law that arises as a result of civil cases, *Dina D'Malkhuta Dina* is applicable. If, as a result of a civil dispute, a Jew was summoned to a Gentile court and was required to take an oath, he was permitted to do so despite the fact that the taking of an oath involves a religious matter.[13] If *Dina D'Malkhuta Dina* decides a civil matter, then all religious laws that are thereafter determined as an indirect result of the civil matter are included in Samuel's precept.[14]

Now let us examine a number of responsa and see how this principle was applied.[15]

In one responsum, written in Egypt at the end of the 15th or the early part of the 16th century, a Jew was given permission to pick *etrogim* in the groves of a Moslem and was permitted to use these fruits to fulfill the commandment prescribed for the holiday of Succot. The fruits or the land while in the hands of the Moslem were not considered stolen goods (*Gezel*), which would disqualify them from use in the performance of the holiday ritual, even though the Moslem or his ancestors had robbed the land years ago. "The law of the kingdom is the law" and the law stated that anyone who possessed a valid deed was the proper owner of the land.[16]

Here, too, the application of *Dina D'Malkhuta Dina* may involve ritual or religious law. However, this is but an indirect consequence of Samuel's principle. Primarily, *Dina D'Malkhuta Dina* decides the proper ownership of the land and once that is established, then the permission or the prohibition with regard to the *etrogim* naturally follows.

In 16th century Palestine, yet another responsum was pen-ned.[17] It, too, falls into the category now discussed. Joseph Caro granted permission to the Jews of a city to purchase the right to set up an *Erub* (*Reshut*) from the king or his appointee and did not require them to do so from each and every non-Jewish home-owner who lived in the city, as did some earlier authorities. The purchase of *Reshut* permitted the Jews of the city to carry things on the Sabbath which would otherwise be prohibited. Caro based his ruling on the precept that *Dina D'Malkhuta Dina,* and the king has definite claims to the land and to the homes of all his citizens.[18]

Once more, it must be clearly understood that Joseph Caro does not here permit or prohibit carrying on the Sabbath, which belongs to the realm of religious law. *Reshut* must be purchased from non-Jewish home owners. The question Caro had to re-solve was—is or is not the king to be considered a rightful owner or at least as someone who has definite rights and claims to all homes of the city? Caro concludes that *Dina D'Malkhuta Dina* definitely gives the king such powers. This aspect of the question deals with civil law alone. The consequence which permits car-rying on the Sabbath is but a natural and indirect result of this decision. It is not *Dina D'Malkhuta Dina* which is applied to re-ligious law.

In some instances, where at first glance it would appear that *Dina D'Malkhuta Dina* was applied to religious law, further in-vestigation reveals that other considerations play their roles. A very good example is the case of the Spanish king who devalued his currency and by a specific government ordinance stipulated the exact rates which were to be operative when repaying a loan. If currency fluctuation brings this rate up above the value of the original loan, one authority of 13th century Spain ordered the pay-ment of the highter rate, even though ordinarily this would con-stitute "increase."[19] By no means does this imply that *Dina D'Malkhuta Dina* was applied to religious law. Quite to the con-trary, the ruling defines the prohibition against "increase" as de-pending upon the intention of the participants involved. In this

127

particular situation there was no intention for "increase" on the part of the creditor or the lender.[20]

Quite similar was the ruling of another authority who stated that a creditor is not obliged to hold a security (*Mashkon*) longer than one year. Once the year is over, he may sell the security in order to receive payment for his loan. This is true even if the value of the security exceeds the amount of the loan. It is not considered "increase," for "the law of the kingdom is the law." [21]

Here, too, *Dina D'Malkhuta Dina* is not applied to religious law. The security a debtor gives to his creditor is given in its entirety and against the entire loan. It matters nought what the value of the security might be. It might be worth only a fraction of the loan or it may be far in excess of its value. By giving the security, the debtor barters the loan for the security. This is the ruling of this authority. It has nothing whatever to do with applying *Dina D'Malkhuta Dina* to religious law.

An individual's or a community's oath or *herem* could not be set aside or disqualified by the civil authorities. Even should a king stipulate that no vow may become final and binding unless it be affirmed and approved by a certain appointed individual, be he even a Jew, such an edict is not to be accepted. "The law of the kingdom" is not operative in religious matters. No one can nullify or affirm another's vow except a husband for his wife and a father for his minor daughter.[22] It is absolute nonsense to rule that a vow may not violate a Mitzvah, the Mitzvah in this case being the maxim of *Dina D'Malkhuta Dina*. Samuel's law cannot be used to abrogate Jewish religious law.[23]

Slavery, still quite common by the 16th century, presented another problem. According to Jewish law, slavery was not merely a civil and economic matter, but entailed religious law as well. To cite but one area involving religious law, we might point out that the status of the non-Jewish slave determines whether or not he may marry a Jewish mate.

Prior to the 16th century, the Spanish authorities ruled that the non-Jewish slave may not convert except with the consent of his Jewish master and then only after he was granted a "bill of manumission." [24] The non-Jew who failed to pay his taxes was to enter into servitude, by order of the king, to him who paid the tax for him. Should he desire to free himself from servitude, it was required that he obtain a "bill of manumission."[25] "The law of the kingdom is the law" and by order of that law the tax delinquent becomes a full fledged slave [26] who requires a "bill of manumission" should he desire to convert to Judaism.[27] Without such a release he could not marry a Jewish spouse.[28]

During the sixteenth century, under Turkish rule, many authorities continued this policy. In Egypt, one authority stated that it was the accepted practice since the days of the early *Negidim,*[29] to deny the secular powers the right to supersede Jewish religious law. *Dina D'Malkhuta Dina* could not be applied to religious law. A "bill of manumission" was not recognized when issued by a Gentile court because slavery belongs not only to civil but to religious law as well.[30]

Up to this point, *Dina D'Malkhuta Dina* was operative only insofar as the status of ownership of the slave was concerned. *Dina D'Malkhuta Dina* allowed the individual who paid the tax to become the master of the delinquent. Similarly, the king may allow a soldier of his army to become the master of any war captive, be that captive Jewish or non-Jewish. "The law of the kingdom is the law" is applicable in this matter.[31] However, there appears one dissenting and very difficult view expressed in a responsum of this century in Salonika. The case involved a non-Jewish female slave whose Jewish master wished to marry her. Since the law of the kingdom was that Jews may not own slaves in the Moslem countries, the decision was rendered that the marriage could take place even without granting the slave a "bill of manumission." [32] Accordingly, it appears that this authority applied *Dina D'Malkhuta Dina* even to religious law. It would be one thing had this master purchased the female slave in Turkey.

Perhaps then it might have been ruled that because of the law of the kingdom, the individual in question never assumed the status of a slave. *Dina D'Malkhuta Dina* would be applied to ownership which is purely civil law. However, the case in question involved a woman who was brought by her master from other lands where the label of slavery as far as she was concerned had already been placed upon her. According to this decision, Samuel's principle removed her status of being a slave which involved religious law.[33]

The 17th and 18th centuries, in the countries under Ashkenazic influence, brought to light yet another circumstance in which *Dina D'Malkhuta Dina* was applied to determine a particular fact, without being influenced by the consequences. The identity of a deceased person may be established by means of *Dina D'Malkhuta Dina* even though a "constrained woman" (*Agunah*) will thereby be released for marriage. A mishnaic ruling deemed testimony to a hanging insufficient to allow the wife to remarry. Testimony must include witnessing death itself.[34] Nonetheless, in the 17th century, the rabbis accepted the fact of death even if the testimony only described the Jew hanging from the gallows. The death penalty was carried out by the secular authorities and secular law demanded that the victim's neck be broken. *Dina D'Malkhuta Dina* was sufficient to establish the fact of death. It determined this fact and had nothing whatsoever to do with the religious aspect of permitting the widow to marry.[35]

In the same manner, we find that a Jew identified the murdered body of a fellow Jew by means of his clothing. However, the garments were by the side of the body and at the time the witness arrived at the scene were not worn by the deceased. An 18th century rabbi ruled that the law of the kingdom demanded a coroner's examination in the case of death by unknown causes, and in order to comply with this ordinance, the deceased's clothing must be removed. Jewish law accepted the fact that the clothing found belonged to the deceased and their identification was tantamount to the identification of the person. The widow would be permitted to marry.[36] Here again, it is a procedural fact which is accepted on the basis of *Dina D'Malkhuta Dina*. Samuel's law does not determine the consequences resulting after the fact. It is not applied to religious law.

A death certificate sent to the family of a Jewish soldier by army officials is recognized as evidence of death. This certificate is equal in legality to the documents issued by a Gentile court. The fact of death is established by *Dina D'Malkhuta Dina*. The consequence of this fact has nothing to do with religious law. The widow may remarry.[37]

A Jewish doctor, descended from the priestly family (*Kohen*) was prohibited from performing such an examination. Biblical law does not permit a *Kohen* to come in contact with the dead. The secular law, demanding that such an examination be conducted, cannot abrogate Jewish religious law. The Jewish doctor of priestly descent must decline to perform such an examination.[38] The same ruling would apply if the government does not permit burial at all without a doctor's certification.[39]

In modern days when post offices exist even in the most remote places of the world, a missing man can always get in touch with his family by letter. The newspapers are an excellent medium of communication which missing persons or their families may utilize. The Austro-Hungarian courts estimated twelve months to be sufficient time for anyone to respond were he alive. Jews could not accept this as proof of death, but utilized the law of the land whenever it might free the *Agunah*.[40]

The Ashkenazic rabbis also recognized that *Dina D'Malkhuta Dina* at times might bring about indirect consequences that would determine religious law. Legal tender which has this status only because of *Dina D'Malkhuta Dina* may be used to betroth a woman. This may be done whether or not the currency actually is worth as much as the government states it is. However, with regard to the redemption of the first born, actual value is necessary. To be sure, a woman must be aware of the amount she receives.

131

However, people in general recognize currency with the value stipulated by the government. This is not so with the redemption of that which belongs to the Almighty.[41]

In this period, it was also recognized that *Dina D'Malkhuta Dina* establishes the ownership of property. Once ownership was established, the resultant consequences, be they even religious in nature, were considered indirect results. It was felt that *Dina D'Malkhuta Dina* had no bearing upon these results. A legal dispute arose when Jews of Moravia informed against their brethren, accusing them of tax evasion. Each time they made out a "bill of sale" for the transfer of "leavened products" prior to the Passover holidays, they ignored the government regulation requiring a tax-seal to be placed upon all legal documents. The Austrian Emperor exempted Jews from complying with this demand, stating that everyone knows that such sales are not effected for business purposes but are concluded for religious reasons. Some authorities argued that "the law of the kingdom" demands that tax-seals be part of every document or else the document be considered invalid. The exemption that such bills of sale were for religious purposes should not be acceptable since *Dina D'Malkhuta Dina.*[42] Others stated the documents are valid since the law only demanded payment for the seal and such a tariff may be excused by the Emperor.[43]

Our concern at the present is not with the decision in this matter but rather with the religious consequences resulting from applying or not applying *Dina D'Malkhuta Dina.* We must emphasize that *Dina D'Malkhuta Dina* is not invoked with regard to determining if the Jew transgresses the biblical law against having "leavened products" in one's possession. *Dina D'Malkhuta Dina* merely determines the validity of the bill of sale which in turn determines whether or not the Jew owns "leavened products."

In another instance, the religious problem of redemption of a first born is dependent upon ownership. A woman sold an animal to a Gentile. After paying for the animal, the Gentile left it in the possession of the Jewess. In the meantime a "firstling" was born. Although *Dina D'Malkhuta Dina* decides that the animal was acquired by the Gentile by means of the payment made or even a handshake, it is but an indirect consequence that the firstling born has no sanctity of a first born and requires no redemption.[44]

The questionable areas are those where religious and civil laws are intertwined. In such cases which first required ownership by a Jew in order for him to fulfil or violate a religious law, such as the redemption of first born, *etrogim,* slavery, leavened products on Passover, wines of a Gentile, etc., the question is if *Dina D'Malkhuta Dina* may be applied. Nowhere can it be found that any authority was even remotely doubtful that *Dina D'Malkhuta Dina* could not be invoked if the secular authorities demanded that Jews violate a strictly religious law. Some matters appear to be civil law because they deal in economic gains and losses but with regard to Jewish thinking are religious in nature. Trade competition may involve monetary consequences. However, Jewish jurisprudence places the matter entirely within the realm of religious law. "A was pursuing his craft in town T when B began to pursue the same craft. A demanded that a ban be issued against anyone beside himself who will engage in that craft. B, however, restrained him from such action until a decision, as to the legality of such a ban, be issued by a rabbi. Subsequently, A bribed the ruler of the town who issued a decree forbidding anyone but A to pursue that particular trade. A again demanded the issuance of a ban, claiming that the Jews are bound to abide by the law of the secular government." [45] The decision came forth that the secular government, according to Jewish law, has no jurisdiction over trade competition. Jews are not bound to abide by their decree since "the law of the kingdom is the law" is not applied to religious law.

To conclude, the talmudic, Gaonic, and later day authorities throughout the centuries stood guard with a watchful eye to prevent the invasion of the secular governments upon their religious

133

beliefs. Although in civil law there were differences of opinion to be found in various eras, and differences to be found between Sephardic and Ashkenazic centers, the Jewish authorities were predominantly united against permitting any intrusion in so far as religious law was concerned. There were forceful invasions of their religious rights but the Jews never recognized these to be lawful. Some Jewish authorities, especially of the Spanish school, were quite liberal in civil matters. They readily harmonized the law of the kingdom with their own way of life. None, however, extended such acceptance directly into the realm of religious law.[46]

CHAPTER XI

Modern Questions of Dina D'Malkhuta Dina

With the political emancipation of the Jews and the granting of citizenship to the Jewish residents of specific nations, numerous problems involving the concept of *Dina D'Malkhuta Dina* arose.

Among these were questions concerning civil marriages and divorces, the problem of military duty that was and is required of all citizens, and questions involving criminal law and civil ordinances.

These problems were a major concern to Jews, especially in the nineteenth century when the thinking of the non-Jewish world changed and Jews were included within the total concept of citizenship. The emotional wave of liberty, equality, and fraternity, begun in France, spread over the continent and Jews everywhere began to feel the need to define their peculiar position of living under a dual system of law. The principle postulated by Samuel rose to the foreground and old and new interpretations flourished. The Jews recognized their new obligations to the State and also reaffirmed their loyalty to their own law. They maintained that the two systems did not conflict. They did not detract from each other. Quite to the contrary, many felt that they enhanced each other, allowing the Jew to live as a better citizen of his adopted land, and at the same time, live as a better Jew.

The Jews of that era were aware that such synthesis could not and would not come about overnight. Greater awareness of the problems before them would help, and education and perhaps revision of thought might be necessary. Here are the words of a Jewish dignitary who wrote to his brethren after the Rights of Active Citizens of France were granted to the Jews in 1791: "At length the day is arrived when the veil, by which, parted from our fellow-citizens, we were kept in a state of humiliation, is rent; . . . We must then, dear brethren, strongly bear this truth in our minds, that till such a time as we work a change in our manners, in our habits, in short, in our whole education, we cannot expect to be placed by the esteem of our fellow citizens in any of those situations in which we can give signal proofs of that glowing patriotism so long cherished in our bosoms. God forbid that I should mean anything derogatory to our professed religion, or to our established form of worship; far from me the idea of proposing any innovation in them. I should consider as monsters those among us, who, from the prospect of some advantages they might expect from the new constitution, would presume to alter the dogmas of their religion . . . No, I shall not believe any of my brethren capable of this . . . But I cannot too often repeat to you how absolutely necessary it is to divest ourselves entirely of that narrow spirit, of *Corporation* [1] and *Congregation,*[1] in all *civil and political matters, not immediately connected with our spiritual laws;* [2] in these things we must absolutely appear . . . as Frenchmen . . . ; to know how to risk our lives and fortunes for the defence of the country . . . ;" [3]

One of the problems with which they had to come to grips was the problem of civil marriage and divorce.

The French Jews at the Assembly of Notables were faced with this situation. The second and third questions proposed by the Emperor involved just these problems. Here is the text of these questions: [4]

"Question 2: Is divorce allowed by the Jewish Religion? Is divorce valid when not pronounced by courts of justice by virtue of laws in contradiction with those of the French code?"

"Question 3: Can a Jewess marry a Christian and a Jew a Christian woman? or does the law allow the Jews to intermarry only among themselves?"

The answer to Question 2 by the Assembly stated that "repudiation is allowed by the law of Moses but it is not valid if not previously pronounced by the French code." [4] The Assembly referred to the "Principle generally acknowledged . . . that, in everything relating to civil or political interests, the law of the state is the supreme law." [4] The members of the Assembly affirmed a position which actual practice had already established, that no divorce could be valid except it be a double divorce—that pronounced by the law of the state and that prescribed by the law of Moses.

The members to the Assembly obviously would not apply *Dina D'Malkhuta Dina* to the process of divorce itself. They recognized the requirements of the State so that a civil divorce would be necessary in addition to the *Get*. In fact, the civil divorce necessarily had to precede the issuing of a *Get*. As far as this additional requirement was concerned, *Dina D'Malkhuta Dina* demanded that Jews comply with the law of the land. However, *Dina D'Malkhuta Dina* was not sufficient; it did not allow the civil divorce to take the place of the *Get*. The Jews would not recognize such a civil document alone to be the substitute for the *Get*. These were religious in nature and the "law of the kingdom" could not apply.

Similarly, the answer of the Assembly to the third question regarding intermarriages stated that marriage "requires religious ceremonies called *Kidushin,* with the benediction used in such cases, no marriage can be *religiously* valid unless these ceremonies have been performed. This could not be done towards persons who would not both of them consider these ceremonies sacred; and in that case the married could separate without the religious divorce; they would then be considered as married *civilly* but not *religiously.*" [4]

Here, too, the express opinion of the rabbis was that marriage is a religious matter. It is sanctification and is not a civil issue. However, they did recognize and make the dichotomy between religious and civil marriages. Although they recognized the powers of the state with regard to civil marriages, they did not

137

allow this power to extend to religious marriages. In reality, of course, it spelled out the fact that the civil marriage was of a different nature and let no one mistake the two.[5] The Jews of that epoch did not regard marriage itself as a civil matter.

The French minister of the Interior, in his report to the Emperor on August 20, 1806, understood the dual aspect of marriage as recognized by the Assembly. In his comments to the answer given by the Assembly to quZestion 2, he wrote: "But this repudiation form of divorce affects only the religious bond, the civil bond remaining intact; moreover the first can easily be made subordinate to the second in dissolving a marriage, as it already is in bringing it about." [6]

Utilizing the answer formulated primarily by R. David Zinzheimer on behalf of the Assembly of Jewish Notables, the Napoleonic Sanhedrin one year later, by virtue of its authority, also made it a religious ordinance that from that time forth no divorce should be issued except after the marriage had been dissolved by a competent civil court and according to the forms prescribed by the civil code. No rabbi might lend his services to the granting of a divorce without first requiring a civil divorce decree; otherwise, the rabbi would be regarded as unworthy of performing future functions. Furthermore, marriages between Christians and Jews, though not invested with religious sanctity, shall not entail any anathema (*herem*).[7]

At the gate which led the Jew into modern life, the possibility of a conflict between religious and civil laws became a greater problem. Harmonization was impossible. All that could be hoped for was that Jews live by a dual code, the one religious and the other the laws of the State.

Towards the end of the century, an Englishman wrote: "We acknowledge the principle laid down in the Talmud: "The law of the country is binding upon us, *Dina D'Malkhuta Dina,* but only in so far as our civil relations are concerned. With regard to religious questions our own religious code must be obeyed.

138

Marriage laws include two elements, civil relations and religious duties. As regard the former, we abide by the decision of the civil courts of the country. We must, therefore, not solemnize a marriage which the law of the country would not recognize; we must not religiously dissolve a marriage by *Get* unless the civil courts of law have already decreed the divorce. On the other hand, we must not content ourselves with civil marriage nor civil divorce. Religiously neither civil marriage nor civil divorce can be recognized unless supplemented by marriage or divorce according to religious forms. Furthermore, marriages allowed by civil law but prohibited by our religious law, *e.g.*, mixed marriages, that is, marriages between Jews and non-Jews cannot be recognized before the tribunal of our religion. Such alliances are sinful . . ." [8]

The authorities hitherto cited attempted to cope with the modern problems facing the Jew. As a citizen of his country, certain duties were required of him. These civic duties combined with his duties as a Jew provided the impetus to many scholars who tried to harmonize the two. As we have stated above, a dual role with dual responsibilities was the result. No particular change in the concept of *Dina D'Malkhuta Dina* occurred.

However, during this same century, the first seeds which eventually led a segment of Jewry to a complete reversal of the concept of *Dina D'Malkhuta Dina* were planted. It was maintained in 1837 that efforts be made for the rabbinical authorities to assume the power granted by the talmudic rule: "Whosoever contracts a marriage, does it on the condition that the rabbinical authorities are in full agreement with the act." [9] Just as the rabbis of the Talmud, by virtue of the above mentioned rule, annulled marriages which led to evil consequences, so let the modern rabbis do the same with marriages dissolved by the civil court.[10]

In 1843 another opinion quite readily agreed to the generally accepted condition that *Dina D'Malkhuta Dina* is applied to civil law alone.[11] The state has not the power to set aside religious law or the religious principles of Jews.[12] However, the laws of the state must be permitted to govern marriages, because marriage is not a religious but a purely civil matter. That is to say, the state of matrimony is a religious institution. However, the acquisition of, and the separation from a wife is achieved by a purely civil process.[13] The Torah and rabbinic law regarding matrimony are rejected. The process is claimed entirely for the modern State.

These conclusions were reached after citing a number of tannaitic and amoraic statements concerning the method of acquiring a wife. The three mishnaic[14] ways of acquiring a wife—money, deed, or cohabitation, were equated with the three methods of acquiring any other object, viz., money, deed, usucaption.[15] Matrimony was a transaction similar to any other purchase. There was absolutely no difference between "buying" a woman or any other commodity. That which the Bible calls "acquisition" (*Kinyan*) was termed "sanctification" by the rabbis.[16] Nonetheless, the act of marriage consummated by means of "money" was described as an "acquisition." [17] Furthermore, a woman of Israelitish descent, who was betrothed to a Kohen, was permitted to partake of *Terumah* because she was "owned" by the Kohen.[18] Finally, the marriage formula *"Harei ott kenuyah li*—Be thou acquired by me" was a legal substitute for the more common *Harei ott me'kudeshet li*—Be thou consecrated unto me." [19] According to this view, the fact that a father was permitted to sell his daughter in her minority or give her in marriage to any man he chose for her shows without a doubt that a wife was considered no more than a "thing." [20]

The second method of acquisition, by means of a "document of marriage," was constantly compared to deeds of sale concerning real-estate, slaves, and cattle. The rabbis of the Talmud at first wanted to ignore this method because it did not compare fully with the instruments drawn up regarding other sales where the seller writes *"Sadi mehura loh*—My field is sold to you," whereas in marriages the purchaser, the groom, writes *"Bitha me'kudeshet li*—Your daughter is consecrated unto me."[21]

The third method, cohabitation, was outlawed by the talmudic rabbis themselves. However, the prohibition against this method did not alter its inherent validity as a legal means of acquisition. There were measures taken against its practice but no attack against its efficacy.[22]

That the consent of the woman was required before her acquisition could take place does not alter the situation. The woman plays a passive role. Once her consent is given she renounces her own will and becomes, in effect, as a thing without an owner, then to be swallowed up by the groom's power of acquisition.[23]

This opinion then concludes that love, sanctity, etc., play no role in marriage at all. It is a civil matter. The acquisition of a wife takes place as a consequence of a man purchasing a woman upon the payment of at least one *Perutah* regardless of the feelings and emotions involved. Even cohabition, physical possession of a woman, is devoid of emotional emphasis. Just as eating of the fruits of a field constitute "possession" with relation to the field, so physical usage of the woman constitutes "acquisition." In fact, marriage was forbidden to take place on the Sabbath or holidays[24] because the acquisition of *any* commodity was forbidden on these days.

The conclusion reached by this view was that marriage and divorce are civil processes and must be governed by the laws of the State since *Dina D'Malkhuta Dina.* However, the overwhelming scholarly opinions reject this entire hypothesis. The methods employed in the process of *Kidushin* are equal and akin to civil purchases. Perhaps in ancient times it was strictly a business matter. However, during the Second Commonwealth, marriage was based upon moral, spiritual law, rather than upon civil law.[25] The husband could not forgive the willful infidelity of his wife. Were marriage but a civil matter, were matrimony but the ownership of an object, the husband would have been within his rights

141

to "forgive and forget" if he so desired. If a wife is but another
item owned as are many other possessions, it would be the prerogative of the husband to do and to decide concerning his "belongings." The act of infidelity goes beyond the realm of "acquisition"
(*Kinyan*) and, for that matter, is a sin that reaches beyond the
status of the husband. It is a sin against morality *per se*.[26] Furthermore, marriage was not considered as merely an "acquisition."
No husband could rid himself of his wife by selling her to another.
Only one method was available to any man during his lifetime by
means of which he could dissolve his marriage and that was a legal
writ of divorce. These writs of divorce were explicitly excluded
from the concept of *Dina D'Malkhuta Dina* by the Talmud. The
laws of marriage and divorce are not civil in nature, and no government was given the right to interfere with them. *Dina D'Malkhuta Dina* does not apply.[27]

Despite the rejection of the former thesis, nonetheless,
one segment of Jewry accepted the idea that marriage and
divorce are civil processes. "Still more expressive of the modern
spirit are the resolutions concerning divorce and remarriage, of
which the one declares divorce to be also from the Mosaic and
rabbinical point of view only a civil act devoid of any religious
character and therefore, valid only when it proceeds from the
civil courts, whereas the so-called ritual *Get* is in all cases invalid
and ineffective." [28]

The thesis that marriage and divorce are civil matters cannot
be accepted, as we have stated earlier. The statements of the
Mishneh which hint at the civil nature of marriage belong to an
early period of Jewish history. The first Mishneh of the tractate
Kiddushin is a very old one. Herein the term *Niknit* was still
used. The second chapter of this tractate makes use of the more
recent concept of sanctification—*ha-Ish me'Kadesh*.

It is also of great significance to note the moral and social
attitude to marriage that developed among the sages of the talmudic period and the Middle Ages. Their sayings reflected either

the prevailing attitude to marriage or at least the goals towards which these teachers aimed. Many talmudic statements, even if agadic in nature, nonetheless, reflect a philosophy of marriage based upon the sanctity of marriage.[29]

Marriage is a religious act and tolerates no interference on the part of the State. That even today one is required to wait for the issuance of a license for marriage merely shows that those officiating comply with the demands of the State. Similarly, in cases where Jewish law permits the issuing of a divorce even against the wife's will, (*e.g.*, when the marriage after ten years did not yield any children), the *Bet Din* can only do so if the government permits such a divorce.[30] However, should a marriage be consummated without a license having been issued, no matter what its civil status, the marriage is valid and is recognized fully by Jewish law. The government cannot set it aside.

Even though, as we have said, all authorities agreed that *Dina D'Malkhuta Dina* applies only to civil law, yet, in November of 1842, the provisional head of the rabbinate in Sachsen-Meiningen, Germany, permitted, nay, urged Jewish students to write their school-lessons on the Sabbath. In response to this question, he cited Samuel's law. Jews are to ignore the laws of the Sabbath where the law of the kingdom demands it. Jews are to accept governmental posts even though they entail the violation of the Sabbath just as they are to serve in the military when called upon. To serve one's country and to fulfill one's duties as a citizen are the obligations of every Jew since "the law of the kingdom is the law." [31]

Opposition came forth mainly from the chief-rabbi in Dresden who vehemently pointed out the errors of such conclusions. *Dina D'Malkhuta Dina* is invoked only when the loyalty of the citizenry is at stake or the welfare of the State is in question. It was in this sense that the Talmud postulated its maxim, but never at the expense of religious law. Let the student attend school, if he must, but he may not violate the Sabbath.[32] Others went even further.

143

The student who attends classes on the Sabbath and does not write, perhaps does not violate the Sabbath but surely does not fulfill its purposes. He is like the man who spends his entire Sabbath sleeping. He violates nought, but neither does he live up to the meaning of the Sabbath. The student in attendance at a secular school does not violate the letter of the law, but neither does he fulfill the spirit of the law.[33]

Modern times and the recognition of the Jew as a full-fledged citizen of his country also brought about a number of responsibilities and duties incumbent upon every citizen. One of these duties was and is to serve the military upon the request of the government. During the Middle Ages, because of mistrust and hatred of the Jew, and the non-recognition of his equal status, he was excluded from partaking in the defense of his nation. Modern times, however, created problems for Jews who wanted to abide by the precepts of Jewish law while at the same time discharging their obligations to their country.

Practically speaking, Jews did serve honorably in the defense of their homelands whenever called upon to do so. Jews distinguished themselves by their loyalty and heroism, and the numerous casualties and dead bear proof of their uncompromising devotion and patriotism to their adopted lands. This was true in 18th century France,[34] during all wars of the United States,[35] in Germany,[36] and in many other countries.

Theoretically, the question was asked each time war broke out and always when peace-time conscription was the law of the land. Since Jews are required to readily answer their nation's call to arms, may they set aside, if necessary, the laws ordinarily governing the Sabbath and holidays? What of the dietary laws? Is there a difference between the standing armies of peacetime and the fighting armies during a state of war? All these questions have been dealt with and it is not our purpose here to resolve them from a *halakhic* standpoint. The purpose is merely to show the

144

application and development of *Dina D'Malkhuta Dina* in these matters which have evolved in the modern age.

Speaking in connection with waging a defensive war, the Talmud states: "Foreigners who attack the cities of Israel to extort money from them are not to be countered on the Sabbath. Should the city be situated at the borders of Israel, even if the attack came as a result of demands for straw, it is to be defended even though the Sabbath be desecrated." [37]

In the Middle Ages, Maimonides added: "It is the duty of every Jew able to come to the aid of his besieged brethren to do so and to help save them on the Sabbath and not to delay his assistance until the Sabbath has concluded." [38] Furthermore, based on the Talmud, he adds: "Once their brethren are rescued, they may return to their homes on the Sabbath while still carrying their weapons in order that they not weaken their defenses for a future time." [39]

In the 16th century, even an attack initiated with the intent for fiscal extortion demanded immediate and prompt defense on the Sabbath. The brigands of their day were not satisfied or appeased, especially when they met with resistance to their demands for money, so that any attack was one which involved the lives of Jews.[40] In modern times, any attack permits the violation of the Sabbath.[41]

An offensive attack must begin at least three days prior to the Sabbath. However, once begun, the attack may proceed on the Sabbath as well.[42] Not only the Sabbath may be set aside, but other religious commands as well. Soldiers on the battlefield in enemy territory who are hungry and have nothing to eat may partake of forbidden foods and drink forbidden wines.[43] The degree of hunger [44] or the question of effort to be expended in the search for permissible food [45] was debated in the 16th century.

The above mentioned passages all referred to Jewish soldiers either defending the land of their forefathers or else attacking in its behalf. Are the same rules and regulations to be in effect when

145

the citizens of the Jewish faith are called upon to serve in the military of their nation?

The opinion of the scholars was and is that it is the solemn duty of Jewish citizens to fulfill these duties in their adopted lands. That which was true for the ancient Judean or the modern Israeli when his State is involved, is true for Jews the world over when their countries are involved.[46] This is true in all nations that require Jews to share the duties of all citizens and grant Jews equal rights and privileges in their armies. *Dina D'Malkhuta Dina* obligates all Jews to defend their nation.

Of course it must be understood, that the laws of the Sabbath or *kashruth* may not be set aside merely because one finds himself in the Army. In peace-time or in nations like the United States where many provisions are made for Jewish soldiers to allow the fulfillment of their religious precepts, *Dina D'Malkhuta Dina* is not sufficient to waive these requirements.[47]

Hitherto the discussion centered about the positive obligations of citizens. The law-abiding citizen also must refrain from committing acts in violation of government restrictions. This, of course, is not the innovation resulting from modern times except that perhaps the areas involved have expanded.

There was an old *takkanah* enacted by the Jews of Jerusalem while under Turkish rule forbidding the purchase of stolen articles. People would buy these articles below their normal cost and reap a healthy profit when they were re-sold. The government forbade such dealings and the Jewish community affirmed this prohibition by instituting a *takkanah* to this effect.[48] Once on the eve of the Jewish New Year when the *takkanah* was to be renewed, the people refused to do so.[49] In fact, one merchant, a Jew, who had come from the diaspora and whose name was Judah, seeing that his business was not successful, began to engage in such illegal activities.[50] The authorities apprehended the culprit and danger loomed over the entire community. The leaders of the city urged the reinstitution of the *takkanah*. One of the leaders pleaded: "If

146

your intentions are honorable, then you must forbid the sale of saffron and the purchase of stolen goods which was forbidden by a royal decree and the "law of the kingdom is the law." [51] The businessmen of Jerusalem refused to heed these warnings. Many religious leaders were involved in their dispute until Elijah Mizrahi was able to bring the matter to a proper solution.[52] Nonetheless, a century later, the following rule was incorporated into the code of R. Joseph Caro of Safed: "It is forbidden to purchase stolen goods, for such an act is a great iniquity. It encourages crimes and causes dishonesty. If there were no receiver, there would be no thief . . . Any article concerning which there is even a presumption that it is stolen, must not be purchased. Sheep from a shepherd, household goods from servants, must not be accepted, for the probability is that the property belongs to their masters . . . It is prohibited to rob or to cheat anyone, even to the smallest extent and the same law applies to the case of a Jew and non-Jew alike."[53]

Well-founded was the antipathy of Jews to summon one another before any but their own courts.[54] Yet, one of the chief medieval formulators of Jewish custom delivered up, of his own initiative, a Jew to justice when he had robbed a non-Jew.[55] In fact, the authorities of the early centuries made it their practice to denounce to the government Jews who bought stolen goods.[56]

Various laws which are instituted by a government for the protection of its citizens or to protect the underdog fall into the category of *Dina D'Malkhuta Dina*.[57] Thus, laws such as the various controls that were enacted in the United States during the war and post-war years, are binding upon Jews. The ordinances against black-marketing, rent-control, smuggling,[58] copyrights,[59] bootlegging,[60] etc., are fair and just enactments and even though they seem to put a burden upon some, as upon the landlord in the case of rent-controls, they are binding. Only laws which are discriminatory in nature are invalidated but not enactments intended for the protection of the majority of citizens. These are valid.[61]

With modern times, and modern problems, modern applications of *Dina D'Malkhuta Dina* were made. The conclusions to be reached, however, are that *Dina D'Malkhuta Dina* is not to be applied when secular law infringes upon religious matters, although in instances where secular and religious law can co-exist, *e.g.,* the requirement of a marriage license prior to marriage, the Jew is required to honor both. The Jew is not to violate civil or criminal law or those ordinances intended to protect the majority of citizens.

The law of Samuel, *Dina D'Malkhuta Dina,* which came into being in the 3rd Century C.E. was constantly developed to meet the prevailing conditions in every nation and at all times. However, neither Samuel, nor the rabbis after him made use of *Dina D'Malkhuta* when dealing with religious law. Only when civil issues were involved, was Samuel's precept invoked.

"The law of the kingdom is the law" was the central factor which guided the Jew along a path true to his ancestral way of life and yet in harmony with the laws of the nation in which he lived.

CHAPTER I

THE TALMUDIC PERIOD

1. Gittin 10b; B.K. 113a; Ned. 28a; B.B. 54b.
2. "Was it not Samuel who has said . . ." ‏והא אמר שמואל‎.
3. Gittin 10b.
4. *Ibid.*
5. ‏תני חוץ מכגיטי נשים‎.
6. B.B. 54b — ‏נכסי עכו"ם הרי הן כמדבר כל המחזיק בהן זכה בהן‎.
7. ‏עכו"ם מכי מטי זוזי לידיה אסתלק ליה ישראל לא קני עד דמטי שטרא לידיה‎.
8. ‏א"ל אביי לרב יוסף מי אמר שמואל הכי והאמר שמואל דד"ד ומלכא אמר לא‎
‏ליקני ארעא אלא באיגרתא‎.
9. *Ibid.*
10. Kid. 26a — ‏נכסים שיש להם אחריות ניקנין בכסף ובשטר ובחזקה‎.
11. The phrase ‏הרי הן כמדבר‎ is explained by RaSHBaM as referring
to *res nullius (Hefker)*. It is difficult to accept this explanation for it
does not explain the contradiction between Samuel's two laws. Accordingly,
there is no answer given by the Talmud. RaSHBaM's attempt to find an
answer in R. Joseph's plea of ignorance is not acceptable. See the commentary of R. Hannanel, who refuses to accept Samuel's law of *Dina
D'Malkhuta* on the basis of this apparent contradiction. However, Dr.
Zeitlin's interpretation solves the problems at hand.

It seems that the reason stated in the Talmud, which is not part of
Samuel's law, ‏מ"ט עכו"ם מכי מטו זוזי לידיה‎, brought about all the difficulties.
Samuel's statements are clear.
12. The phrase ‏כל המחזיק בהן‎ does not mean "first come, first served,"
as does the phrase ‏כל הקודם זכה‎. It has a literal meaning. The one who
has possession is the one who acquires the land.
13. Mishneh, Ned. 3:3.
14. ‏נודרין להרגין ולחרמין ולמוכסין‎.
15. ‏למכס שאין לה קצבה‎.
16. ‏למכס העומד מאליו‎.
17. B.K. 113a.
18. B.B. 55a.
19. *Ibid.*
20. Differences between the two applications will be discussed in a
subsequent chapter.
21. B.K. 113b.
22. Yeb. 46a — ‏א"ל ר' פפא לרבא חזי מר הני דבי פפא בר אבא דייהבי זוזי לאינשי‎
‏לכרגייהו ומשעבדי בהו כי נפקא צריכי גיטא דחירותא או לא‎.
23. ‏מוהרקייהו דהני בטפסא דמלכא מנח ומלכא אמר מאן דלא יהיב כרגא משתעבד‎
‏למאן דייהיב כרגא‎.
24. Different opinions are found as to whether the one who fails to

149

pay the head-tax was a Jew or a non-Jew. Rashi, the Tosafists, and others were of the opinion that the one redeemed was a Gentile, whereas Maimonides and others maintained that both individuals involved were Jews.

25. B.M 108a.

26. See note 2.

27. B.B. 55a.

28. B.K. 113a; Ned. 28a.

29. J. Z. Lauterbach, *Rabbinic Essays,* p. 295 ff.

30. B.B. 115b; Pes. 54b; etc.

31. Furst and Rapoport, *Literaturblatt des Orients,* 1847, #3, p. 39 and *ibid* p. 196.

32. M.K. 26a.

33. B.M. at the end.

34. B.B. 115b; Pes. 54b; M.K. 26a.

35. B.B. 10b.

36. B.M.at the end.

37. Kid. 39a; Hul. 78b; Men. 38b; Shab. 53a.

38. Rashi, Men. 38b; See also *Ozar Tob,* 1878 p. 67—Samuel Ibn Nagdela in his letter to Hananel on the death of his father, Hushiel, eulogizes the rabbi for having merited such a son as Hananel. He refers to him as *Aryok* and *Shabur Malka* among other complimentary titles such as סיני עוקר הרים. These laudatory terms referred to Hananel's scholastic prowess and his eminence as a recognized talmudic scholar. These titles would not have been used if the intent had been to connote "closeness to the royal court" as Lauterbach would have us believe. וטובך רבנא חושיאל דאיתנגדית ושבקת דורכנא בברא אלפאנא שכלולא דאוריתא שיחורא דתלמודא אריוך ושבור מלכא סיני עוקר הרים •••. See also *JQR,* Vol. 9, p. 166.

39. Men. 38b.

40. Nazir 24b.

41. M.K. 26a. The text of the Talmud appears to be corrupt. The phrase ברוב צבור is vague and may be a later insertion into the text. We do not find this phrase applied except with reference to an assembly of Jews, (e.g., for a quorum necessary for a religious service). This difficulty was noted by the rabbis of the Middle Ages. Maimonides, *Mishneh Torah, Ebel 9,* required that a majority of Jews would actually have to be killed ere *Keriah* be required. Nahmanides, merely required a majority of Jews to be present when any number of Jews are killed for *Keriah* to be mandatory. They did not know what the phrase ברוב צבור meant. Terms such as רוב ישראל, רוב עם would refer to individuals, whereas ברוב צבור, refers to an assembly.

42. Josephus, *Wars* II:8.

CHAPTER II

THE GAONIC PERIOD

1. Abraham Ibn Daud, *Sefer haKabbala* and Zacuto, *Sefer haYohasin*, ed. Shulem — ורב האי סוף הגאונים.

2. S. Zeitlin, "Rashi and the Rabbinate," *JQR*, Vol. 31, 1940.

3. B.B. 89a.

4. B.K. 59a — סבור יוהרא הוא אתיוהו וחשבוהו.

5. Sanh. 5a — א״ר האי מאן דבעי למידן דינא ואי טעה מיבעי למיפטריה לישקול רשותא מבי ריש גלותא.

6. Ber. 64a; Hor. 14a — ...א״ר אבין הלוי כל הדוחק את השעה שעה דוחקתו מדרבה ורב יוסף... שלחו להתם סיני ועוקר הרים איזה מהם קודם, שלחו להו סיני...

7. Erub. 11b — When the head of the academy differed with the Exilarch he was fearful of the Exilarch. Once, the head of the academy cautioned a colleague not to reveal to the Exilarch that their opinions clashed.

8. Sanh. 5a; *Midrash Ve'hizhir, Mishpatim* — ...אלא אני נוטל רשות ור״ח ...מר׳ הקדוש.

9. Sherira, *Letter* — ed. Hyman — ובאלין שני כלהון גאונים דהוי במתא מחסיא לא נהירנא להו שפיר על הסדר ואית בהון חנופתא ונטורתא דנשיאים דמעבריך להון ומהדרין להון.

10. Sherira, *Letter* 3:6 — וביומיה סליק רב אחא משבחא לא״י דמר רב נטרוי שמעיה הוה וכד אדברינהו נשיאה עלוהי סליק להתם.

Also, Abraham Ibn Daud — אבל לא נסמך רב אחא משבחא זה לגאון מפני שנאת ראש גלות שבאותו הדור שהיה שונאו.

11. Nathan the Babylonian in *Sefer haYohasin* — ועוד משהיו משלחין אגרות זה לזה ראש ישיבת פומבדיתא כותב יתקרי הדין דיסקא קמא גאון ורבנן דסורא וריש ישיבת סורא יתקרי הדין דיסקא קמי רבנן דפומבדיתא, ואינו כותב לו גאון.

12. *Ibid.* — שלא יהא גאון פומבדיתא אלא מסורא ע״פ ראש הישיבה שלה.

13. *Ibid.* — ועוד כשימות ראש גלות כל הרשויות שלו ינתנו לראש סורא ואין בהן לראש ישיבת פומבדיתא חלק כלל Again, וכשימות ראש גלות כל הרשויות שלו ינתנו לראש ישיבת סורא.

14. Graetz, Vol. V, Note 13 — "*Freilich schweigt Scherira darüber, und wie es scheint geflissentlich, weil . . . Scherira nur die Metibta von Pumbedita verherrlichen wollte.*"

15. Abraham Ibn Daud, *Sefer haKabbala* — ...וענן זה מבית דוד היה. והכירו בו שמץ פיסול ומפני זה לא נסמך לגאון וגם לא סייעוהו מן השמים להיות ראש גלות.

16. Sherira, *Letter* — בימי דוד בן זכאי הנשיא אישתפלו מן שולטנותא דמלכא.

17. Harkavy, זכרון לראשונים וגם לאחרונים — כך ראינו כי המנהג בבבל שבית דין הגדול הן ממנין דיאנין בכל פלך ופלך וכותבין לו לדיאן איגרות רשות...

18. Nathan, the Babylonian, in describing the appointment of the Exilarch stated that he was chosen and approved by the heads of the acad-

151

emies. Nathan wrote in the 10th century and his narrative describes the inauguration of the Exilarchs when their authority had greatly diminished. The Geonim had already assumed great authority.

19. Sheb. 6b — ‏כגון מלכא ואלקפטא רופילא וריש גלותא‎.

Graetz, Vol. IV: 15, p. 252 — *"er war einer der Würdenträger des persischen Reiches und Nahm auf der Stufenleiter der persischen Grossen den vierten Rang nach dem Könige ein."*

20. This was also true later on during the rule of Islam. See Sherira, *Letter*. — He uses the phrase ‏שולטנותא דמלכא‎, a phrase synonymous with ‏הורמנא דמלכא‎ used frequently to connote the concept of *Dina D'Malkhuta*. See also Rashi, R. Joseph Ibn Habbib to Sanh. 5a — ‏שיש: את העם‎ ‏שרודין‎ ‏להן כח ורשות ממלכי פרס‎. See also Maimonides, *Mishneh Torah, Sanh.* 4:13 — ‏ראשי גליות שבבבל במקום מלך הן עומדים ויש להן לרדות את ישראל בכל מקום ולדון‎ ‏עליהן בין רצו ובין לא רצו...‎. The phrase ‏במקום מלך‎ refers to the kings of the nations of the diaspora.

See also R. Solomon Duran, *Responsa,* 353 — ‏והא ריש גלותא בהורמנא‎ ‏דמלכא הוא‎. Also, Barfat, *Responsa,* 271.

In the dispute between Saadyah and David b. Zaccai, the latter was deposed. Although the effects of this dispute greatly diminished the authority of the Exilarch, nevertheless, his official position was still significant. Using the authority of the secular government, David was able to remove his brother Josiah, whereupon Saadyah had to flee for his life. — See Ibn Daud, *Sefer haKabbala.* See also Sherira, *Letter* 3:4 — ‏והכין נהיגא מלתא‎ ‏הדין עד שיעור מאתן מן השתא האויל והוה להון לריש גלותא מרות קשה ושולטנותא‎ ‏רבתא בימי פרסים ובימי (ובראש ימי) ישמעאלים‎.

21. Sherira, *Letter* 3:1 — Based on Sanh. 5a — ‏לא יסור שבט מיהודה‎ ‏ואעפ״כ היו מרביצין תורה הכא והוה להו ראשי‎. Sherira writes: ‏אלו ראשי גליות‎ ‏גלותא מבית דוד‎.

22. The office of the Exilarch was often bought from the kings. See Sherira, 3:4 — ‏דהון זבנין ליה לראש גליותות בדמים גדולים והוה בהון דמצערי טובא‎ ‏ומעיקי להו‎.

Also, see Ibn Daud, *Sefer haKabbala* — ‏כי ראשי גלות אלו לא היו בעלי‎ ‏אמת והיו קונים נשיאותם‎.

Again, ‏אבל מימי ישמעאלים לא נהגו ראשי גליות שררה כהוגן אלא קונין אותה‎ ‏בממון רב מן הישמעאלים כמו מוכסים‎.

23. The Exilarch was able to order the confiscation of materials essential for his use. See Sukkah 31a.

24. See Sanh. 5a where *Mumhin* are required; also 7b; Maimonides, *Mishnah Torah, Sanh.* 4:15 — ‏מי שאינו ראוי לדון מפני שאינו יודע או מפני שאינו‎ ‏הגון שעבר ראש גלות ונתן לו רשות או שטעו ב״ד ונתנו לו רשות אין הרשות מועלת לו‎ ‏כלום עד שיהא ראוי...‎.

25. Nathan, the Babylonian, writing when the Exilarch had lost his authority, stated that the Exilarchs would read from the Torah but that

the Geonim did not read after them since this was beneath their dignity. וחזן הכנסת מוריד ספר תורה לראש גלות ... וקורא ... ואחריו ראשי כלות אבל ראשי הישיבות עצמן אינן קוראין באותו היום מפני שקדמן אחר.

26. Abraham Ibn Daud, *Sefer haKabbala.*

27. *Ibid.* — דהוה זבנין ליה לריש גלותא בדמים יקרים.

28. S. Zeitlin, "Rashi and the Rabbinate," *JQR*, Vol. 31 — Dr. Zeitlin speculates that they were accused by their enemies of "scheming to set themselves up as rulers of the Jews and even aspired to become the Messiah."

29. Sherira, *Letter* 3:4,5 — והויין שני שמד וצרות בסוף מלכות פרסים.

Ibn Daud, *Sefer haKabbala* — עד שגברה מלכות ישמעאל והשמידום מתחת השמים וקודם לכן הפך ד' לבם לשנוא עמו. He also states that the schools closed because מפני שנאת מלכי פרס ושמדותיהם.

30. *Teshubat haGeonim,* Harkavy, 297-8.

31. L. Ginzberg, *Geonica* II, 87: וכן כל הפיך ושאלה אשר יהי לכם מצד המלכות הגד תגידוהו לפנינו כי אז נצוה את בעלי בתים חשובים אשר בבגדד אשר אנחנו יושבים ביניהם ... ואז ישיבו לכם מאת המלך.

32. *Teshubat haGeonim,* Harkavy, 346; L. Ginzberg, *Ibid.* II, 5; see chapter on taxes for more detailed discussion. *Teshubat haGeonim,* Coronel, 26.

33. A method often employed by the secular authorities to force individual Jews to relinquish their money or property was to coerce a community into taking an oath that they have no knowledge of the whereabouts of a fellow Jew or of his money. The Geonim ruled that the members of a community so threatened may oblige the authorities by taking the oath, and do not have to deliver the victim. *Teshubat haGeonim,* Coronel, 26.

Rab Shashna made the distinction between *herem* and an oath. He felt that an oath may not be broken by a community. See *Halakot Pesukot,* 121; *Toratan Shel Rishonim* P.I., 13; *Shaarei Teshuba,* 195; R. Samuel Ibn Adret VII, 453; Ibn Zimra, *Lilshonot haRambam,* 63; S. Duran, 38; R. Meir of Rothenburg P. 813; *Teshubat haGeonim haKezorot,* 26 — ואם אמרו דד״ך לא על כזה המעשה רק להטיל מכס על האנשים ולקחת מהם לעשות גשרים וצרכי רבים לכן המלך והשלטון ובעל מכס אחד שמשער בקהל מחרימין בשביל חפציו וצרכיו ואי אפשר שלא להחרים.

34. L. Ginzberg, *Geonica* II, 5 — ולפנים להראות לשלטון נעשתה ולא לגרשה גירושין גמורין.

See also, Harkavy, *Teshubat haGeonim,* 346 — ראובן היה מצטער הרבה מעונש השלטון וכשהיה יוצא מעירו תופשין את אשתו במקומו ומצערין אותה מחמת העונש, יעצוהו מקצת בני אדם לכתוב גט פסול לאשתו ולאתפושה כל מקרקעי שיש לו בכתובה ולצאת כדי שלא תהא אשתו נתפשת תחתיו, ויש מבני אותה העיר שעושין כן להבריח את עצמן מעונש השלטון.

35. J. Mann, *JQR,* Vol. 10, quotes the תקנת מורדת, a *takkana* instituted by the Geonim which voided a talmudic law with regard to a rebellious wife. (Sherira, *Letter* — states that this *takkana* was instituted in the days

of Mar Rab at the end of the 7th — beg. of the 8th century.) See Ibn Daud ואחריו מר רב רבא שתקנו בימיו לתת גט לאלתר לאשה —. According to the talmudic law a woman who refuses to remain with her husband must wait twelve months before her husband is forced to divorce her. This period was to serve as a "cooling off" period during which conciliation might be effected. The Geonim, however, feared that a woman in such a position would "attach herself to a powerful Gentile" or to a non-Jewish court and by such means force her husband to grant her a divorce sooner. A divorce issued under duress (by Gentiles) is considered a גט מעושה and is not valid. The Geonim, therefore, ordered the elimination of the talmudically prescribed twelve month waiting period and forced the husband to issue the divorce immediately.

Mann concludes that the fear of secular interference in religious matters induced the Geonim to issue their edict. Jewish religious autonomy was threatened.

The key phrase in this responsum is בנות ישראל נתלות בגוים והולכות ליטול להן גיטין באונס מבעליהן. To say that נתלות בגוים refers to the non-Jewish courts appears to be inaccurate. The term ערכאות or אגירות would have been used. We are then left with the other interpretation given by Mann, namely, that נתלות בגוים refers to powerful individuals who could force the granting of a divorce. It seems unlikely that the Geonim would institute a *takkana* which actually negated talmudic law for what could at best be a rare occurrence. One cannot conceive that individuals became so powerful and that their interference became so frequent and widespread as to prompt Gaonic action to circumvent these intrusions.

The interpretation given by Sherira Gaon, R. Asher, Ket. V, 35; Mordecai and *Shiltei Gibborim, ibid.* seems far more accurate. Recognizing the possibility of the deterioration of the morals of women, especially under circumstances where they are merely marking a year's time until their divorce is issued, the Geonim feared the promiscuity to which the talmudic edict might lead. The Gaonic *takkana* tried to remedy such a situation and had nothing at all to do with governmental interference. נתלות בגוים refers to promiscuity on the part of women with non-Jews.

36. Lewin, B.K. p. 99; A Jew, who of his own accord testifies on behalf of a Gentile suing another Jew in a Gentile court is to be excommunicated. This penalty is only applied to a single witness. Jewish law does not recognize the testimony of one witness in such matters. האי בר ישראל דידע סהדותא לכותי ולא תבעו מיניה ואזל ואסהיד ליה בדיני דכותי על ישראל חבריה משמתינן ליה מ״ט דאינהו מפקי ממונא אפומא דחד ולא אמרן אלא בחד אבל בתרי לא.

37. *Ibid.* Also *Shaarei Zedek* 4; Ibn Adret, 137; L. Ginzberg, *Ginzei Schechter* p. 127—A Jew who refuses to pay his debt and no *Bet Din* is available, may be taken to a Gentile court (if the court is honest). Witnesses not only may, but are urged to testify before that court. Ginzberg and Mann misunderstood this responsum and stated that Hai and Sherira

urged the creditor to go to a Gentile court. Actually, the responsum states
that the witnesses are urged. שיש להן רשות ומצוה לעשות כך.

38. The Geonim did not recognize the Gentile courts because generally
they were corrupt and were not to be trusted. See Marmorstein p. 59;
Harkavy, *Teshubat haGeonim*, 278 — (פקיעין) אבל בדורות הללו שאנו בקיעין
בהן שכל עיסקיהן שקרנות וכזבנות אין ללמוד משטרותיהן כלל שכולן בחזקת זיוף הן.

39. Lewin, *Ozar haGeonim*, B.K. p. 99 — הכין חזינא כי המדינה הזאת שאנו
עכשיו בתוכה והיא בגדאד אין מקבלין בערכאות של גוים אלא עדים פקחים וגדולים
ועשירים שלא עלה (נתלה) עליהן גזל ולא דברי שקר ולא דברי שוא ושמצוויינין בדתם...
כגון אלו אם העידו על שטר מכר או הלואה וסידרו את העדות בערכאות שלהן וקיבלן
השופט שלהן אף אנו נמי דנין באותו השטר וכשר הוא אצלנו. וכן מנהגנו עכשיו מעשים
בכל יום. ויש מקומות וכפרים ומרחקים שאינן כך אלא שקרנות וכזבנות ידועה בהן
וגומלין הן ונהגין מעדיותיהן כגון אלו אין אנו מכשירין שטרותיהן.

40. See subsequent chapter on non-Jewish courts.

41. *Teshubat haGeonim*, Harkavy, 440.

42. *Shaarei Teshuba*, 9.

43. *Ibid.*, 182.

44. B.K. 84b.

45. J. Mann, *JQR*, Vol. 10; also Alfasi, B.K. 84b — מנהג שתי ישיבות
שאע"פ שאין גובין קנס בבבל מנדין אותו עד דמפייס ליה לבעל דיניה וכד יהיב ליה
בתשובת הגאונים :שיעור מאי דחזי ליה שרו ליה לאלתר Also R. Asher, *ibid.* 2 and 3:
נשאל ממר צמח גאון ז"ל אלו נערות שיש להן קנס... והשיב כלל אמרו אין מגבין קנסות
בבבל... אלא משום שלא יהא חוטא נשכר... שכיון שיודעים שאין גובין קנסות בבבל
שולחים יד זה זה נהגו חכמים אחרונים לנדותם עד שיפייסו בממון... ומעשה באחד...
וגידוהו מר רב צדוק גאון ז"ל... In the European countries, France and Italy,
the Jewish courts continued to impose fines. They interpreted the talmudic
statement אין גובין אותו בבבל to refer to Babylonia exclusively. The Babylonians considered that they did not possess *Semikha* and therefore could
not impose fines. The Franco-German centers followed the traditions of
the Palestinians and continued the chain of authority that began with
Moses. They imposed fines. See S. Zeitlin, "Rashi and the Rabbinate," *JQR*,
Vol. 31.

The Geonim, following in the traditions of Babylonia, felt that if
Babylonia was excluded from levying fines, then certainly all other parts
of the world did not possess this right.

We must note that R. Tam also ruled that fines could be imposed
anywhere. אנן שליחותייהו קא עבדי. He felt that the courts of the diaspora
are merely carrying out the wishes of the Palestinian courts. R. Tam ex-
tends the ruling of the Talmud (B.K. 84b) which permits the courts of
the diaspora to impose and collect fines whenever a particular violation
occurs frequently and incurs a monetary loss to the victim. Tosafot B.K.
84b; Sanh. 3a — ומעשים בכל יום שאנו דנין דיני גזילות. See also Tosafot, Gitt.
88b where the same ruling is listed in the name of R. Isaac of Dampierre
(Ri).

46. *Teshubat haGeonim*, Asaf תש״ב p. 75 or perhaps to R. Samuel b. Hofni.

47. Gittin 10b — ‏ואב״א תני חוץ מכגיטי נשים.

48. *Ibid.*

49. ‏אלא כיון שתירצו תירוץ [שני וא]מרו ואי באעית תני חוץ מכגיטי נשים נכנסה‏
‏אף המתנה בכלל גיטי נשים.

50. According to Jewish law, a man whose property was lost at sea relinquishes his right of ownership and the rescuer assumes said right. Comp. Joshua Starr, *The Jews in the Byzantine Empire*, who cites R. Hanannel b. Paltiel who asked permission of the king of Africa to cross to Italy. He and the other fugitives who fled Oria at the time of her capture took along their household goods and whatever funds they could rescue. R. Hanannel went to Constantinople and petitioned King Basil II to grant a decree allowing him to travel throughout the cities of the realm and recover his family possessions.

The sages at Bari contested his right to these articles and cited the following: "If a man saved some articles from an invading army or from a flood, or from a fire, they are his . . ." See B.K. 10:2. R. Hanannel replied: ". . . our rabbis ruled that 'the law of the kingdom is the law' and here is the document with the seal the king gave me."

51. *Hakmei Zorfat ve'Lotir*, 97.

52. Similarly, if a ruler forbids a Jew to collect his debt, the *Bet Din* will not intervene and collect his debt for him. The recognition on the part of the creditor that he cannot override the ruler's decree, forces him to give up hope of ever collecting his debt. See חצ״ו, 34; R. Meir of Rothenburg, L. 381; Miller, *Einleitung*, who claims that this responsum was formulated by Rashi or R. Tam.

53. The "divine right of kings" is the belief that monarchs derive the right to rule directly from G-d, rather than from the consent of their subjects. So far as the people are concerned, the king can do no wrong.

54. *Teshubat haGeonim*, Asaf תש״ב p. 75 — ‏ראשון אמר שמואל דד״ד...‏
‏ואילו ע[מד]ן לנו תירוץ זה לבדו היו המתנות אשר בשטר...כי כן היתה מאמר שמואל‏
‏כי כאשר השליט הקב״ה את המלכויות בעולמו כך השליטן על ממון בני אדם לשלוט בו‏
‏כרצונם.

55. *Teshubat haGeonim haKezorot*, 26 — ‏ואם אמרו דד״ד לא על כזה‏
‏המעשה רק להטיל מכס על האנשים ולקחת מהם לעשות גשרים וצרכי רבים...

CHAPTER III

RABBINIC ATTITUDES TOWARD GOVERNMENT

1. RaSHBaM, B.B. 54b — כל המסים וארנוניות ומנהגות של משפטי מלכים
שרגילין להנהיג במלכותם דינא הוא שכל בני המלכות מקבלים עליהם מרצונם חוקי המלך
ומשפטיו והלכך דין גמור הוא ואין למחזיק בממון חבירו ע״פ חוק המלך הנהוג בעיר
משום גזל. Hayyim b. Isaac *Or Zarua*, 34; *Abkat Rohel*, 72, and many others.
Berthold Altmann, in his article "Medieval German Jewish History," *Proceedings of the American Academy for Jewish Research*, Vol. X, renders
an incorrect translation of the above commentary. Altmann writes: "There
is a legal rule that all inhabitants of the kingdom should voluntarily submit
to the king's laws and decrees." Altmann misread the text, placing the words
דינא הוא together with the subsequent words. Thus, he read שכל הוא דינא
בני המלכות . . . without realizing that this rendered the tense of מקבלים
completely wrong. By misplacing a comma, he arrived at a faulty meaning
of the text. See I. Agus, *R. Meir of Rothenburg*, Intr. p. XXI footnote 3.

2. Compare I. Agus *op. cit.*; also, his *Teshubot Baalei Tosafot*, p. 18.

3. The "social contract" theory goes back to Plato (*Republic* Book
II, *Gorgias*) but was fully expounded much later by Rousseau. In his book
"The Social Contract," Rousseau states: "The clauses of this contract are
so determined by the nature of the act that the slightest modification would
make them ineffective, so that, although they have perhaps never been
formally set forth, they are everywhere the same and everywhere tacitly
admitted and recognized, until, on the violation of the social contract, each
regains his original rights and resumes his natural liberty while losing the
conventional liberty in favor of which he renounced it" (Book I, chap. IV).
See also Convention Parliament of 1688 which accused James II of having
"endeavored to subvert the constitution of the kingdom by breaking the
original contract between king and people."

According to this theory, the state should not be controlled by power.
The only rightful rulers are those freely chosen by the people of the land.
A monarch's right to rule is given him by the people and not by G-d nor
may it be taken by force. The citizens of a nation enter into an agreement
with a king whereby they surrender some of their rights and submit themselves to a supreme government.

One major criticism of this theory of government has been the fact
that we have no historical evidence of any such social contract. Indeed
the evidence of history seems to be contrary to this theory.

It may now be shown that R. Samuel and the numerous rabbis who
accepted his views, translated this theory into practice. Many Jewish communities accepted or rejected the law of the kingdom based upon the social
contract. The king's laws were considered binding as long as these laws

lived up to the social contract. Whenever the king acted contrary to the contract; whenever he arbitrarily or wantonly overstepped the boundaries prescribed by the social contract, he was considered to be committing "royal robbery" and such edicts were internally ignored. — (דינא דמלכותא גזילא דמלכותא). See Nissim Gerondi Ned. 28a; Tosafot, *ibid.*; the terms גזילא דמלכותא and חמסנותא דמלכותא were used throughout the entire rabbinic literature and may be found countless times referring to a king who acted in a high-handed manner. Comp. B. J. Bamberger, "Individual Rights and the Demands of the State: The Position of Classical Judaism," *CCAR-Yearbook*, Vol. LIV, 1944, pp. 229-234.

4. Ibn Adret, VI, 149 — לפי שהארץ של מלך היא ומי שבא לגור בארץ ע"ד וכ"ש במדינות שהארץ כולה שלו ויכול הוא לעשות — 22 *haMeyuhosot*, וְכן הוא בא בה חוקים כמו שירצה שע"מ כן הוא מחלקה להם וע"פ חוקי המלך קיבלוהו יושביה. See also I. Agus, *Teshubot Baale Tosafot*, 130, responsum of R. Isaac b. Aaron — דע"מ כן מתיישבין תחת השרים שיהא גופם וממונם כרצון המלך לגבות מהן והיינו טעמא דדיניה — 110 ,34 .Also, Hayyim b. Isaac *Or Zarua*, כפי רצונו דינא שהארץ שלו היא ואין רשאי אדם שיעמוד בארצו אם לא במצותו. See Note 3.

5. Maimonides, *Mishneh Torah, Geselah* V:18 — בד"א במלך שמטבעו יוצא באותן הארצות שהרי הסכימו עליו בני אותה הארץ וסמכה דעתן שהוא אדוניהם והם לו עבדים אבל אם אין מטבעו יוצא הרי הוא כגזלן בעל זרוע...

6. See *Hoshen Mishpat* 369, 2; *Tur, ibid.;* Mordecai Jaffe, *Lebushim,* 369; *Zemach Zedek, Hoshen Mishpat,* 2.

7. *Shiltei Gibborim* to B.B.

8. Actually R. Eliezer of Metz—see Ibn Adret in his commentary to Nedarim 28a; also, Nissim Gerondi, *ibid.*

9. וכתבו בתוספות דדוקא במלכי עכו"ם אמר דד"ד מפני שהארץ שלו ויכול לומר להם אם לא תעשו מצותי אגרש מן הארץ אבל במלכי ישראל לא לפי שא"י כל ישראל שותפין בה.

10. E.g. extortionate taxes, freedom of motion, etc.

11. R. Asher b. Yehiel, Ned. 28a — והיינו טעמא דדינו דינא שהארץ שלו היא ואף הדיוט שיש לו קרקע כך דינו שלא יהנה אדם מארצו אלא מדעתו ובקצבתו.

12. See *Hesronot haShas* to Ned. 28a — אין זה ד"ד אלא גזילא דמלכותא.

13. David Ibn Zimra, III, 533 — בנ"ד שלקח המדינה בכח המלחמה שהרי הבעלים בעצמן חייבין לו מיתה וקיי"ל כל הרוגי מלכות נכסיהם למלך.

14. I. Agus, *Teshubot Baalei Tosafot* — דהפקיעו חכמים ממון במנהג והמלכות כדרך שהפקיעו מפני תקנת השבים (ב"ק צד:) ומפני תיקון העולם (גיטין לד:) ומפני דרכי שלום (גיטין נט:) וכן הא דתלאה וקדיש (ב"ב מח:) וההיא עובדא דהוי בגרש יבמות קי.) שהפקיעו קידושי תורה). Comp. *Shittah Mekubezet,* quoting R. Jonah, B.B. 546 — וכענין הפקר ב"ד הפקר.

15. I. Agus, *op. cit.*—who considers R. Tam's statement as a reason for Samuel's law.

16. Ibn Adret P. III, 54 — שאין ... כי כל מה שעשו הב"ד לא עשו כהוגן לב"ד רשות בנכסי בני אדם כלום למכור ולמשכן וכ"ש להפקיר בלא טענה ידועה מן הדברים שניתן רשות ביד ב"ד לפרוע בעל חוב בחובו ולאשה בכתובה או מחמת

מזונות או להפקיר ממון לעונש וכיוצא בזה אבל למכור או למשכן נכסי אחרים מדעת
עצמן וכ"ש להפקירם שלא בטענה טעות הוא זה וכ"ש בתי דינין של עכשיו דלא אלימי
לאפקועי ממונא.

17. See Asaf, *Teshubat haGeonim* p. 75 (תש"ב); Maimonides, *Mishneh
Torah, Malveh veLoveh* 27:1; Abraham Ibn Daud, *ibid.; Tur,* 68:1; *Hoshen
Mishpat, ibid.;* R. Asher b. Yehiel, *Responsa,* 18:2; *Abkat Rohel,* 72; Sam-
uel b. Modena, *Hoshen Mishpat,* 304, 350; *Shiltei Gibborim* to Gittin 10b;
Joseph b. Solomon Colon, 18; R. Solomon Luria, *Yam Shel Shlomo,*
Gittin, 22.

18. R. Jonah Gerondi, B.B. 54b — שאם יכול ישראל לכוף את חבירו בדיני
ישראל ואין המלך כופה אותו לדון באותן דינין שלו והנהגות שהנהיג נמצא שלא פקע
זכותו של ישראל מחמת אותו ד"ד אא"כ הלך חבירו לדון בפני ערכאות שלהם כיון שלא
קבע המלך אותם דינים אלא בערכאות שלהם. The outstanding exception to this
viewpoint is R. Tam.

19. Nahmanides, see *Shiltei Gibborim,* Gittin 10b; also M. Katzenellenbogen, *Responsa,* 54 — שטרות העשויין בנוטורי"ן של מלכות פי' ע"י סופרי
המלך ואפי' אין עדים חתומים בו אלא אחד ממונה ע"פ המלכות כשר ולא מן הדין אלא
וכיון שבדיניהם היה לו דין אע"פ שבדינינו לא היה — Trani, III, 100 משום ד"ד
לו דין... הוה ליה כמלך שכעס על א' מעבדיו ולקח שדהו שאינה גזל ואין הבעלים
מוציאין אותו מיד ישראל שלקחה מן המלך ולא גרע זה שהיה יכול להוציאו בדיניהם
החקוקים להם מן המלך שאין לו דין אלא מצד ד"ד...

20. Because of factors which would disqualify its usage—see following
chapter.

21. E.g., writs of gifts.

22. Ibn Adret VI, 254 — וא"נ במה שישראל עושה עם ישראל חבירו מדעת
עצמו כאותה שאמרו... כל השטרות העולות בערכאות... שאע"פ שמצד דיני המלך
אינו מועיל כיון שבמתנה אין בו תועלת למלך כיון שזה מדעתו עשה מתנתו בערכאות
הרי קבל עליו לילך בזה בדיני המלכות... ובדבר שבממון יכול לשעבד עצמו וליתן
משלו שלא מן הדין.

23. *Hatam Sofer, Yoreh Deah,* 127 — ועוד לא דמי לדהתם שחק מחק מס
המלך ומחק פרנסת חייליותיו דמדאורייתא דד"ד וכיון שנכתב ונחתם בטבעת המלך בספרו
אין להשיב ונקנה קנין גמור טפי מכל השטרות בעולם אבל הכא פס"ד שלהם איננו קנין
לא עדיף מפס"ד של ישראל דלא קני.

24. See Graetz Vol. VI, 5 — Yussuf Ibn Teshufin was bribed by the
Jews to revoke his demands for the conversion of an entire Jewish community. *"Indessen brachten ihn die von den Juden Luccena's zusammenge-
brachten Summen."*

25. Graetz, Vol. VI, 7 — *"Sie besassen nicht bloss Häuser sondern
auch Acker und Weinberge die von ihnen selbst oder von christlichen
Knechten bearbeitet wurden."* See Joseph haMekane.

26. Graetz, Vol. VI, 7 — *"Der jüdische Prevôt wurde von der Ge-
meinde gewählt und von dem Könige oder dem Baron, dem die Stadt
gehörte, bestätigt.* Also Meir of Rothtenberg. See also Benjamin of Tudela

‎Rimon was ‎(...) ‎ושם‎. ‎הנשיא אבא מרי בר׳ יצחק והוא פקיד השלטון רימון‎ —
Raymond V who lived during the 12th century and died in 1194. See Ibn
Verga, *Shebet Yehuda* — ‎רימון שלטון מת‎ (‎קנ״ה‎) ‎קל״ה שנת‎.

27. Graetz, Vol. VI, 8 ff.

28. Tosafot, Ned. 28a; B.K. 113a; Also, *Sefer Hasidim*, 421; Moses
of Coucy, *Semag*, 73.

29. Tosafot B.K. 58a — ‎אי נמי‎: ‎ואומר ר״י ששאם בא ישראל וקנאם מיד השר‎
‎מחזירה לבעלים ונוטל מה שהנהו דאין זה ד״ד כי ראינו במדינה שבסביבותינו שמשפט‎
‎היהודים לעמוד כמו פרשים בכל מקום שירצו ובדין מלכותא היו תופסין שלא יחזיק‎
‎המושל בנחלת היהודים כשיצאו מעירו וכן היו נוהגים בכל ארץ בורגוניא‎.

30. R. Meir of Rothenburg, L. 313, Pr. 661 — ‎ואם ברח יהודי מעירו‎
‎והגיח קרקעותיו והחזיק בם השר‎...‎ נראה לר״י שאין לישראל אחר לקנותם שקרקע‎
‎אינה נגזלת‎...‎ כי הדין הוא בכל המלכויות האלה שכשהיה יהודי יוצא מן העיר שבדין‎
‎מלכות לא היו המושלים מחזיקין בביתו לפי שמשפט היהודים ללכת אנה ואנה בכל מקום‎
‎שירצו ואם שעוותו את הדין אין זה דין מלכות אלא גזל מלכות‎.

31. R. Hayyim b. Isaac Or Zarua, 179; Meir of Rothenburg L. 114 —
‎ועוד מזקנים נתבונן דר״ת עשה תקנה אחת‎...‎ וז״ל ועל כן בן ברית איש ואשה גזרנו‎
‎באלה אשר יתערב נגד השרים היושבים תחת השלטון הצרי משיקוע כל אדם ואם ח״ו‎
‎יעבור על גזירתינו‎.

32. R. Asher b. Yehiel, B.K. 58 — ‎כי המנהג הוא בכל המדינות וחק ישראל‎
‎הוא על פי השרים והמלכים לילך ולדור בכל מקום שירצה ולא יעכב משלהם כלום‎.

33. Joseph Ibn Habbib and Mordecai *ad. loc.;* Ibn Adret, V, 198 —
‎לפי שהדבר ידוע בדיניהם שדין יהודים כדין הפרשים לדור בכל מקום שירצו וכיון שכן‎
‎אם בא איזה מלכות לשנות את הדין ולעשות דין לעצמו אין זה ד״ד‎.

34. Tosafot, Ned. 28a; B.K. 113a; *Semag* II, 43d; Solomon Luria,
Yam Shel Shlomo to B.K., 18.

35. Barfat, 2 — ‎במוכס‎ ‎מוקמינן בגמ׳‎ ...‎ דכי תנן בפ׳ ד׳ דנדרים נודרין להרגין‎
‎שאין לו קצבה ר״ל ששואל דבר שלא מן הדין או במוכס העומד מאליו והכי הוו כמו‎
‎אונסי׳ אבל במכס שהוא מחוק המלך אסור לעבור עליו ואין זה נקרא אונס דדד״ד אבל‎
‎כשהדבר מחמת אונסין או שהמלך מעליל שלא כדין כדי להעניש ממון כמו שעושה עתה‎
‎בממון האנוסין שברחו לעשות תשובה או ממון היהודים היוצאים מארצו לארצות הפרשים‎
‎או למלכות אחרת שאין זה מן הדין אלא שנותן עליהם חקים לא טובים להתגולל עליהם‎
‎לקחת ממונם בזה מותר להערים או בנדר או בשבועה‎.

36. See *supra* footnotes 5 and 6.

CHAPTER IV

SAFEGUARDS TO SAMUEL'S LAW

1. B.K. 113b.

2. *Ibid.* 113a; Ned. 28a.

3. *Ibid.*

4. See previous chapter. Although the Geonim ruled in this matter according to what has been stated, there were many rabbis who, later on, reversed the Gaonic decision and allowed Gentile writs for gifts to be properly processed and honored in a *Bet Din*. See below.

5. Eliezer of Metz quoted in Mordecai b. Hillel Ashkenazi, B.K.; *Or Zarua* III, B.K. 447; *Sefer Eben ha-Ezer,* ed. Albeck, 112; *Rabyah,* B.K.; Hayyim b. Isaac, *Or Zarua,* 110, 253 — ולי נראה דלא אמור דיניה דינא אלא דוקא בקרקעות במשפטים שהם תלויים בקרקעות והיינו טעמא דדיניה דינא שהארץ שלו היא. Also, *Sefer ha-Terumah* quoted in *Abkat Rohel,* 6 — כגון ענייני דרכים והמסים והטסקא שלו.

6. Hayyim b. Isaac, *Or Zarua,* 110 — ואין רשאי אדם שיעמוד בארצו אם לא במצותו.

7. *Ibid.,* 253.

8. Joseph Colon, 191, in the name of Mordecai b. Hillel Ashkenazi. Samuel de Modena states that this is also Colon's decision as found in responsum, 188. This responsum deals with an entirely different matter. In 191, Colon cites Mordecai and states: בשלמא לענין קרקע שיהיה נקנה בשטר שלהם כדין קרקע שנגקנה בשטר שייך לומר דד״ד... אבל לענין יד בעל חוב על התחתונה או על העליונה וכיוצא בזה פשיטא דלא שייך דד״ד. However, Colon disagrees with this view.

9. Ibn Zimra, V, 2076 — כיון דד״ד... נמצא שהכל הוא משועבד מלמלכות וחשבי ליה כאלו הוא גבוי.

10. Maimonides, *Mishneh Torah, Malveh ve-Loveh* I — והרי עליו שטר חובות לעכו״ם ואמר הרי כל נכסי משועבדים לעכו״ם... אין שומעין לו.

11. *Abkat Rohel,* 47.

12. Ibn Adret, I, 1132 — זו היא שורת; III, 165 — שהדרך של מלך הוא. הדין זולתי אם יש חקי המלך כמו שיש במקצת המקומות שכל כיוצא בזה הולכין אחר חקי המלכות; IV, 35 — וכ״ש אם יש דין המלכות שם להיות כל הדרכים שלו.

13. *Ibid.,* 111 — שכל הדרכים של המלך הם וכך הוא בחוקי הממלכים ואין לאדם בהם זכות אלא במה שהוא חק המלכות... וכל שייש בו מנהג הכל הולך בכיוצא בזה אחר מנהג לפי שבכל כיוצא בזה דד״ד.

14. Ibn Adret, *Torat ha-Bayit,* 134, 292 — ומה גם שהשוקים והרחובות הם למלכים והם יכולים לסגור ולבנות ברחובות עיר כן ראוים אותם נוהגים כן אם נתן המלך לאלו לעמוד להם דלתות עושין דדד״ד.

15. Levi Ibn Habib, 44 — אמנם אם מחוק המדינה או המלך שאין אדם יכול

להוציא בנין על דרך הרבים פשיטא שהדין עם ראובן ויכול למחות בו דבהאי מילתא
דד״ק אליבא דכ״ע כי דרך הרבים הוא למלך ודינו דין...

16. Joseph Ibn Migash, B.B. — דכיון דאכול מדינתא הוא דקא רמי לה הוי
ליה ד״ק.

17. Maimonides, *Mishneh Torah, Gezelah*, V, 14 — כללו של דבר כל
דין שיחזקוק אותו המלך לכל ולא יהיה לאדם אחד בפני עצמו אינו גזל. Also, Isaac
b. Aaron, quoted by I. Agus, *Teshubot Baalei Tosafot*, 130 — כללו של
דבר כל שיחזקה המלך לכל ולא יהיה לאחד בפני עצמו אינו גזל רק דין דין המלך.

18. Ibn Adret, V, 198 — שאם גזל המלך לאחד מבני עמו ממוגו שבא עליו
בעלילה דחמסנותא דמלכותא מיקרי אבל במאי דעבד בכל ארעיה הורמגותא דמלכא הוא
ודינא הוא.

19. Hayyim b. Isaac, *Or Zarua*, 110 — לא אמרי׳ דד״ק אלא כשהמלך משוה
Mordecai, מידותיו על כל בני מלכותו אבל אם משנה למדינה אחת לא הוי דיניה דינא
B.K. in name of Eliezer of Metz — דלא אמרי׳ דד״ק אלא כשהמלך משוה מידותיו
בכל בני מלכותו. See also, Joseph Caro, *Shulhan Aruk*, 369; *Siftei Kohen*,
73:39; *Hatam Sofer*, 126 — וכשיהיה החק שוה לכל עם ולכל אדם.

20. *Or Zarua*, bases his views on Mishneh, Gittin 5:7 — לא היה
סיקריקון ביהודה בהרוגי מלחמה. The law of סיקריקון was valid because of
the power and force of the king, but *Dina D'Malkhuta Dina* did not apply
since it involved individuals and was not equally applicable to everyone.

21. R. Nehemiah, at end of the responsa of R. Meir of Rothenburg —
ואפי׳ בחקים נמי דוקא שיעשה בהרמגא דבני מלכותא וכשיהיה שוה לכל.

22. Ibn Zimra, V, 2248 — אם היו קהל טריפול מלכי האדמה לא היה בידם
כח לזה שאין הדבר שוה לכל בני המלכות דד״ק אמרי׳ ולא גזלנות...

23. Joseph Habbib, *Nemukei Joseph*, B.B. — ד״ק שצריך שיהיה אותו
החוק כללי לכל בני המלכות ואפ״י שהיה חק חדש לבד שיהיה כללי ולא פרטי אמרי׳ דד״ק.
See also, *Abkat Rohel*, 6.

24. Moses Isserles, *Hoshen Mishpat*, 369:8.

25. Asher b. Yehiel, B.B. — כל המשפט חרוץ שתקן והנהיג המלך על כל
בני מדינתו ואין בו משום גזל המחזיק בממון ע״פ המלך. See also, Joseph Caro,
Hoshen Mishpat, 369:8.

26. Solomon b. Simon Duran, 47 — ע״כ אם המלך צוה לשלול העיר שמרדה
בו כדין עשה והזוכה בשללה זכה מן הדין שזה מחוקי המלוכה היא.

27. R. Yom Tob b. Abraham Ibn Ashvilla, 53 — ומ״מ למדנו מזה
שדברים אלו הם כפי המנהג והסכמת שופטי המלך בזה אינו מעלה כלום אלא א״כ הוא
חק קבוע מן המלכות על כל המלכות ואפי׳ על היהודים דקיי״ל דד״ק.

28. *Abkat Rohel*, 80 — דשטרי כתובות הנעשו בעש״ג היו כשטר מכר והלוואה
שהם כשרים לכ״ע דכיון דעיקר השטר של כתובה שכותבים בפניהם הוא כמו שטר חוב...

29. *Hatam Sofer, Eben ha-Ezer*, 126 — הייתי רוצה לומר... אינו בכלל
דד״ק כי סבור הייתי שאין כתובה קבוע אלא לבנות ישראל נמצא אינו כולל לכל עם ועם
בשוה רק לעם לבני ישראל ובזה לא אמרי׳ דד״ק.

30. Moses Isserles, *Mapat ha-Shulkhan*, 369 — Isserles quotes the responsum 195 of Joseph Colon. The writer could find no such reference.

31. The requirement for equality in law preceded the requirement for all laws to be within the established, traditional law. The law of equality was first proposed by Ibn Migash in the 12th century, whereas the first to mention the need for established law were the scholars of the 13th century.

Solomon Luria, *Yam Shel Shlomo*, B.K. 18 quotes Maimonides, *Mishneh Torah, Gesela*, V:13 — כללו של דבר כל דין שיחקוק אותו המלך לכל ולא יהיה לאדם אחד בפני עצמו אינו גזל וכל שיקח מאיש זה בלבד שלא כדת הידועה לכל שלא כדת הידועה לכל אלא חמס את זה הרי זה גזל. Luria points to the phrase and claims that Maimonides already stipulated the need for established, traditional law. The phrase can only be understood in context with the entire ruling of Maimonides. He is speaking of the law of equality. The phrase "known to all" refers not to established traditional law, but is known to all because it applies to everyone and involves all citizens. The law requiring precedence was instituted later on.

32. Ibn Adret, VI, 254.

33. *Ibid.* — דיני המלכות שכל עם ועם יש לו חוקים ידועים... וד"ד אמרו דיני דמלכא לא אמרו. Also, *ibid. Torat ha-Bayit*, 356; R. Nehemiah, at end of responsa of R. Meir of Rothenburg; Joseph Habbib, *Nemukei Joseph*, B.B. Meiri, — הלכך כל שנטל השר ממון יהודי שלא מחוק המלכות הקבועים חמסנותא הוא quoted by *Shittah Mekubezet, ad. loc.* — וזה שאמרו ד"ד ולא אמרו דינא דמלכא; Yom Tob b. Abraham Ibn כלו' דינים הראוים לו מצד המלכות אבל מה שהוא מחדש מחמת אונס... כנגד דינים שלנו אינם בכלל זה שא"כ כל דיני ישראל בטלים הם Ashvilla, *ad. loc.*, Ned. 28a; Asher b. Yehiel, *Responsa*, 86:9 — דע"כ לא קאמרי ד"ד אלא דוקא אם הוא תקנת המלך וניימוס מפורסם... אבל כיון שאין נימוס דמלכותא; Nissim Gerondi, Gittin 10b — המלך ואבותיו אין זה ד"ד אלא גזילה דמלכותא; Solomon ולליישנא דדינא דמלכותא הכי משמע [כלומר מה שהמלך עושה מחוקי מלכות] b. Simon Duran, 212 — לפי סברות האלו אין אומרים בנדון הזה דד"ד כיון שלא; Solomon דינא דמלכותא ולא דינא דמלכא — *Abkat Rohel*, 6; נהגו בו הראשונים Luria, *Yam Shel Shlomo*, B.K. 18.

34. Ibn Adret, *ibid.* — אעפ"י שיאמר עכשיו המלך כן אינו דין. See also L. Finkelstein, *Jewish Self-Government in the Middle Ages*, II, p. 332 — "The commissioners shall endeavor to obtain a decree from our lord, the King, that the Community should not be compelled to pay any salary to the tax-collectors or *Asignaciones* since their pay used to come from the treasury of the king and not from the communities." שלא תהינה הקהילות מוכרחות לפרוע שום שלארי לנוגשי המס והא שיקנסי אונש באשר שכרם היה מאז על גנזי אדו' המלך יר"ה ולא על הקהלות.

35. *Ibid.* — הדינין הידועין or חוקים ידועים; Asher b. Yehiel, 86:9 — וניימוס מפורסם; Joseph Habbib, *Nemukei Joseph, ibid.* חוקים ידועים. Also, Ibn Adret, *ibid.* — שהוא וכל המלכים אשר לפניו נהגו כן; Asher b. Yehiel, *ibid.* —

Solomon b. Simon Duran, שלא נהגו בימי האבות — שאין נימוס המלך ואבותיו —
ibid. — שלא נהגו בו הראשונים.

36. Ibn Adret, ibid. — Yom Tob; והם כתובים בדברי הימים ובחוק המלכים
b. Abraham Ibn Ashvilla, Ned. 28a.

37. Ibn Adret, ibid. — דכי אמרי׳ דד״ד היינו כגון הדינין הידועים למלך בכל
מלכותו שהוא וכל המלכים אשר לפניו נהגו כן והם כתובים בדברי הימים ובחוק המלכים
אבל מה שהמלך עושה לפי שעה או חק חדש שהוא עושה לקנוס פעם במה שלא נהגו בימי
האבות חמסנותא דמלכותא הוא ואין דנין באותו הדין.

38. Tosafot, B.K. 58a — ובדין מלכותא היו תופסין שלא יחזיק המושל בנחלת
. Also, Meir of Rothen-היהודים כשיוצאו מעירו וכן היו נוהגים בכל ארץ בורגוניא
burg L. 313; Pr. 661 — שבדין מלכות לא היו המושלים מחזיקים בביתו לפי שמשפט
היהודים ללכת אנה ואנה בכל מקום שירצו ואם שעוותו את הדין אין זה דין מלכות אלא
גזל מלכות.

39. Solomon b. Simon Duran, 212.

40. Ibid.

41. Asher b. Yehiel quoted by Solomon b. Simon Duran, ibid.; Tur
and Agudah, quoted by Solomon Luria, Yam Shel Shlomo, B.K. 18.

42. R. Moses ha-Kohen, quoted by both sources mentioned in the
previous note; Nahmanides, quoted by Solomon Luria, ibid.

43. Abraham Ibn Daud of Posquieres — דמדקאמר דמלכותא ולא אמר
דמלכא נראה שלא אמרו אלא בחקי המלכות הקבועים להם כגון מסים וטסקא אבל שר
. Also, Joseph Ibn Habbib,שגזל שדה בדרך חמס הרי הוא כשאר גזלנים ואין דינו דין
Nemukei Joseph, B.B. — מדאמר ד״ד משמע דלא אמרו אלא בדברים שהם חוקי
המלכים שלכל המלכים יש חוקים ידועים אבל מה ששר אנס נוטל בזרוע אינו דין הלכך
Nissim Gerondi, כל שנטל השר ממון יהודי ׳שלא מחוק המלכות הקבועין חמסנותא הוא
וללישנא ד״ד הכי משמע [כלומר מה שהמלך עושה מחוקי מלכות] ואי עביד — Gittin
הגמון שלא כדין חמסנותא הוי ולא דינא.

44. Ibid.; Joseph Habbib — וישראל שלקח ממנו לא זכה וכגזל הוא אצלו.
In a situation where the government confiscated the property of B to pay
for a debt which A owed, two opinions arose. The Spanish authorities
ruled that A must reimburse B for his expenditure when the confiscation
was deemed a legal one. See Maimonides, Hobel U'Mazik, 8:6 — מי שנתפס
על חבירו ולקחו עכו״ם ממון ממנו בגלל חבירו אין חבירו חייב לשלם לו מי שנתפש
על חבירו ויהיה חייב לשלם לו מן הנתפש׳ מפני המס הקצוב על כל איש ואיש בכל שנה.
On the other hand, the French and German authorities reversed the process. Only when B saves A from incurring a loss must he be reimbursed.
However, a legal debt must be paid and it is not considered a loss. Therefore, only when the king illegally confiscated property must A repay B.
See Tosafot, B.K. 58a; B.M. 31b — מה ההפסד דמה מן מצילו אין נמי דהתם ויי״ל. ולפי״ז
שמלוה טורף ממנו אין זה הפסד שהרי נתחייב לו ולכך חשיב ליה מבריח ארי...
אם השר גזל ביתו של ישראל ובא חבירו ישראל ופייס אותו בדמים מועטים אם ירצה
בעה״ב ליקח ביתו ישלם דמים לחבירו וכן פסק רבינו גרשום. Also Meir of Rothenburg, B.K. (59) — שהרי לו לפרוע חייב שפדאו ההפסד מן דהצילו כיון בנ״ד וא״כ.

164

היהודי לא היה חייב בדין לעכו"ם שתפשו והאי גזלנא הוא ולא הוי דינא כמוכס שאין לו
קצבה ... וא"כ חייב לשלם לו דמי פדיונו .See also, Isaac b. Samuel of Lemberg,
16.

45. Ibn Adret, *ha-Meyuhasot*, 22 — דכל שיש טעם במה שהמלך מצוה
ומנהיג דבר לתקון הנהגת המדינה יכול הוא לומר ממון שראוי להיות לזה מן הדין יהא
לחבירו ולא אמרי' חמסנותא הוא ... ויש כח למלך להפקיע ממון בכי הא דתקון מדינה
הם, ... ועושים מעשה בכל יום.

46. Joseph Caro, *Hoshen Mishpat*, 369.

47. Joseph Habbib, *Nemukei Joseph*, B.B. 54b — ד"ד אמרו דינא דמלכא
לא אמרו ... אע"פ דלא שייך ביה מלכא אלא הוא תקנה ותועלת לבני המלכות אמרי' ד"ד
Ibn Adret quoted by Joseph Colon in responsum 637; Joseph Caro, *Bet
Joseph*, 26; Moses Isserles, *Hoshen Mishpat*, 369.

48. Maimonides, *Mishneh Torah, Malveh ve-Loveh*, 27:1; see *Magid
Mishneh ad. loc.;* Nissim Gerondi, Gittin 10b; Ned. 28a; Ibn Adret, VI, 254
— וכן אינו דין אלא במה שיש לו למלך תועלת Asher b. Yehiel, 103:1; Meir of
Rothenburg, Ms. שזח"ה, 889; Samuel de Modena, *Hoshen Mishpat*, 224;
ibid. Samuel Halevy and Joseph Taitozok; M. Isserles, *Hoshen Mishpat,*
369; *Darkei Moshe,* 11.

49. *Ibid.*

50. Ibn Adret, V, 194 in name of Abraham b. David of Posquieres —
שלא נאמר דד"ד אלא בדברים שהם עסקי המלך כעניני המכסים והטסקאות שלו אבל עסק
שבין אדם לחבירו לא. Also, Joseph Caro, *Abkat Rohel*, 81 in name of *Magid
Mishneh* — ה"מ במה שהוא תועלת למלך בעניני המסים שלו ומה שהוא מחוקיו אבל
בדברים שבין אדם לחבירו אין דינו בהם דין.

51. *Abkat Rohel*, 72, 6 — כי בכאן יש תועלת למלך יר"ה.

52. Joseph Caro, *Bet Joseph, Hoshen Mishpat*, 26.

53. *Ibid.; Hatam Sofer, Yoreh Deah*, 315.

54. *Ibid., Hoshen Mishpat*, 142.

55. Ibn Adret, III, 34, 40; V, 198; Barfat, 197 — וכיון שהמלך צוה
בפרוש שכל אדם יקח בכל מלכותו המטבע החדש הגרוע בערך היפה וישוכלו לפרוע בו
חובותיהם לפי הערך היוצא ודאי דד"ד ואין זה חמסנותא דמלכותא לפי שענין המטבע
הוא מחוקי המלוכה. Nahmanides, quoted in *Hatam Sofer, Eben ha-Ezer*, 126;
Siftei Kohen, Yoreh Deah, 165:8; *Hoshen Mishpat*, 74; *Hatam Sofer, Hoshen Mishpat*, 58, 178 — כל המעיין בצדק יראה שכן דעת כל הראשונים והאחרונים
הלא בספרתם דלענין מטבע לפחות ה"ל דד"ד. Apparently he did not see the authorities who disagree; Samuel de Modena, *Hoshen Mishpat*, 75.

56. Meir of Rothenburg, Ms. שזח"ה, 889; Asher b. Yehiel, 103:1 —
ומה שכתבת ... כשהמלך גזר על המטבע ... אם דד"ד או לא לא ידענא מה שייך להזכיר
בכאן ד"ד ואם המלך עשה מטבע חדש ... בשביל זה לא גזר להפסיד למלוה שהלוה מטבע
טוב שיקבל גרוע המלך אינו מקפיד אלא שיהא מטבע הראשון נפסל ומעובר מן העולם ...
ואינו חושש אם יפרוע למלווה כפי ערך מטבע הראשון כי בזה אין המלך מפסיד כלום.

57. Solomon Luria and Joel Sirkis considered the problem a ספיקא דדינא
(המוציא and only he who was able to substantiate his claim could prevail
מחבירו עליו הראיה).

165

58. Nahmanides, Ned. 28a and quoted in *Hatam Sofer, Hoshen Mishpat*, 58, 65; Nissim Gerondi, Gittin 10b; Ned. 28a; Joseph Habbib, *Nemukei Joseph*, B.B. 55a — ושמעינן משמעתין דד״ר אפי׳ במילי דלא שייך ליה למלכא מידי; ביה כי הכא דמאי איכפת ליה למלכא אי קני ארעא באיגרתא או לא; Bezalel Ashkenazi, *Shittah Mekubezet, ad. loc.;* Ibn Adret, I, 895.

59. Gittin 10b.

60. *Ibid.*

61. Yom Tob b. Abraham Ibn Ashvilla, 38; Ibn Adret, I, 895; III, 63, 66, 69, 79; VI, 218; *Torat ha-Bayit*, 213; *Novellae,* Gittin 10b; Barfat, 51, 203; Nissim Gerondi, Gittin 10b; Ibn Zimra, I, 67, 541; Solomon b. Simon Duran, 219; Joseph Caro, *Bet Joseph,* 66; Solomon Luria, *Yam Shel Shlomo,* Gittin 22.

62. Gittin 10b.

63. Alfasi, Gittin, mentions both solutions. Two opinions arose as to which of the two answers Alfasi accepted. Ibn Ashvilla felt that Alfasi did not make any decision. Ibn Adret stated that Alfasi ruled according to the last answer or else why mention it. Comp. Ibn Zimra, I, 67; *Teshubat ha-Geonim,* Asaf (תש״ב) p. 75; Maimonides, *Mishneh Torah, Malveh ve-Loveh,* 27:1; *Maggid Mishneh ad. loc.;* Joseph Caro, *Hoshen Mishpat,* 68:1; Joseph Colon, 18, 161.

64. Nissim Gerondi, Gittin 10b, Mordecai, *ad loc.; Maggid Mishneh, Malveh ve-Loveh,* 27:1; Joseph Caro, *Abkat Rohel,* 72; Samuel de Modena, *Hoshen Mishpat,* 304; Solomon Luria, *Yam Shel Shlomo,* Gittin 22; *Hatam Sofer, Hoshen Mishpat,* 58 claims that whenever there is a matter which directly concerns the king, then "the law of the kingdom" is to be applied even if it contradicts Jewish law. Samuel's principle is not necessary when the law of the government coincides with Jewish law. ותו ממ״נ אי נימא דמיירי באופן שאין קפידא כלל א״כ פשיטא שמצוה לשמוע למלך ולא למרות פיו ואין זה נוגע כלל לענין ד״ד כיון שאינו נגד דין תורה...

65. Ibn Adret, VI, 254 — וא״נ במה שישראל עושה עם ישראל חבירו מדעת עצמו כאותה שאמרו... כל השטרות העולות בערכאות... אע״פ שמצד דיני המלך אינו מועיל כיון שבמתנה אין בו תועלת למלך כיון ש׳זה מדעתו עשה מתנתו בערכאות הרי קבל עליו לילך בזה בדיני המלכות... ובדבר שבממון יכול לשעבד עצמו וליתן משלו שלא מן הדין.

66. Ibn Ashvilla, 38; Nissim Gerondi, Gittin 10b; Barfat, 203; Samuel de Modena, *Hoshen Mishpat,* 304; Solomon Luria, *Yam Shel Shlomo,* Gittin 22; Solomon Luria states that in 16th century Poland there was no such demand on the part of the king, and therefore, a writ for a gift was not accepted when it was issued by a Gentile court.

67. Asher b. Yehiel, 18:3; Nissim Gerondi, Gittin 10b; *Abkat Rohel,* 72 — אבל אם היה מקנהו המתנה באחת מהדברים שניקנית בהם המתנה והיה כותב לו שטר מתנה לראי׳ בעלמא שהשטר כשר וכ״כ רבינו ניסים בפ׳ המביא גט.

68. Asher b. Yehiel, 18:2 — אבל נראה שבזמן הזה אין רגילים בדיני ישראל

ולא בערכאות של ישמעאלים לקנות בשטר לא במכר ולא במתנה... הלכך כלהו כשרים בערכאות של ישמעאלים; Barfat, 51; *Hatam Sofer, Eben ha-Ezer*, 95.

69. Barfat, 484 — ואיך ימשכנגו בגופו שצריך לבקש פרנסתו בשוקים וברחובות ומה שטען שמעון המלוה בזה דד"ד אינו ענין לזה כלל ישאין דינא דמלכות ואף לא דינא דמלכא שיהיה אדם נתפשט בעד הלואה אלא באלפרד"א לבד הוא המנהג והדין ואם זה התנה להתחייב בהלואתו כפי חק ההוא ומדין תורתינו אין תנאי זה מועיל והמלך מה יעשה לו.

70. See chapter III.

71. Meir of Rothenburg L. 313 — אם שר אמר מעצמו איני חפץ ששום יהודי ידור בעיר הזאת אלא ברשות ראובן בהא ודאי מודינא לך שראובן יכול לעכב עליו מדינא דמלכותא.

72. *Ibid.* — כיון שהשר לא גירשו לזה ישמעון אלא מחמת שביקש אותו ראובן על ככה לאו כל הימנו להפסידו בדורו שאל"כ לא שבקית חיי לעניים מעשיר כי יתן לשר דבר מועט כדי לגרש כל העניים שבעירו.

73. *Ibid.* — אם שר אמר מעצמו.

74. Mordecai, B.K.; Ibn Adret, V, 244 — דאין חרם מבוטל ע"י כך שאין ביד שום אדם לבטל שבועות ונדרים וחרמות ישל אחרים ולא להתיר זולתי איש לאשתו ואב לבתו. See also M. Isserles, 52.

75. Maimonides, *Mishneh Torah, Gezelah*, V:13 — מלך שכעס על אחד מעבדיו ושמשיו מבני המדינה ולקח שדהו או חצירו אינו גזל ומותר ליהנות בה... שזה דין המלכיב כולם ליקח כל ממון שמשיהם כשכוטסין עליהם והרי המלך הפקיע שעבודן ונעשית חצר זו או שדה זו כהפקר... אבל מלך ישלקח חצר או שדה של אחד מבני והוא אמר — Also, Mordecai, B.K. (215). המדינה שלא בדינין שחקק הרי זה גזלן שמואל דד"ד: המלך שכעס על עבדיו ושמשיו מבני המדינה ולקח שדהו או חצרו אינו גזל ומותר ליהנות בו והלוקח אותו מן המלך הרי הוא שלו ואין הבעלים מוציאים מידו שזהו דין המלכים שלוקחים כל ממון שמשיהם כשכוטסים עליהם והרי המלך הפקיע שעבדו ונעשה שדהו כהפקיר וכל הקונה אותו מאת המלך זכה בה. Also, Isaac b. Aaron, I. Agus, *Teshubot Baalei Tosafot* — שזה דין המלכים כולם ליקח כל ממון שמשיהם.

76. *Ibid.*

77. Ibn Adret, V, 286 — הדין עם תובע משום דקי"ל דד"ד ומדין המלכים הוא שכל מי שדר בעריהם שיעלו להם מס... Note that no distinction is made between a head-tax and a land-tax. The Talmud, B.B. 55a made such a distinction. Furthermore, confiscation as a result of the failure to pay land-tax which was considered legal by the Talmud and by the medieval authorities, was denied later on when kings no longer owned the land. See Joshua Falk, *Sefer Me'irat Enayim*, 369:10; See also David Halevy, *Turei Zahab, ad loc.*

78. Meir of Rothenburg L. 381; Ibn Adret, *Torat ha-Bayit*, 369; Mordecai, B.K. (215); Maimonides, *Mishneh Torah, Gezelah*, 5:13; Contr. Samuel de Medina, *Hoshen Mishpat*, II, 55.

79. Ibn Adret, *ibid.*, 225; M. Trani, III, 128.

80. As in many instances where under ordinary circumstances "the law of the kingdom" was not invoked because the matter was of no direct

concern to the king, if in any nation the king insisted that the law be obeyed, and thus made it his concern, then Samuel's law prevailed. Consequently, Ibn Ashvilla ruled that where the king demanded that property should be confiscated upon the failure to repay a debt, such confiscation was legal and whosoever purchased such property from the creditor cannot be accused of theft. See Ibn Ashvilla, 127 — אם נתברר לב״ד כי הגובײנא ההיא שנעשית לגוי היתה כראוי ע״פ ב״ד של ישראל או אפי׳ ע״פ ערכאות של גוים במקום שדין המלכות הוא לעשות כן ולדון עם ישראל בדיניהם הא קײ״ל דד״ד...If the king makes restitution to A for properties stolen from him, but unknowingly includes property belonging to B, such property must be returned to B. The law of the kingdom was to restore the stolen articles to their rightful owners. Such must be done even if such owner had already resigned himself to his loss. Ibn Zimra, I, 460 — ותו דאפי׳ תימא דיאוש׳ כזה נקרא יאוש בשלמא אם היה מציל שמעון מיד הגייס בעצמו דין הוא שיהיה שלו אבל בנ״ד לא הציל אלא מכח משפט המלך יר״ה ומשפטו הוא שיחזיר הגזל לנגזל יהיה מי שיהיה שהרי אין להם דין יאוש ודד״ד. Religious books confiscated by order of the king belonged to him who redeemed them. See Maimonides, *Responsa*, ed. Sasportas, 131: אם זה השללי היה בגזרת המלך הרי קנה הוא הכל...אמנם אם נגנבו שלא בגזירת המלך... ויחזרו אותם הספרים למקומן הראשון.

81. *Hakmei Zorfat ve'Lotir*, 34; Meir of Rothenburg L. 381; Ibn Adret, I, 1105.

82. Meir of Rothenburg Pr. 677.

83. M. Trani, I, 194.

84. Joseph Caro, *Abkat Rohel*, 47 — וכמו ישבעניגינו ראינו שכל מלך סותר בתים שאצל החומה בשעת חירום כדי שלא יכנסו הצרים הצוררים בבתים .. וזה ד״ד ואינו גזל וכאלה רבות מקרים בכל יום מזה המין ומימיניהם אחרים לצורך המלך.

CHAPTER V

AGENTS OF THE KING

1. B.K. 113b — שלוחא דמלכא כמלכא.

2. *Ibid.*

3. Joseph Caro, *Orah Hayyim,* 391; *Bet Joseph, ad loc.; Abkat Rohel,* 47. Some of the rabbis preceding Caro ruled otherwise. Caro quotes Ibn Adret, I, 626; V, 168; *ha-Meyohosot,* 218 and others who ruled that the kings have no rights with regard to the homes in a city. Consequently, "the law of the kingdom is the law" cannot be cited as justification for the act of purchasing *Reshut.* The king who oversteps his rights and claims authority over property in a city is guilty of royal theft. It is incumbent upon the Jews residing in such a city to purchase *Reshut* from each Gentile resident separately. It cannot be achieved by means of a "package deal" via the king. Comp. Meir of Rothenburg quoted by Mordecai, Erubin (509) and Adret, V, 4; *Kol Bo,* 33; Maimonides, *Erubin* — שני יהודים הדרים בכרך אחד אין די להם במה שקונים מהשר לעשות עירוב אלא צריכים לשכור מכל בית ובית שיש להם; *Tur,* 391; *Baal Halakot Gedolot in Semag, Mitzvot deRabonon;* Jacob b. Aaron, *Mishkenot Jacob, O. H.,* 112 — ה"ה באנשי חיל אף דמד"ד יכולים לבא לבתינו אין זה ענין שתהא נקראת ברשות הישמעאלי' שהרי לא קנו ולא שכרו אותה רק מטעם המלך יש להם לדור בבית ולהשתמש בו אבל עיקר הרשות נשאר לבעלים... Joseph Caro differentiates between instances where the king has certain rights in these cities and those wherein he enjoys no rights at all. Most kings have rights such as quartering soldiers, seizing or razing homes in times of war, or the authority to make use of any home whenever he so desires. In such cases, it is sufficient to purchase *Reshut* from him or any agent. — המלך יש לו רשות להשתמש בכל בית ובית שבעיר כשירצה ומשתמש בשעה שצריך א"כ יכולים היהודים לקנות רשות כל העיר ממנו שהרי ד"ד שבכל בית ובית מן המדינה חונין שמה עבדיו ופרשיו ויכול להפקיר (להפקיד) כליו בכל שעה שירצה.

Where even such rights are denied the king, then it is necessary to purchase *Reshut* from each homeowner individually. See *Bet Joseph,* 391. It is obvious that everyone agrees that when the king actually owns the homes of a city it is sufficient to purchase *Reshut* from him alone. See Simon b. Zemach Duran, II, 281; *Bet Joseph, ibid.* — שהרי יש' שר שכ"ע יודע שיקנו רשות ממנו והוא שר שהבתים שלו והשכירם.

First, it should be noted that only Adret speaks of a city containing a substantial Jewish community. The others speak of a few (שני יהודים הדרים) individual Jews residing in a Gentile city. In the latter case the problem was not as pressing. Adret lived at a time when Jews desired to limit the power of the king as much as possible. We have shown in the previous chapter why this was so. The overall situation warraned their ruling against recognizing and granting broader rights to the king. Even though in this

169

particular instance the rights granted to the king would facilitate matters for the Jews of a community, in the long run the powers granted the king would have harmed them.

On the other hand, 16th century Palestine under Moslem rule had no such fears. The Jews lived interspersed with Gentiles, although Jewish sections existed (שכונות ישראל). They enjoyed autonomy and were not anxious to curtail the powers of the king since these kings did not over-step their bounds. The problem of Jews living next door to Moslems be-came acute with regard to the Sabbath and Caro re-interpreted the earlier *halakah* to ease the burdens created by the new situations. — דלא מיירי בתשובותיו כי אם בשר ומושל העיר דאין היכולת בידו לעשות דבר קטן וגדול מבלי דעת ורשות מנהיגי וגדולי העיר. Caro considered the potential right of the king to requisition the homes of his citizens, as if it were an actual right of ownership.

4. Adret, I, 1105 — אבל עכשיו כל שר ושר במלכותו הוא כמו מלך; *Shiltei Gibborim,* B.B. 54b — וכל שלטון ושר וממונה בעיר ומושל במקומו דינו דין והוא ממש דמלך דומיא מקומו מחוקי שעושה כ״ז דד״ד בכלל בעירו; *Hoshen Mishpat,* 369. Furthermore, the Jews' fear of churchmen following the rules and regula-tions set forth by the Church, rather than the more liberal statutes of the secular government, prompted N. Gerondi (Gittin 10b) to exclude the legal acts of bishops. — ודוקא במה שהמלך עושה מחוקי מלכותו אבל מה שהגמון עושה שלא כדין לא... זאי עביד הגמון שלא כדין חמסנותא הוי ולא דינא. 5. *Ibid.* — ומיהו נראה דצריך שיהיה שליח מהמלך ממש לאפוקי שאם אחד מן החצרנים וההדרנים ויועצים מן המלך עשה שאין זה שלוחי דמלכא כמלכא...

6. R. Yom Tob Ibn Ashvilla, 44 — והטעם שאם אנו באין לדון הדין שלפנינו כדיני ישראל שאין אדם מקנה לחבירו דשלבל״ע... אלא מאי אית לך למימר דמתנה זו שנתן המלך לזקנו של ראובן היה במתנה כדיניהם של גוים וכדיני המלכות אע״פ שבדינינו אינה מתנה לית לן בה דאנן כדיניהם של גוים דייננו ליה... Comp. also Ibn Adret, *Torat ha-Bayit,* 213. However, should the recipient, A, attempt to sell these privileges to B, there was a difference of opinion. Ibn Ashvilla allowed the resale even if it did not comply with all conditions required by Jewish law. All facets concerning this transaction are to be governed by secular law and are validated by *Dina D'Malkhuta,* — וכיון שרצה ראובן שיזכה שמעון... הרי שמעון זוכה בו בכח חותם המלך כאילו היה דבר שבא לעולם כפי דיניהם של גוים..., whereas, Ibn Adret denies this leniency. A may only acquire these privileges by means of *Dina D'Malkhuta* but cannot sell them in turn, unless all conditions of Jewish law are fulfilled. — ואם יטעון שהוא זכה זכה משום ד״ד שעושין ונותנין בחסד וקיים אבל הוא אינו יכול להקנות לאחרים אלא באחד מדרכי הקניות של תורה והוא זוכה ואינו מזכה לאחרים. Comp. *Siftei Kohen, Hoshen Mishpat,* 356:10.

7. The *Herem Hayyishub* was introduced in the Middle Ages in order to give the dwellers of a city the prerogative to restrict the settling of newcomers. The *herem* had nothing at all to do with any laws governing trade competition. In fact, the *herem* could be applied to all newcomers

to a city, regardless of their intention to trade, or not to trade, there. It dealt strictly with the prevention of new settlers into a community. Dr. Zeitlin already stated (*J.Q.R.*, 1944, pp. 381-8): "Whenever the rabbis had to promulgate a new law for which they had a clue in the Talmud they never resorted to a *herem*. They declared a new law on the basis of the Talmud. Only where there was no clue in the Talmud or in the Gaonic literature did they invoke a *herem*."

The above thesis may be substantiated by a statement made by Mordecai b. Hillel Ashkenazi (B.B. 22) — ולכן נהגו הקדמונים להטיל חרם על הישוב דמשום דמן הדין לא מצי מעכב. In other words, it was only on the basis of the *herem* that the communities could refuse newcomers to settle but not on the basis of the law. Comp. S. Zeitlin, "The Herem Hayyishub," *J.Q.R.*, XXXVII, pp. 427-431, 1946-47.

8. Solomon Luria, *Responsa*, 36 — ועוד מצינו... שהיו קונים חזקת הישובים מן השר... ואף שג"כ אין ממש בקנין מן השר... אלא רשות ושלטנ' במתא חשוב כמו שקנה גוף העיר לאותו שולטנות... שקנה בית לדירה. See Joseph Saul Nathanson, *Shoel u'Meshib*, I, 18; Hayyim Ozer Grodzensky, *Ahiezer*, III, 79.

9. *Ibid.* — ומה שרגיל אדם לקנות מן שולטני העיר שאוזלינן בתרייהו בד"ד וידוע הוא בכל המלכות שקונים המכסים... או יין שרף... ושולטנות בעיר על הקניין ע"י שטר ארנדא. The arrangements between *Arandar* and landlord varied in different times and places. Thus, R. Menahem Mendel of Lubavitz, *Zemach Zedek, Hoshen Mishpat*, 78 writes that the *Arandar* was not considered an agent of the Emperor but rather merely paid a tax for the right to sell in a particular territory. — ולא שייך לומר כלל שהאוארענדא היא של הקיר"ה ושמוכרה לו דא"כ היה מקבל סך רב אלא רק שהקיר"ה מקבל מזה מס וזה לא נק' כלל בא מכחו דאטו מי שמשלם מס מאיזה דבר חשוב מוחזק באותו דבר.

10. *Hatam Sofer, Hoshen Mishpat*, 175 — דהרי דד"ד והשר גזר על הדברים תחת ממשלתו ובכלל מס שלו הוא זה שלא יהיה רשאים לקנות שום משקה כ"א מזה ששכר הארענדא ממנו והעובר ע"ז גונב את השוכר שעומד עפ"י ובמקום השר.

11. See Zeitlin, "Rashi and the Rabbinate," *JQR*, Vol. XXXI, pp. 28-32.

12. Finkelstein, *op. cit.* — חרם תקנת הקהלות ששם רבינו גרשם מאור הגולה דאין לישא שתי נשים אין להתירה רק במאה אנשים מג' ארצות ומג' קהלות. Also, S. Zeitlin, *op. cit.*

13. *Ibid.*

14. See footnote 11 above.

15. Adret, V, 126; A. Neuman, *Jews of Spain*, Volume II, p. 48.

16. Adret, I, 729 — וכל ציבור וציבור במקומן כגאונים וכל שתקנו כמה תקנות לכל וקיימות לכל ישראל. Also A. Neuman *op. cit., ibid·*

17. Ibn Adret, V, 279, 270; A. Neuman, *op. cit.*, p. 50.

18. Ibn Adret, V, 279; Barfat, 249; A. Neuman, *op. cit., ibid.*

19. Ibn Adret, VII, 453.

20. *Ibid.*, 454, see also A. Neuman, *op. cit.*, p. 57-8.

21. Ibn Adret, III, 388 — הרי שיש לקהל חותם מצד המלכות שיברו שנים
או שלשה ברורים יהודים בעניני התרעומות שידינו בין יהודי ליהודי ושיהיו מוכרחין
להודיע לגזבר המלך... ועניז החותם הוא כן שכל מי שיבוא לפני הממונים ההם...
שהרשות נתונה להם מצד המלכות שיראו ויחקרו העניז אם ירצו אבל לא בהכרח אבל
אם יתחילו בעניז החקירה מיד הם מוכרחים להודיע לגזבר.

22. Ibid. — וכל מי שנשבע לשקר מחוייב למלך בק' דינרי.

23. Ibn Adret, I, 612 — אם השלטון הזה יש בו כח לעשות חקום בעירו דינו
דין דקי"ל דד"ד ומי שמענשין המקלקלים כגון הגזלנים והגנבים והרצחנים וכיוצא בזה
ממשפטי המלוכה והאדנות הוא זה ודנין בכל אלו וכיוצא באלו דין ולפיכך בין שנטל
האדון בעצמו עונש הנענש או המעשר ממגו ונותנו לפקיד בין שיצוה לעגוש ליתן ליהודי
פקידו מותר לו לפקיד.

24. Barfat, 271 — ושאר המלכים במלכותם כמו מלך פרס בימים ההם בארצות
ההם.

25. Barfat, ibid. — ואיברא שאין לאדם ליטול רשות מן המלך שלא ברצון
הקהלות ומי שעושה כן הוא מצער את הציבור ועתיד ליתן את הדין וכ"ש אם אינו ראוי
לדון מפני שאינו יודע או מפני שאינו הגון שזה אין רשות מועלת לו כלום ואפי' נתן
Simon b. Zemah ;לו הרשות ראש הגולה או הנשיא... אין הרשות מועלת לו כלום
Duran, 158-162; Samuel b. Simon Duran, 533 — והראיה דלא אמרי' דד"ד דהא
ריש גלותא בהורמנא דמלכא הוא וקאמרי דלא מהני רשותא אלא למי שהוא מומחא דגמיר
וסביר... Isserles, ibid. — ומיהו כתבו שצריך להיות ראוי לכך והוי מרצון הקהילות;
שנתמנה עליהם.

26. Ibn Adret, I, 475 — בארצינו יש רבנים מצד המלכות ואינן יודעים לקרוא
כהוגן.

27. Samuel b. Simon Duran, 533 — אבל במגוי דייגות אם אינו הגון וידעו
בו שאיגו הגון לא ימנוהו אלא יטעים לומר שהוא הגון... והרי איגם מקפידים.

28. The fact that all rabbis asked for official sanction from the government was not the same as seeking official appointments to the rabbinate. This approval was sought so that no one be accused at the hands of informers (פושעי ישראל) of rebelling against the authority of the crown by administering justice without the king's consent. Samuel b. Simon Duran, ומה שהיו חכמי הדורות שואלין הורמנא דמלכא לא מחמת שיועיל להם לעניז דינה —533 דהגהו גמירי וסבירי וחשיבי אלא כדי שלא יאמרו עליהם פושעי ישראל איכא דדאין בלא הורמנא דמלכא ויעלילום. Comp. A. Yaari, *Igrot Eretz Yisroel*, p. 105.

29. Barfat, ibid. — ומי שעושה כן הוא מצער את הציבור ועתיד ליתן את הדין.

30. *Takkanot* such as at the Synod of Castile in 1432. "We further ordain that no officer may appoint any judge or any other officer without the consent of the community, or the majority thereof, and that the proposed officer must be mentioned by name (before the electorate). Any election held in any other way than that prescribed is hereby declared void." Finkelstein, *Jewish Self Government in the Middle Ages*, p. 357-8.

31. Samuel de Modena, *Orah Hayyim*, 156 — נראה שזה החי שעשה כדבר הרע הזה איגו ראוי להקרא ח'.

32. *Ibid.*

33. Barfat, 271.

34. *Ibid.*

35. *Ibid.*

36. Barfat, 272 — ואם יעמוד משה ושמואל ויגזרו או יתקנו בדבר קטן יחייבו
את ראש שונאיהם למלך כמורד במלכות.

37. *Ibid.* — ואף תלמיד חכם אינו רשאי לנדות בזאת הארץ כי אם בהורמנא דמלכא.
The excommunicated person could apply to the secular authorities for an
injunction restraining the rabbi from putting the *herem* into effect. This
could mean that the restraint was not a right granted to the government,
but was effected by means of force. However, were this to be true, some
form of protest would have been registered. See Barfat, 395 — וגם בקש
מן הגזבר יכריח אותי להבטיחו לבל אעשה דבר כנגדו במעשה או בדבור. Interesting
are the decisions of M. Isserles, 123 and *Hatam Sofer*. Isserles, living in
16th century Poland, and Sofer, in 19th century Hungary, both were influenced by the Franco-German School and yet recognized the appointment
of a rabbi by the government. Isserles stated: נראה דודאי אמרינן (דד״ד)
דהשררה והשולטנות שלהם ומחוקי המלך למנות שררה מושלים למי שירצה וראייה מעזרא
ונחמיה בן חכליה שהיו מושלים ע״פ כורש מלך פרס וכן שאר מלכי ישראל בבית שני.
Hatam Sofer concurred.

38. The communities of Spain were subjected to a Chief-Rabbi appointed by the kings. Local authorities were responsible to this official,
known as *rab de la corte*. He was usually a man without any rabbinical
qualifications. See Baer, I, p. 212; II, 287, 360, 365; A. Neuman, *Jews in
Spain*, p. 114.

39. Barfat, 61.

40. Duran, I, 161 — ...שהוא סדר ותקן שלא יהא רשות לדיין אחר לדון
ויש בזה עכוב מצוה שהוא מעכב ביד אחרים מלדון.

41. Duran, 158-162 — ויצא לנו מכל זה שאין אומרים בו דד״ד חדא שאין זה
מחוק המלכות למנות שופט ישראל... וכל שאינו מחוקי המלכים דינייהו לאו דינא...
42. *Ibid.*

43. *Ibid.* 162 — ולפי שנשתנו העתים לטובה לא כתבתי יותר וגם זה העלמתי ולא
הראתיו מפני כבוד ומפני דרכי שלום.

44. Comp. A. M. Hershman, *R. Isaac b. Sheshet Perfet and his Times,*
pp. 52, 55 — who writes that the phrase "conditions had changed for the
better" refers to Duran's recognition that Barfat would not abuse his
powers as the sole religious authority of Algiers. It is difficult to say that
this would be considered an improvement of "conditions." ולפי שנשתנו
העתים לטובה refers to the fact that the exclusive powers of Barfat were
rescinded.

45. *Ibid.,* 160. A grandson of Simon Duran states that a *takkanah*
was instituted to excommunicate anyone accepting a religious position by
royal appointment and that this *takkanah* was instituted by Simon Duran
and Barfat together. See *Yakin U-Boaz*, I, 17 — וכבר תקן א״ז הרשב״ץ עם
מורינו הרב יצחק בר ששת זלה״ה התקנה בכח חרם נדוי שלא יקבל אדם בעולם מינוי
אחד בענייני הקהל בהורמנא דמלכא הלא כתובה אצלינו אעתיק לכם נוסחתא ב״ה.

This appears difficult to accept for in doing so Barfat ruled against himself. Some maintain that Barfat in his old age changed his ruling to agree with Duran. See C. Lauer, *Jahrbuch der Jüdisch-Literarischen Gesellschaft*, Vol. XVI.

46. Barfat, 272 — ...אלא כל קהל וקהל בהורמגא דמלכא עושין תקנותיהם
ואם יעמוד משה ושמואל ויגזרו או יתקנו בדבר קטן יחייבו את ראש שונאיהם למלך כמורד
אם היו קהל טריפול מלכי האדמה לא היה — Ibn Zimra, V, 2248; ...במלכות
בידם כח לזה כיון שאין הדבר שוה לכל בני המלכות דד"ד אמרי' ולא גזלנות'.

47. See I. Agus, *Meir of Rothenburg*, p. 71, footnote 85 who points to the justification of the practice of capital punishment given to R. Asher, *Responsa*, 17:8 — ואמרו לי כי הורמגא דמלכא הוא. Dr. Agus states: "No scholar of Germany or France would ever give such a reason. R. Asher who was still steeped in the customs and manners of legal thinking of his native land found great difficulty in accepting a king's patent as a legal basis for the competence of a Jewish court; other reasons were therefore given to him. In cases, however, where the German and French communities also resorted to capital punishment, R. Asher was not hesitant any longer; his logic was clear, his proofs were based on sound Jewish law and his decision was straightforward and final."

48. Mordecai, B.M. 257 — וגם מפני תקנות הקהלות צריך שמעון להחזיר
...האבדה לראובן אפי' אם גתייאש ראובן דהפקר ב"ד הפקר שנא' וכל אשר לא יבא
ולייכא למימר דוקא בדורו של שמאי והלל או של ר"ג שהרי אמרו חכמים למה לא נתפרשו
שמותן של זקנים שלא יאמר אדם פלוני כאלדד ומידד פלוני כנדב ואביהו ואומר וישלח ד'.
Solomon Luria claims to have used a parchment written by Meir of Rothenburg; also see S. Zeitlin, "Rashi and the Rabbinate," *JQR*, Vol. 31, p. 42.

49. L. Finkelstein, *Jewish Self Government in the Middle Ages*, p. 154:
גזרנו ונדינו והחרמנו שלא יהא אדם רשאי ליטול שררה על חבירו ע"י מלך שר ושופט;
Simon b. Zemah Duran, I, 142.

50. Meir of Rothenburg, Pr. 137; Cr. 190; Mordecai, B.K. (107) —
לא טוב עשה להמגות ש"צ דרחמנא ע"פ הדוכוס ובארצגו היו מקפידים מאד על כיוצא בזה.

51. The responsum deals with any office, rabbi or cantor. The interchange of words and the ability to fine would indicate this. See also statement: *Hatam Sofer, Hoshen Mishpat*, 19; Meir of Rothenburg, Pr. 137. See also S. Zeitlin, "Rashi and the Rabbinate," *JQR*, Vol. 31, p. 44 —
ועוד גזרנו ונדינו והחרמנו שלא יהא אדם רשאי ליטול שררה על חבירו (לא) ע"י מלך
וכל מי — Also Finkelstein, *op. cit.* p. 154; *ibid.* p. 227 — שר ושופט (ולא ע"י).
שיעמיד חזן (סגן) או גלילת (ספר) התורה או כל צרכי (הקהל) צבור ע"פ גוים יהא בנידוי
אין למגות ש"צ ע"פ שר עובד גלולים אף — *Orah Hayyim*, 53; ובשמתא ובאחרמתא
שרוב הציבור חפצים בו.

52. Barfat, 271 — ומעת נעדר מהר"ר מתתיה נ"ע ועד עתה שהם כחמש שנים
הלך מהר"ר יוחנן בדרכי אביו נ"ע יושב בישיבה ומורה הוראה ודן את הדין.

53. See note 51.

54. Barfat, 271.

55. *Ibid.* — ראשונה ... היה ראוי למגות נוהג בשררה ההיא מהר' יוחנן

לפי שאביו מהר״ר מתתיה נ״ע נהג בה כבר ברצון הקהלות ובהורמנא דמלכא... ומן
הדין בנו קם תחתיו.
56. *Ibid.* — שנית... כיון שכבר היה נוהג בשררה ההיא שקבלה מעצמו והחזיק
בה זכה בה.
57. *Ibid.* — שלישית... שכבר נתמנה... בהסכמת קהלות צרפת וקבלוהו עליהם
ומעתה אין מורידין אותו דמעלין בקדש ואין מורידין.
58. *Ibid.* — רביעית... שנתמנה בהורמנא דמלכא ודד״ד...
59. *Ibid.* — תחלת כל דבר צריך לבאר מה זו סמיכה שנהגו בצרפת ואשכנז
שהרבנים נסמכים והם סומכים אחרים... ועתה כבר בטלה הסמיכה.
60. B. H. Auerbach, *Brit Abraham,* p. 6.
61. Barfat, 271; C. Lauer, "R. Meir Halevy aus Wien und der Streit
um das Grossrabbinat in Frankreich," *op. cit.* Vol. XVI pp. 1-42.
62. *Ibid.* p. 21.
63. Weiss, *Dor,* V, pp. 170-1 — אמנם רבי ישעיה חשב לעשות לרבי יוחנן
נבלה גדולה אשר כל איש אמת ידבר עליו משפט מרשיע... האין זה עול וחמס..
Also, Graetz, VI; S. Zeitlin, "Opposition to the Spiritual Leaders appointed
by the Government," *JQR,* Vol. XXXI, pp. 289 footnote 8.
64. C. Lauer, *op. cit.* p. 21 — *Wie ist es denkbar, dass der grosse
R. Meir Halevy . . . einem habsüchtigen Rabbiner mit Ordination und
Titel ausstaten und ihn dazu ermächtigen konnte, einen fremdem Lande
seit Jahren amtierenden Rabbiner zu entthronen?*
65. *Ibid.*
66. *Ibid.* — *"Unbegreiflich is es, dass R. Jochanen . . . in einer
schwulstigen Sprache zwei Briefe, einen an katolonischen Rabbiner und
den andern an Ribasch abfasst, in welchen er gewaltige Phrasen drischt,
meisterhaft schimpft, aber keine einzige Stelle ausdem Talmud . . . anzu-
führen weiss, die für seine . . . gerechte Sache zeugen."*
67. *Ibid.* p. 22 — *"Wie konnte der Grossrabbiner von Frankreich in
einem Kampfe unterliegen, in welchen er die Hilfe der Regierung, die ihm
in dieses Amt eingesetzt hatte, anzurufen vermochte? . . . Es scheint aber,
dass R. Jochanen die ihn "schützende Hand" eben nicht hat anrufen
können."*
68. *Meir of Rothenburg,* M. Mintz, 102; Graetz, *Geschichte,* Vol. VI,
181; Vol. VII, 21; also quoted above note 57.
69. C. Lauer, *op. cit.* p. 30 — *"R. Jochanen dagegen, wie gesagt,
konnte keinem bessern Anwalt für seine "gerechte Sache" finden als R.
Isaak b. Schescheth, der später selber von der Regierung zum Grossrabbiner
ernannt wurde."*
70. Dr. S. Zeitlin, "Opposition to the Spiritual Leaders appointed by
the Government," *JQR,* Vol. XXXI, pp. 294-5.
71. A. M. Hershman, *op. cit.*
72. Finkelstein, *op. cit.* pp. 357-8.

CHAPTER VI

TAXES

1. B.K. 113a; Joseph Caro, *Hoshen Mishpat*, 369:2.

2. B.K. 113a; Ned. 28a — במוכס שאין לה קצבה.

3. Meir of Rothenburg, A., II, 128; Mordecai B.B. (480); *Terumat ha-Deshen*, 341; Nehemiah b. Isaac found at end of Meir of Rothenburg (Am. Ed.) — וא״ת דד״ד ומלכא אמר לפרע צורבא מרבנן הא ליתא שכבר כתבו הראשונים דכל מידי דלא דינא ומלכא אמר דלעבדו דלא מתקרי דינא דמלכא אלא חמסנותא דמלכא שלא אמרו דינא דמלכא אלא ד״ד ואפי׳ ד״ד לא אמרו אלא בחקי מלכות ואפי׳ בחקים נמי דוקא שיעשה בהרמנא דבני מלכותא...; J. Caro, *Hoshen Mishpat*, 4; Joseph Saul Nathanson, *Shoel u'Meshib*, I, 21 — כיון דמצד הדין ת״ח פטור אין זה ד״ד רק חמסנותא.

However, money set aside for charity was taxable. See Nissim Gerondi, *Responsa*, 2 — ...וגם ראיה דבמסים וארנוניות אזלינן אחר דעת המלך משום דד״ד דלאו משום דינא אלא משום שכן דעת המלך... וא״כ בהיות דעת המלך הנהנה מהקרקע וכל מאן דאכיל ארעא ליהב טסקא מה איקפד לן אם הוקדש לעניים.

4. Ibn Adret, *Novellae*, B.K. 113a.

5. Maimonides, *Gezelah*, 5:11 — בד״א שהמוכס כליסטים בזמן שהמוכס עכו״ם. Also Joseph Caro, *Hoshen Mishpat*, 369:6; perhaps Maimonides, living in Moslem countries, was more prone to blankly disqualify non-Jewish tax farmers because the Moslems in general were more avaricious and cared little if the money was legally or otherwise acquired. In 16th century Salonika Samuel de Modena testified that the profit accrued by tax farmers was considered stealing from the king. *Hoshen Mishpat*, 156 — שכפי האמת במלכות שאנו עומדים בו הריוח שהמוכסין מרויחין אינה אלא גזלה שגוזלין מהמלך ירי״ה. Compare interpretation of this Maimonidian statement made by R. Hayyim Volozin, *Hut Hameshulosh*, 14, 16.

6. Nissim Gerondi, Ned. 28a — במוכס שאין לו קצבה: וכיון שכן לאו דינא הוא אלא חמסנותא וחמסנותא דמוכס (חסרונות הש״ס — דמלכא) לאו דינא.

7. Ibn Adret, V, 178.

8. Hayyim b. Isaac, *Or Zarua*, 253.

9. *Ibid.*

10. Ibn Zimra, II, *Lilshonot ha-Rambam*, 164; IV, 54 — וכיון שזה המוכס אינו לוקח יותר מהקצוב אע״פ שמרויח לפי שלוקח בזול מן המלך אסור להבריח ממנו.

11. He is not barred from giving testimony because he may be guilty of theft for taking more in taxes than he is legally permitted. Were theft the reason for disqualifying him, the Mishneh (B.K. 113a) would not have to list separately the tax collector. He could be included in the category of *Gaboin* who are barred because they put their hands into the public till. See Samuel de Modena, *Orah Hayyim*, 152.

12. B.K. 113a; Ned. 28a — מוכס העומד מאליו.

13. Solomon Luria, *Yam Shel Shlomo,* B.K. 18 — היינו ששר אחד תקיף
מוציא דבר חדש ובודה מלבו להוסיף חקים בין הוא לצורך עצמו בין הוא לגזבר המלך
כל מה שלא תיקן המלך מעצמו אפי׳ עכשיו רואה המלך ושותק אין זה אלא עומד מאליו.

14. Ibn Zimra, II, *Lilshonot ha-Rambam,* 164 — והארכתי בזה לפי שראיתי
בני אדם מורים היתר לעצמם בדבר זה ואומרים כיון שהוא הולך מעצמו לקחת המכס
מהמלך נקרא מוכס העומד מאליו והא והאי ליתא שאם לא יעמוד זה אחר היה עומד...
ואסור לגזול מנת המלך.

15. Ibn Adret, I, 644; *Abkat Rohel,* 205 — אבל עתה שהמלך חלקם ודד״ד
נתבטלו כל הטעמים והרי הם כשני קהלות בשתי עיירות בפני עצמם ואין א׳ צריך לסייע
לחבירו בשום מס...

16. Asher, 6:15.

17. It was the right of the German Emperor to relieve Jews from
paying for a "seal" (*Stempel*) on the bills of sale for leavened products
prior to Passover. The exemption was justified on the grounds that these
sales were not for business purposes but were rather of a religious nature.
See subsequent chapters that deal with the problems this ruling engendered.
Hatam Sofer, Orah Hayyim, 113.

18. Of course, the communities accepted privileges which would benefit them all, even if they were awarded to a specific court favorite. For
example, among the taxes to be paid by the individual was a tax on
bread. It was only by special royal privilege bestowed upon one court
favorite that permission was granted to bake bread at home or for the
community to bake *Matzah* for the Passover instead of being required to
utilize the royal bakeries. Adret, IV, 139.

19. Sometimes the communities themselves conferred a tax exemption
upon an individual. See Ibn Adret, I, 967 — הקהל עשו שטר שחרור עולמי
לראובן מקרקע... However, this subject continually served as a source of
irritation and litigation as will become evident from the responsa to be
cited. See also A. Neuman *op. cit.* Vol. II, p. 102 — "At the Cortes of
Valladolid, in 1312, it was charged that five thousand of the richest Jews
of the country were tax free. Considering the source of the complaint,
it may be assumed that this figure was a gross exaggeration. But there
was undoubtedly, enough truth in the claim to prove grievous the plight
of the *Aljamas* as a result of the king's reckless grants of exemptions."
See *Meshal ha-Kadmoni,* ed. Venice 10b; ed. Zamora p. 46; Baer, I, pp.
92-93; Isaac Ibn Sahula of Gualalajara lists those who receive shares from
kings as not meriting a share in the world to come.

20. B.B. 55a; *Tur,* 163 — א״ר אשי פרדכת מסייע מתא והנ״מ דאצילתיה מתא
אבל אנדיסקי סיעתא דשמיא היא.

21. Joseph Habbib, *Nemukei Joseph, ad. loc.* in the name of *Hai Gaon:*
דדוקא שעשה לו המלך החותם קודם שעשה תביעתו או קודם שקבע המס על כלל העיר
אבל אחר שהטיל המס על כלל העיר פטרו אינו נפטר מחלקו שכבר חל החיוב עליו.

22. Joseph Colon, 2 — שהרי הלכה רווחה היא בישראל שאין הבורחים אחרי
שאילת המס פטורים בשביל כך מלפרוע חלקם מן המס.

177

23. B.M. 8:9.

24. השותפין שמחלו להן המוכסין מה שמחלו מחלו לאמצע ואם אמרו בשביל פלוני מחלו מה שמחלו מחול לו.

25. R.Simha quoted in Mordecai B.K. (177) — אלימא דמחלו סתמא פשיטא דמה שמחלו מחלו לאמצע. Also, quoted by Asher, B.K. (25); Tur, 178; R. Yeruham, Mesharim Netib, 27:1; R. Menahem Mendel Lubavitch, Hoshen Mishpat, Zemah Zedek, 28.

26. Ibid. — אלא מיירי שביקש אחד מן השותפין שימחלו לו וע״י בקשתו מחלו לו ואפ״ה מחול לאמצע דאין שותף חולק שלא לדעת חבירו ודרך השותפין לטרוח בשביל חביריהם.

27. Ibid. — ואם אמרו בשביל פלוני.

28. R. Simha quoted by Mordecai ad loc. and Samuel de Modena, Hoshen Mishpat, 364 — שאמרו מעצמם ר״ל בלא בקשתו מה שאנו מוחלין אנו מוחלין בשביל פלוני זכה הוא לבדו ולא זכו חביריו עמו. Comp. Mahariah quoted in Hagaoth ha-Oshri B.B.

29. Ibid. — הרי אמרו על דודי ה״ר קלונימוס הפרנס שאחר שהיו הקהל מתפשרים היה בא אצל ההגמון... וכסבורין היינו שמדת חסידות היה עושה ועכשיו אני רואה דמדת הדין הוא.

30. Meir of Rothenburg, ibid. — שבקש מהם למחול סתם וקמ״ל אע״פ שלא היה שם אלא הוא מחלו לאמצע כיון שמחלו סתם. Jacob b. Joseph Reischer, Shebut Yaakob, Hoshen Mishpat, II, 181.

31. Ibid. — אבל אם אמרו בשביל פלוני מחלנו מחלנו על ידי בקשתו מה שמחלו מחול לו.

32. Ibid. — דאם כבר פשרו הקהל עם השר ושוב בקש אחד לפושרו מחלקו הציל לעצמו ופטור אבל אם קודם הפשרה בקש יהודי אחד מן השר לפוטרו וכן עשה ופטרו חייב לתת מס.

33. Meir of Rothenburg L. 358 — ומה שכתבתי שאם השר מעצמו הקיל ע״ז והכביד על זה שהרשות בידו ה״מ קודם שנתפשרו עמו... Also Mordecai ad loc.

34. Ibid. — אבל אם כבר נתפשרו ושוב רצה להוסיף לזה ולפחות לזה לאו כל כמיניה...

35. Ibid. — גם השר הבא לשנות את הדין אין שומעין לו דלא אמרי׳ בכה״ג דד״ד ולאו כל כמיניה זה מזה... הוא אלא גזילה הוא ולא הוי דינא. Also, ibid. A., I, 122 — השר להפרידה זה מזה... ולאו היינו ד״ד אלא גזילה דמלכותא כמו מכס שאין לה קצבה.

36. Terumat ha-Deshen, 341 — כיון שדרים יחד בצבור ונושאים תדיר בכל מיני עולים לא שייך כאן לומר שותף חולק שלא מדעת חבירו.

37. Hayyim b. Isaac, Or Zarua, 80, 253, 206 — ועוד נ״ל שאפילו אם לא ביקש מהמלך להפרידו והפרידו המלך אפי׳ קודם ששאל את המס אמר פלוני יתן לי כך ואתם תגו לי כך ומתוך כך מקיל על זה יותר... שאין כח ביד המלך להפרידה שאין זה ד״ד שלא קבלו עליהם בני המלכות חוקי המלך ומשפטיו אלא כמו שהנהיגם הוא ושלפניו אבל הוא רוצה לשנות ומפרידם זה מזה... אין כח ביד המלך שאין זה ד״ד...

38. Finkelstein, op. cit. p. 332 — כי בהביא הקהלות את כספם אל גנזי המלך ימצאו חן בעיניו ובעיני יועציו ושריו. A takkanah of Aragon 1354.

39. Meir of Rothenburg, A. I, 122; Cr. 222; L. 358; Ibn Adret, I, 841: אם מדעת הקהל נחלק מהם הרשות בידו אבל בלא דעת הקהל אינו רשאי להפרד מהם...;

ואח״כ נתפשר בפני עצמו עם השר בכך וכך ושלא להשתתף עם הקהל אם מדעת הקהל נחלץ
מהם הרשות בידו אבל שלא בדעת הקהל אינו רשאי להפרד מהם שלא לישא בעול עמהם;
Agudah, B.K. 144; *Maharil*, 71; M. Mintz, 61; *Terumat ha-Deshen*, 341.

40. Adret, V, 279; A. Neuman, *op. cit.* p. 104.

41. Finkelstein, *op. cit.* p. 368.

42. *Ibid.*

43. Ibn Adret, I, 841 — ולאו כל מיניה דהשר להפרידם זה מזה לשנות מנהג
שהנהיגו היהודים שבעירו ולאו היינו ד״ד אלא גזילה דמלכותא כמוכס שאין לו קצבה.

44. Meir of Rothenburg A. I, 122 — ה״מ כשהמלך אמר כך מעצמו מבלי
בקשת אבולי אבל בנ״ז שע״י בקשתו שבקש מן השר להפרידם מן היהודים רוצה להפרידו
לאו כל כמיניה.

45. Joseph Colon, 186 — הא לא הכביד עולם לא היה מסייע מתא כלל ואפי׳
היו לו אוצרות כסף וזהב כיון ישאינו עושה ריוח בעיר הרי נמצ״ל שאפי׳ יש לו כל
כסף וזהב שבעולם אינו חייב להם כלום.

46. Samuel de Modena, *Hoshen Mishpat*, 364.

47. R. *Asher and Tur, Hoshen Mishpat*, 389 — אע״ג דבימיהם היה שייך
למחלוקת זה והיה מנהג זה נוהג בזמנו... אבל בזמן הזה מנהג פשוט הוא.. הילכך
עפ״י המנהג המצוי ביניגו ישתנה הדין... א״כ זכינו בדין שיש לחלק הדין כפי המקום
וכפי הזמן.

48. Samuel de Modena, *Hoshen Mishpat*, 364 — שכל מה שנחבטו אלו
החכמים ר״ש והנמשכים אחריו ומהר״ם אין ללמוד מהם למקומות אלו ומלכות הגדול
הזה יר״ה דאותם המקומות היו ישראל במקומות מועטים מעטי הכמות כלם עוברים תחת
השבט כצאן ע״י מונה אין נמלט מהם ובאותם המקומות היה בהם כל החשש שאמרנו
שמה ישהמלך או השר ומה שיקל מזה מחמיר על זה ואין גורע מחקו הקצוב באומד דעתו
דבר ועל כן נכנסו אלו החכמים ז״ל לדקדק כל כך באותם המקומות אבל במלכות הזה
יר״ה רחב ידים אין נמשכים הדברים כל כך בדקדוק ופוק חזי כמה איכא בשוקא שאין
עליהם משא מלך ושרים.

49. Solomon b. Abraham ha-Kohen, II, 147 — ...וזהו דד״ד בכל העולם.
ובהא גוונא למדין מדיני הנכרים לישראל.

50. Maimonides, *Pirush le-Mishnayot* Ned. — אבל אם העמידו המלך הנה
העיקר אצלנו דד״ד ואין מותר לו לברוח מן המכס ואיך ישבע עליו... Also *Gezelah*,
V:11 — ולא עוד שהוא עובר המבריח ממכס זה מפני שהוא גוזל מנת המלך. Evasion
of a proper tax law is a violation of the commandment "Thou shalt not
steal." *Hoshen Mishpat*, 369-6. Also, R. Bahye b. Asher, *Kad ha-Kemah*,
Gesel p. 20 — ואין צריך לומר מי שאינו נזהר להביא חוקו בעניו המס עם יתר חבריו
אנשי מקומו שהוא גוזל את הרבים ומראה עצמו שאין לו אמונה ושאינו מאמין בעונש
השם חלול יש בזה אחד נגע עוד ...וישכר. Baer, I, pp. 229-30 — "He who does
not take meticulous care to contribute his share of the taxes along with
his fellow members in the community robs the public and betrays his want
of faith and his lack of trust in Reward and Punishment, denies the existence of a personal Providence and seeks to deceive the Lord as did Cain,
the villain, who said there was no law and no judge . . . There is robbery
of the public which alone is a criminal offense, and the public also contains the poor, the orphaned and the widowed . . . It includes yet another

179

sore—blasphemy of the Lord. It involves perjury, for whoever swears to
pay the tax faithfully and fails to do so is guilty of sin and *Lèse-Majesté* ...
How many impecunious persons are there of insecure livelihood and heavy
obligations, who shed their life-blood and pay taxes with their marrow and
blood ... and here comes the wicked and villainous rich man who says in
his heart, 'There is no God,' and wants to fill his chambers 'out of the
oppression of the poor and the sighing of the needy' in order to make his
own burden lighter and the yoke of the indigent, the orphaned, and the
widowed heavier."

51. Asher, 68:10 — אבל במס המלך נהגו הקהלות לתפוס כל מי שאינו פורע
‏...מס המלך ודד״ד.

52. Barfat, 2 — דכי תנן בפ׳ ד׳ דנדרים נודרין להרגין וכו׳ מוקמינן בגמ׳ במוכס
שאין לו קצבה ר״ל ששואל דבר שלא מן הדין או במוכס העומד מאליו והכי הוי כמו
Solomon אנסי; אבל במכס שהוא מחוק המלך אסור לעבור עליו ואין זה נקרא אונס דד״ד
b. Abraham ha-Kohen, II, 81 — כי דבר המכס הוא ד״ד עד שמטעם זה אמרו
שאסור להבריח מן המכס עוד יש בזה עבריינות של שבועה כי מי שנשבע להביא את
המלך .Also, Solomon b — המס בנאמנות ואינו עושה כן הרי זה עבריין ומבזה את המלך
Simon Duran, 64.

53. Samuel de Modena, *Yoreh Deah*, 71 — מכל הני משמע דאם משביעין
אותו כדין על דבר צווי המלך שאינו יכול לעבור על נדרו ולא על שבועתו אפי׳ אונסין
‏...אותו.

54. Zevi Hirsh b. Jacob Ashkenazi, *Hakam Zevi*, 72 — אבל לאחר
ההברחה אם יש לחוש שיענישוהו יותר מהסך הנוגע למוכס מטעם שעבר על המכס יש
פנים לכאן ולכאן דא״י כיון שהקנס הוא ג״כ ד״ד אסור לישבע ואי״ל כיון דאין לקנס קצבה
הו״ל בענין קנס כמוכס העומד מאליו ... ועל כל פגים אסור להורות היתר דמסרכי מילתא
‏...ואתו לזלזולי בשבועות.

55. Meir of Rothenburg, L. 246 — ויפה כתבת שלא לסמוך על דברים שבלב
‏.אלא גבי נודרין להורגין וכו׳ ... ולמוכס שאין לו קצבה דגזילה דמלכותא היא לאו דינא

56. Barfat, 2 — אבל כשהדבר מחמת אנסין או כשהמלך מעליל שלא כדין כדי
להעניש ממון כמו שעושה עתה במממון האנוסין שברחו לעשות תשובה או ממון היהודים
היוצאין מארצו לארצות הפרשיים או למלכות אחרת שאין זה מן הדין אלא שנגתו עליהם
חקים לא טובים ... בזה מותר להערים או בנדר או בשבועה .Also, *ha-Hadoshot*, 9;
See also Asher; Joseph Habbib, *Nemukei Joseph*, B.K. 55a; Nissim Gerondi,
8:10, Ned. 28a; Moses Isserles, *Hoshen Mishpat*, 369:7; Comp. Maimonides, *Responsa*, 146, ed. Freiman — יכול ראובן להשבע שבועה גדולה שהחנות
שלו ... וזה תשמרו אותו שכל דבר שיהיה לגוים הפסד על ישראל אפי׳
פרוטה א׳ שלא כדיני ישראל ... יתחייב להכחיש אמיתת זה הדבר וישבע בה׳ אלקי ישראל
על האופן אשר יצילהו מההפסד. *Ibid.* 299.

57. Moses b. Joseph Trani, I, 261 — מוכס שאין לו קצבה ומרבה ליקח
‏.יותר ממה שהמלך חפץ הילכך כולו גזל

58. *Ibid.* — אבל הכא שהמכס עצמו אין בו חיוב אלא מצד דד״ד כיון שזה מוסיף
מדעתו ... הרי הוא נחשב לגזלן ונסתלק ממנו דד״ד ... ולכן מותר להבריח ממנו המכס
‏...בכל מה שיוכל.

59. Ibn Zimra, *Lilshonot ha-Rambam*, II, 164 — ומסתברא לי שגם בזה

אסור להבריח וכי מפני שגוזל את אחרים יהיה מותר לגזול את שלו. See also his
commentary to Maimonides, *Shebuot*, III:2.

60. Meir of Rothenburg L. 246; I. Agus, *Meir of Rothenburg*, 174 —
ויפה כתבתי שלא לסמוך על דברים שבלב אלא גבי נודרין להורגין... ולמוכס שאין לו
קצבה דגזילה דמלכותא היא לאו דינא אבל אם יצוה המלך שלא לגזוז המטבע דין גמור
(הוא) ובלא ציווי המלך דין הוא...

61. A different interpretation of this talmudic text is rendered by
Rashi, *ad. loc.* He writes that the dispute between Rab and Samuel concerns merchandise which is given to another who is to repay the donor
with money. Since the agreement expressly calls for money, Rab rules
that the currency in use at the time of payment must be utilized. That
which had been invalidated by the king no longer can be considered money.
Samuel, on the other hand, considers any currency money as long as it
has value anywhere. However, according to this interpretation, in the case
where money was lent, both Rab and Samuel agreed that the old, albeit
voided, currency may be used.

62. B.K. 97a — המלוה את חבירו על המטבע ונפסלה המטבע רב אמר נותן לו
מטבע היוצא באותה שעה.

63. *Ibid.* — יכול לומר לו לך הוציאו במישן.

64. *Ibid.* — א"ר נחמן מסתברא מילתא דשמואל דאית ליה אורחא למיזל למישן
אבל לית ליה אורחא לא.

65. *Hatam Sofer, Hoshen Mishpat*, 58 — ואי ס"ד דד"ד א"כ הרי מן הדין
צריך לשמוע לדברי המלך ואיך נאמר לו לך עבור על דברי המלך. Perhaps this is why
a whole array of rabbis of the Middle Ages disregarded Samuel's decision
and ruled with Rab. R. Tam, RaSHBaM, Ri, Mordecai, B.K. (111-113)
state the debtor is to pay with currency in use at the time his debt is due
because such was the demand of the king and "the law of the kingdom is
the law." See also Meir of Rothenburg Pr. 1000.

66. Comp. *Tosafot*, B.K. 97a המלוה ד"ה; also Meir of Rothenburg
Pr. 353 — כיון שיוצא במישן שם מטבע עליו.

67. Comp. *Hatam Sofer, Hoshen Mishpat*, 62.

68. *Ibid.* 64.

69. *Ibid.* 144.

70. Ibn Adret, IV, 287; Ibn Migash, 195; Asher, 103:1.

71. *Ibid.* III, 34, 40 — ומ"מ אם יש מאמר המלך בזה שיגזור במה יתן הלוה
למלוה בהתחלף המטבע נראה שהדין כמו שיגזור המלך... וכיון שכן קיי"ל דד"ד.

72. *Ibid.* V, 198 — אף בזה דינו דין שהתוספות הזה שלא בתנאי ושלא ברצון
הבעלים הוא נפרע ואלמלא דינו של מלכות אינו בכלל רבית אלא בכלל גזל אלא שדינו
של מלך דין והפקרו הפקר ואין כאן גזל ואין כאן רבית.

73. *Tosafot*, B.M. 70b תשיך ד"ה — יש להתיר לפי שיש עלינו מס ...אור"ת
מלך ושרים והכל הוי כדי חיינו. Under Peter IV, the Jews of Aragon petitioned
against the excessive cruelty of the tax collectors. ". . . Whereas the tax
collectors have of late gone beyond all bounds making sorrowful the souls
of our brethren . . . and they have bound them in affliction and in irons . . .

181

the commissioner should endeavor to obtain a decree from the king, forbidding his tax collectors . . . to cause anyone bodily pain, except in the
manner which the king and his ancestors have been in the habit of em-
ploying heretofore." Finkelstein, *op. cit.* p. 332 — עוד ישתדלו מאשר נוגשי
המס עתה מקרוב פרצו ויעבור להאדיב נפש אחינו על דבר נגישתם ולתחם אסירי עני
וברזל ... הסכמנו שישתדלו להפיק חותם מאת אדו' המלך יר"ה, לבל ינגשו נוגשיו הרודים
בעמינו על דבר המס לענות נפש כי אם על הדרך אשר נהג הוא ואבותיו מאז.

74. *Tosafot, ibid.* — ועוד שאנו שרויין בין האומות ואי אפשר לנו להשתכר
בשום דבר אם לא נישא וניתן עמהם הלכך אין לאסור רבית ... Comp. Isaac b. Samuel of Dampierre and RABIAH quoted in *Or Zarua,* ed. Jerusalem, p. 59;
Eliezer b. Nathan, *Eben ha-Ezer* p. 97a; Asher, B.M. (52) — הלכך אין
לאסור רבית שמא ילמוד ממעשיו יותר משאר משא ומתן; Meir of Rothenburg, Pr.
796; Jacob Weil, 38.

75. Comp. A. Neuman, *op. cit.* pp. 194-7.

76. Ex. 22:24; Ezek. 17:13; Ps. 15:5.

77. Comp. A. Neuman, *op. cit. ad. loc.*

78. Asher, 79:7 — דודאי אם היה ד"ד מה שהכותים תובעים ממנו מצי שמעון
לומר החזיר לי הממון שנתתי לך כי לא היה שלך ומשל אחר היה ואני צריך להחזירו
מן הדין.

79. *Ibid.* — אבל ידוע שגזל הוא ואנס מה שהכותים אונסים את היהודים בלא משפט
אלא עול הוא כי חוק לישראל עד היום הזה ליקח רבית מכותים.

80. In Castile, in the early part of the 14th century, a royal decree
outlawed loans on interest extended by Jews. The Jews refused to accept
the legality of this statute. It was discriminatory in nature. They called it
"the scourge of the land." *Ibid.* — דמכת מדינה היא שלא כדין.

CHAPTER VII

COURTS AND JUDGES

1. Exodus XXI — ‏ואלה המשפטים אשר תשים לפניהם.‏

2. *Baraita,* Gittin 88b — ‏ותניא היה ר״ט אומר כל מקום שאתה מוצא אגוריאות‏
‏של עכו״ם אע״פ שדיניהם כדיני ישראל אי אתה רשאי להיזקק להם שני׳ ואלה המשפטים...‏
‏לפניהם ולא לפני עכו״ם...‏ In *Sheiltoth* to Genesis, the same statement was
made in the name of R. Meir and in Sifre to Exodus 21 in the name of
R. Eliezer b. Azariah. Contr. Holdheim, *Autonomie Der Rabbinen,* p. 66 ff.

3. As we have seen in Chapter 2.

4. *Teshubat ha-Geonim,* Harkavy, 278; and above chapter 2.

5. Lewin, *Ozar ha-Geoni*m B.K., p. 99. The Hebrew text may be
found above chapter 2, footnote 39.

6. *Shaarei Zedek,* 4; Harkavy, *Teshubot ha-Geonim,* 233; Joseph b.
Samuel Bonfils quoted by *Haga'oth Maimuni;* Maimonides, *Sanhedrin,*
26:7; *Sefer Ha-Terumot,* 62; *Semag,* II, 74d; L. Rabinowitz, *Jews of Northern France in the XII-XIV Cent.* p. 77; Joseph Colon, 132, 172; Meir
Katzenellenbogen gave permission to one of the children of Don Samuel
Abravanel to hail his two brothers to a non-Jewish court because they
refused to come before a Bet Din. See A. Marx, "R. Joseph Arli and R.
Johanan Treves," *Studies in Memory of Moses Schorr,* p. 218 — ‏בג׳ אגוסטי‏
‏ש״ז הסכים בפאדובה עם פסק מהר״ם ליתן רשות לדון יצחק אברבנאל לילך אל ערכאות‏
‏הגוים בריבו עם אחיו דון יעקב ודון יהודה.‏

7. Finkelstein, *op. cit.* p. 153 — ‏ונמנונו וגזרנו והחרמנו על כל איש ואשה‏
‏קרובים ורחוקים אשר יביא את חבירו בדיני גויים או יכופנו על ידי גוים הן שר הן‏
‏הדיוט הן מושל הן סרדיוט אם לא מדעת שניהם בפני עדים כשרים.‏ Also, Meir of
Rothenburg L. 248, 334; Pr. 717, 979, 994.

8. *Ibid.*

9. Contr. Finkelstein, *op. cit.* p. 156, who states: "It is evidence of
the greater tolerance that was arising among the French rabbis that they
do not include Christians in the category of idol-worshipper. The only
reason for keeping Jewish litigations in Jewish tribunals was the fear of
injustice on the part of the Gentile courts. Therefore, where both parties
agreed, the rabbis of France could see no reason for hesitation in bringing
matters before them."

Comp. D. M. Shohet, *The Jewish Court in the Middle Ages,* p. 85
who agrees with the above: "We cannot but marvel at the tolerant spirit
manifested by the Jewish authorities towards the followers of other reli-
gions, despite the persecutions of an intolerant medieval Church. If here
and there, as we shall see later on, an attitude other than generous seems
to pervade the responsa, this is due not to an inherent contempt for the
Christian world." See also G. Kisch, "Jewish and Christian Courts," *Historia Judaica,* Vol. XXI, part 2.

183

We submit that the *takkana* of R. Tam had nothing whatever to do with "greater tolerance that was arising among the French rabbis." The Geonim evaluated non-Jewish courts on the basis of their honesty and reputation for fairness. As a result, the courts of Bagdad, because of their honesty, were recognized. Also, in civil matters, an individual may do with his money as he chooses. The parties involved may accept the decisions of a non-Jewish court as binding. The Talmud has a similar situation when the "courts of Syria" (ערכאות שבסוריא) were permitted to be utilized if both parties agreed. See Sanhedrin 23a.

Comp. D. M. Shohet *op. cit.* p. 101, who tries to prove that Jewish and non-Jewish judges sat together at trials. He writes "That Jewish judges sat at trials together with non-Jewish judges, appears from the fact that the Roman court in Palestine had Jews among its personnel and even the defendant or the debtor was granted the right of preference in the selection of a tribunal for litigation." Shohet cites a talmudic passage, Sanh. 23a, dealing with ערכאות שבסוריא and Rashi *ad loc.* A number of difficulties arise with Shohet's interpretation of the cited talmudic text. The Talmud defines that these courts consisted of men who were "ignorant of Jewish law," judges who were not *Mumhin.* Rashi *ad loc.* states: שלא היו בקיאין בדין תורה. *Or Zarua,* quoted in *Haga'oth ha-Asheri, ad. loc.* has the following: ואוקמא ר' יוחנן בערכאות שבסוריא דהיינו יושבי קרנות. Comp. also Ibn Adret, II, 290 who also maintains that such courts consisted of Jews, albeit ignorant of Jewish law. Whether these courts consisted of ignorant Jewish or non-Jewish judges is really outside of this discussion. The main point is that nowhere is it stated that these courts did have a mixed group of judges sitting together.

Furthermore, the statement made by Shohet that "even the defendant or the debtor was granted the right of preference in the selection of a tribunal for litigation" is not substantiated by the source cited. On the contrary, in the case of ערכאות שבסוריא the debtor was merely granted the right to *refuse* to submit his case before that court. In all other circumstances, it was the creditor who determined which court was to hear their dispute. See Sanh. *ad. loc.* — והאמר ר' אלעזר לא שנו אלא מלוה אבל לוה כופין אותו ודן בעירו.

Shohet also states that "the judges in these courts were, it seems, regularly appointed by the Roman authorities." For his source, Shohet cites *Or Zarua* quoted in the glosses to Asheri, Sanh. See Shohet, *op. cit. ad. loc.* footnote 3. The source quoted has no mention of such appointments. There is found a passage from *Mahariah* but one which does not state that such appointments were made regularly or that the Romans were the ones who made them. Finally, Shohet also writes: "If a Jew accepted (and the acceptance was strengthened by a *kinyan* — symbolical delivery) a Gentile to act as one of the judges trying his case, the decision of the court could not be invalidated on the plea of the presence of a Gentile trial judge, even if he were suspected of having taken bribes." Here again, Shohet wishes to demonstrate that a mixture of Jewish and non-Jewish judges sitting at a trial was valid. He cites as his source Mordecai, *Nezikin*, 686. If Shohet had not quoted the passage of Mordecai out of context, he would have noticed that the responsum of R. Meir of Rothenburg, quoted in Mordecai, refers to accepting a Gentile as a witness and not as a judge. — פסק האלפסי ראם קבל עליו חד קרוב או פסול כבי תרי וקני מיניה לא מצי הדר ביה וכן פסק המיימוני וכן בא מעשה לפני רבי מאיר באחד שאמר נאמן עלי אותו נכרי וקנו מיניה וכשהרגיש שהיה (הנכרי) מטה דבריו וקבל שוחד רצה לחזור בו ופסק דלא מצי הדר ביה . . .

It becomes obvious that the phrase נאמן עלי אותו נכרי refers to accepting upon oneself a Gentile, who otherwise would be disqualified to serve as a witness. Comp. I. Agus, *R. Meir of Rothenburg*, II, pp. 409-410 (421) who properly translated this responsum. The same responsum appears in Cr. 245; Pr. 284; *Or Zarua*, I, 752.

10. Meir of Rohenburg, Cr. 185; L. 334; and quoted in *Agudah*, Sheb. 22; Mordecai B.K. (195) — ונהי שרבי אפרים לא טוב עשה בעמו וראוי למתוח אותו על העמוד כי הלך בערכאות כותים . . .

11. *Ibid.* — . . . לא היה לו לעשות הדבר אלא ע"פ קהלו או ע"פ הגדולים שבמלכות.

12. Meir of Rothenburg, Pr. 103, 247, 717, 994 — ומה שמגזם אפילו אם תפטור אמו שרוצה לקבול עליה בפני הדוכוס תפס חבלא בתרי ראשי . . . ראוי לנדותו על הדבור ולהבדלו מעדת ישראל . . . כ"ש וכ"ש אם ילך בערכאות של גוים ;Cr. 185 L. 334; Mordecai B.K. (55), (195); B.M. (27); Comp. Finkelstein, *op. cit.* p. 237 who states that this was a *takkanah* which is usually attributed to R. Paltoi Gaon. Contr. Joseph Colon, 126 who states that even a mere threat to utilize a non-Jewish court suffices to disqualify anyone from giving testimony.

13. *Ibid.* L. 247-8; Mordecai B.K. (195) — . . . ועוד הא דאמרינן המסורין הני מילי קודם שמסר . . . ואפילו בשעת רדיפתו . . . נ"ל אם היה יכול להציל באחד מאבריו בחתיכת לשונו או בסמוי עינו אסור להרגו . . .; M. Mintz, 44; D. Kaufmann, "Jewish Informers in the Middle Ages," *JQR* (OS), Vol. VIII, pp. 217-228.

14. A *takkanah* of the early 13th century, probably of Mayence, Finkelstein, *op. cit.*, 221 — אם יגזם אדם את חבירו בפני עדים אני מפסיד את ממונך אם יפסיד אותו היהודי יחייבו את המגזם לפרוע כפי אשר נשבע הנפסד שהפסידו ואם יש עדים כמה הפסיד יפרע לו המסור והמלשין יהא פסול לשבועה.

15. Meir of Rothenburg, quoted by Mordecai, B.K. (195); some have said that the *takkanah* of R. Tam did not include one who denounces an individual who has previously denounced him to Gentiles. See Rabiah, *Agudah* to B.K. — גם לא תחול על השם מלשין ששם א[ות]ן בידי גוים והיכא דתקפה בדין גוים לעצמו אף דאין לעשות כן מ"מ לא דייניגן ליה דין מסור ואפי' אם הפסיד אותו שתקפה מידו הרבה כגון שהעלילו הגוי והענישו הרבה אפ"ה אין לו על התוקף דין מסור . . .,דלא מצינו בתלמוד אלא המתכוין להזיק חבירו אבל נתכוין להוציא את שלו R. Meir of Rothenburg denies that the communities would promulgate such a *takkanah*. He understood that someone acting in a "moment of passion" might be freed of any punishment which the community would

otherwise inflict. However, the offender who has acted to revenge himself, gains nothing for himself but the satisfaction of revenge by equally damaging his opponent. *Ibid.* 196 — ושכתבתי שיש שפוטרין את רבי יואל לפי שאין

אדם נתפש על צערו כיון דבשעת חימום הוה שאותו קם עליו והעמידו בערכאות של כותים נהפך גם הוא לתגין לעשות לכשנגדו כאשר זמם לו ולא כאשר עשה ותולין הדבר בתקנת הקהלות איני סבור שתקנו הקהלות הקהלות דבר זה שאם השני חזר בו ומסר את הראשון והתכוין להפסיד את ממונו ובזה לא הציל עצמו רק שנתכוזן לנקום עצמו בכך ודאי כל כה"ג לא פטרו אותו הקהלות אלא מן הקנס שלא לנדותו או להלקותו על המסירה שמסר את חבירו כי יחם לבבו אבל מלשלם ההפסד שהפסיד לחבירו דבר פשוט הוא שלא פטרו...

16. Meir of Rothenburg, Pr. 717; see also a similar case *ibid.* 994; contr. with R. Hayyim b. Isaac, *Or Zarua,* 25, 142 who understood the *ṭakkanah* to free the offender when such offense came as a result of the "heat of the moment."

17. Meir of Rothenburg quoted by Judah Mintz, *Mabik,* 7 — סוף דבר כל צרכי הקהל יעשה על פיהם ככל אשר יאמרו ואם המיעוט יאמנו ויעמדו מלשמור ולעשות ככל הכתוב יש כח ביד הרוב או מי שימנו הרוב עליהם לראשי להכריח' ולכפות אנו רוצים עד שיאמרו בין בדיני ישראל בין בדיני האומות — Also, Jacob Weil, 147 כמבואר בתקנותינו שהרבים יכולים לכוף היחידים בעש"ג ובלא תקנותינו כבר פשוט מנהג זה בכל מדינות אשכנז...

18. One questions the decision of Zevi Hirsh b. Jacob Ashkenazi, *Hakam Zevi,* 14, in Amsterdam in the early part of the 18th century, who ruled that *Kahal* may avail itself of the power of the secular court to enforce its decision but only after it received the consent of the Bet Din. In a dispute between the *Kahal* and an individual, the *Kahal* may confiscate the individual's property in order to assure his appearance before a Bet Din. — הרשות ביד הקהל לכופם בין בדיני ישראל בין בדיני או"ה ברשות דייני ישראל... שכן דונו והורו הלכה למעשה אפי' בין יחיד ליחיד כ"ש בין צבור ליחיד... הרשות ביד הקהל יצ"ו לעכבם עד יבואו פה ויעמדו למשפט... ומעשים בכל יום... וכן נוהגים בכל הארצות אשר שמענו שמעם. Whether this ruling, which granted *Kahal* no greater powers than an individual and which made *Kahal* subservient to the Bet Din by requiring the latter's permission, was prompted by the gradual decline of the power of *Kahal* and the natural shift of power to the Bet Din or whether it was due to the personal quarrels which *Hakam Zevi* had with his *Parnasim* remains doubtful.

19. Meir of Rothenburg, Pr. 357; Cr. 175, 246; Am. II, 30; L. 126-7; Mordecai B.M. 276.

20. G. Kisch, "Relations between Jewish and Christian Courts in the Middle Ages," *Historia Judaica,* Vol. XXI, part 2, pp. 89-90. Also, Sol Landau, *Christian-Jewish Relations,* p. 22. Comp. Menahem Merseburg in the appendix to the responsa of Jacob Weil, ed. Hanover, p. 74a, ff. who lists numerous cases of Jews informing against their neighbors to the Gentile authorities. In one case, the Gentiles so severely beat a Jew that he died. Menahem required the informer to seek atonement for his misdeed. וראובן צוה לתפוס בעל ריבו בידי גוים והכהו ומת... וצריך כפרה כמו רוצח —

In another instance a Jew informed against his own son-in-law that he intended to escape from his creditors. Perhaps the Jews involved only informed to the Gentile authorities but not to the Gentile courts since the court is nowhere mentioned. See also Jacob Weil, 147 — who cites the case of a known informer. — ועוד האי גברא זימלין הוחזק בכך להביא חביריו לפני גוים כאשר עשה ליוסף לוי ולאחרים ומה שתבעו מזימלין שממסר יוסף והביאו לפני האיינגיער ר"ל דיין העיר...

21. *Baal ha-Terumot* — אפילו בדיני חבלות שאינם מסורים לנו בזמן הזה אסור למסור ביד גוים.

22. Finkelstein identifies Baruck b. Isaac as the author of the *Sefer ha-Terumah*. Comp. Joshua Starr, "Jewish Life in Crete Under the Rule of Venice," *Proceedings of the American Academy for Jewish Research,* Vol. XII.

23. *Ibid.*

24. Finkelstein *op. cit.* p. 268 — עוד לדעת ... יען כי רבים מבני עמנו יקבילו את אחיהם היאודים בע"ש ובעיו"ט לפני המשפט באופן כי יאחר שם עד סמוך לקדוש היום והם נמנעים מצרכי שבת ומ﹩שמחת יו"ט והסכמנו לתקן את אשר עותו רוב אחינו בשבתות וחדשים ובמועדים והמקודשים שמכאן והלאה כל איש ישראל הנמצא בינינו לא יורשה בקנס ברכה לקבול את חבירו הישראלי בשום מקום המשפט הן אצל גוים הן אצל יאודים בע"ש ובעי"ט וזה למען לא ימנע מ﹩שמחת י"ט שיכין ג"כ צרכי שבת לה' ולא תהיה עדת ה' כצאן אשר אין להם רועה.

25. *Takkanah* at Synod of Frankfort, *ibid.* pp. 257-8.

26. *Ibid.*

27. *Ibid.*

28. R. Isaac Alfasi, *Responsa* quoted by Isserles, 52 — אחד מבעלי דינים שרוצה לדון לפני גוים צריך לנדותו.

29. *Ibid.* 221 — אסור לבר ישראל להזדמן אצל שופטי עכו"ם ואפי' היה הדין שוה עם דיני ישראל.

30. Maimonides, *Sanhedrin*, 26:7 — כל הדן בדייני עכו"ם ובערכאות שלהן אע"פ שהיו דיניהם כדיני ישראל הרי זה רשע וכאילו חרף וגדף והרים יד בתורת משה רבינו. See *Responsa,* 295 and 296, ed. Freiman for *takkanah* initiated by Maimonides, Menashe b. Joseph, Samuel b. Saadia, Isaac b. Sasoon in 1187 — Also, Joseph Caro, עוד הסכימו כי יהיה ריב בין אנשים שלא ילכו בערכאות של גוים *Hoshen Mishpat,* 26:1.

31. *Ibid.* — היתה יד העכו"ם תקיפה ובעל דינו אלם ואינו יכול להוציא ממנו בדייני ישראל יתבענו לדייני ישראל אם לא רצה לבא גוטל רשות מב"ד ומציל בדיני עכו"ם מיד בעל דינו. Also, Joseph Caro, *ibid.*

32. *Ibid.*

33. Ibn Adret, VI, 254 — ומ"מ לנהוג כן מפני שהוא משפט גויים באמת נ"ל שאסור לפי שהוא מחקה את הגויים וזהו שהזהירה תורה לפניהם ולא לפני גויים.

34. *Ibid.* — ואומר אני שכל הסומך בזה לומר שמותר משום ד"ר טועה וגזלן הוא... ואם נאמר כן בטלה ירושת בנו הבכור דכל הנחלות ותורת הבת עם הבנים.

35. *Ibid.;* V, 171; VI, 140; Asher, 18:4, 5, 6 — ולא עוד אלא אפי' לעמוד לפניהם לדין אפי' בדבר שדיניהם כדין ישראל... איך נתנו יד לכלל דברים אלו שאסרתן תורה שלמה שלנו.

36. Ibn Adret, VI, 254 — ובכלל עוקר כל דיני תורה השלמה ומה לנו לספרי
הקודש המקודשים שחברו לנו רבי ואחריו רבינא ורב אשי ילמדו את בניהם דיני הגויים
ויבנו להם במות טלואות בבית מדרסי הגויים חלילה לא תהיה כזאת בישראל ח"ו שמא
תתגור התורה עליה שק.

37. *Ibid.* III, 109; VI, 149 — כך ... אלא כמו שאנו יש לנו משפטי מלוכה
בשאר האומות דינין ידועים יש למלכים ובהם אמרו דדיניהם דין אבל דינין שדנין בערכאות
אין אלו כמשפטי המלוכה אלא הערכאות דנין לעצמן כמו שימצאו בספרי הדיינין שאם
Yom Tob b. Abraham Ashvilla, ;אין אתה אומר כן בטלת חס ושלום דיני ישראל
ומ"מ למדנו מזה שדברים אלו הם כפי המנהג והסכמות שופטי המלך בזה אינו — 53
מעלה כלום אלא א"כ הוא חק קבוע מן המלכות. See also Levi Ibn Habbib, 44 —
ובתנאי שיהיה חק המדינה או ממשפטי המלך שאם אינו כן אלא שהששופט הערבי דן את
הדין כפי דינם אינו נקרא ד"ד ואין דנין אותו בדיניהם כי אם בדינינו... וכבר כתב
הרשב"א ז"ל דא"כ בטלת כל דיני ממונות...

38. Asher, 68:13.

39. Adret, VI, 149 — שזה בא ומחדש ומפרש דינין לפי דעתו ושכלו ואחר
בא ומהפך דבריו ואין למלך בזה הקפדה כלל אא"כ הם נימוסין ידועין עשויין מצד המלכות
שלא על דיני עכו"ם אמרו דד"ד שאין — Barfat, 228; וכמצוה שלא ידונו אלא כך...
המלך מקפיד על דינין ידועים שזה בא ומחדש ומפרש דינים לפי דעתו ושכלו ואחר בא
ומהפך דבריו ואין למלך בזה הקפדה כלל אלא א"כ הם נימוסין ידועין עשויים מצד
המלכות... Contr. I. Epstein, *The Responsa of R. Solomon b. Adreth of
Barcelona*, p. 47 who writes: "Side by side with the Jewish law courts
there were civil ones, and the Jews could bring their affairs to either —
the ordinance of R. Tam (twelfth century), prohibiting Jews from dragging
their litigants before non-Jewish tribunals, not having been accepted in
Spain." The evidence presented from the responsa of Adret does not bear
out this statement.

40. Ibn Adret, V, 171 — אבל אם היה אנס וב"ד של ישראל מתייראין מלכתוב
עליו אדרכתא זה בכלל רשעים הוא ומתרעם ממנו בב"ד של גוים ואינו חושש לשל ישראל
ד"ד... ;שהוא מתחייב למלכות חדא דד"ד Nahmanides, *Seforon Shel Rishonim*, 63
(186); Asher, 18:4.

41. *Ibid. Toldoth ha-Adam*, 84.

42. Ibn Adret, *ibid.* — וא"נ במה שישראל עושה עם ישראל חבירו מדעת עצמו
כאותה שאמרו... כל השטרות העולות וכו' אע"פ שמצד דיני המלך... כיון שזה מדעתו
עושה מתנתו בערכאות הרי קבל עליו לילך בזה בדיני המלכות... ובדבר שבממון יכול
לשעבד וליתן משלו שלא מן הדין. Contr. Nahmanides, *Commentary*, Ex. 21:1
who forbids such an agreement. — ואע"פ שהזכירו חכמים שתי הכתוב האלה
כאחת יש הפרש ביניהם שאם רצו שתי בעלי הדין לבא לפני הדיוט... אבל לפני הכנענים
אסורים היו לבא לפניו שידון להם ביניהם לעולם ואפילו היו דיניהם כדינינו באותו הענין.
Also Joseph Caro, *Hoshen Mishpat*, 26:1.

43. Asher, 18:4 — אבל כל זמן שאומר הנגבע אני מזומן לירד עמך בדיני
ישראל... אין התובע רשאי להביאו לפני הערכאות... וגם דייני ישראל לא ידונו לו
אלא מדין תורה. Comp. I. Epstein, *op. cit.* p. 48 who in connection with this
subject writes: "The Spanish civil law courts would often pay deference
to the jurisdiction privileges of the *aljamas* . . . even when the civil law

court had adjudicated in a litigation between Jews, and had even given
its verdict, it would allow the dispute to be transferred to the Jewish law
courts." For his source, Epstein cites Adret, I, 1148. The reading there is:
ופייסו את החצר שיעמיד את שמעון על דיני ישראל, and refers to a decision to be
rendered on the basis of Jewish law. It does not mean that the case be
transferred to a Jewish court. We often found that Gentile courts were commanded to decide according to Jewish law. See Barfat, 305, 239, 413 —
בפני דיין נתמנה ע״ז מכח המלכות לדון בד״י.

44. Adret, III, 384-5 — וזה אינו מענין תביעתו ומלשינות הוא כי הודיע
ולפי הנראה לנו מלשין הוא כיון שהגבררים — 388 ;לפאירש שהוא חייב להם בקנס הגזבר
ואם יתרעם עליו בפני האומות הע״א — Asher, XVII, 4 ;הם מוכרחים להודיע לגזבר
יש לו דין מסור.

45. Asher, ibid. — דאמרינן אפילו בדין שעכו״ם דנין כדיני ישראל ההולך לפני
הערכאות ׳של עובדי אלילים מחלל שם שמים.

46. Ibn Adret, II, 290 — כיצד נעשה בעיירות שאין שם מי שיודע אפילו אות
אחת ואנו צריכים להמידן לדון ולפשר על כרחן של בעל דבר ואם לא נעמדו גמצאו
הולכין לערכאות של נכרים.

47. Ibid. — ורבו האנסין.

48. Asher, 68:13 — דאפי׳ אם הלוה והמלוה עומדין בפנינו ואמר הלוה למלוה
אם תרצה תתבעני בדיני האומות מחינן במלוה ואמרינן ליה שלא יתבענו אלא בפני ישראל
ואי לא ציית משמתינן ליה.

49. Adret, VII, 142; Asher, 18:5, 6; A. Neuman, op. cit. p. 151.

50. Barfat, 102, 216 — צריך להחרים ולנדותו המחזיק ביד ההולך לדון דיני
גוים.

51. Finkelstein, op. cit. pp. 361-2.

52. Ibid. p. 364.

53. Ibn Adret, II, 3, 19, 84 — אבל אם יש לו עליו דין שיעכבהו ע״י החצר
כדי שלא ישמטנו ויברח מדינו אינו רואה בזה דין מסור ומעשים בכל יום שמעכבים את
לגבות — Ibid. 225 ;בעלי דינין שלא ישמטו מממון אחרים וילך למדינת הים...
ואם יעמוד — Asher, 21:9 ;כדינא דמלכותא כנהוג שם אכוף את המבריח על ידי המלך
במרדו ולא ינהיג דין מנודה בעצמו אני גוזר עליו במצות המלך יר״ה... Also Barfat,
395.

54. Ibid. 239 — דדין המעושה בנכרים שהכריחו את ישראל לדון עם חבירו
בבית דין של ישראל או שהכריחו את הב״ד לדון בין שני ישראלים אותו הדין ׳שדנו ע״י
אנס זה אם דנוהו כהלכתו ולאמיתתו דין כשר הוא.

55. Adret, II, 225 — ואחר שאין אתם רוצים לכופו אלך לאדוני הארץ ויכוף
הסית עליו ראובן כל העיר ומסרו בערכאותיהם עם — Ibid. 244 ;אותו וכן עשה...
חברותי והוצרך לפזר ולשחד ;Ibid. III, 3; V, 171; VI, 4, 92; Asher, CVII, 6 —
והוחלפו כמה מונים מדין ישראל לדין או״ה ומדין או״ה לדיני ישראל.

56. Ibid. CVII, 6 — ועתה נתגלגלה הדבר שבאי הלום בצווי גבירתינו המלכה
מב״ת והביאו לי כתבה שהיא צותה עלי ׳שאקח כל שטרי... ושאדון ע״פ טענותיהם הללו
ממה שיראה לי מקו היושר והאמת. See also A. Neuman, op. cit. pp. 154 ff.

57. Barfat, 305 — וכבר אנו רואים בעינינו ׳שכל מלכי ארגון נותנין רשות לדון
תורתנו ומצוים לשופטיהם שידונו כן בין יהודי ליהודי.

58. *Ibid.*

59. Ibn Adret, III, 141; *Terumat ha-Deshen,* 354 — ראובן הרשה את
שמעון שיהיה טוען בעדו בעסקיו בערכאות העכו״ם הנקרא בלשון העכו״ם אדבוקאט;
והוצרך ליקח מליץ שיטעון בעדו. — Asher, 18:5

60. A. Neuman, *op. cit.* pp. 147-8.

61. G. Kisch, *op. cit.* pp. 91 ff. He cites the privilege extended by
Bishop Rüdiger of 1084 for the Jews of Speyer which "bestowed upon the
Jewish court the right of exclusive jurisdiction in legal disputes between
Jews . . . Only if the Jewish court regarded itself unable to pass judgement
was the suit to come up for decision, before the Bishop or his chamberlain."
Also, he quotes the privileges extended by Emperor Henry IV in 1090 to
the Jews of Speyer and Worms. Here, again, "the exclusive character of
the Jewish courts' jurisdiction was pointed out with even greater distinct-
ness. Jewish litigants shall be convicted and judged by their equals and
not by others . . . according to their own law." The *Meissener Rechtsbuch,*
III, 17, 41 states that Jews of the last part of the 14th century were to be
tried by their own courts. In Breslau, the courts considered excommunication by a Jewish court equal to excommunication of any other ecclesiastical
court and would not recognize any petition of an individual under the ban.

62. Meir Katzenellenbogen, 154 — דאפי׳ אם אינו עושה שום מעשה רק
כופיהו בד״ג שיעמוד בד״י ראוי למותחו.

63. Joseph Colon, 154.

64. *Ibid.* 161.

65. *Ibid.* 172, 132; Meir Katzenellenbogen, 154.

66. Finkelstein, *op. cit.* pp. 314-5 — ראינו שערוריה פה פיסארו כי יריבון
אנשים ונגשו אל המשפט בערכאות שלהם ושפטום ואם יטילו השופטים שבועה על א׳
מהם המשביע לחבירו ילך ויביא במקום המשפט שלהם חפץ של מצוה כגון תפילין או
אחד מספרי הקדש ... ומפני שהם לא ידעו את ערך הקדושה ... הרואה אותם מזלזל
בהם והרצועות שבהם ידמו בעיניהם כאלו יהיו שרוך הנעל ... ונמצא שם שמים מתחלל
ח״ו לכן אנחנו ... גזרנו שלא יוכל שום [אחד] מבני ישראל להשביע ... רק ישביענו על
הקולמוס כמשפטם ואם לא יתקרר דעתו ... יבואו בעלי הריב ... בפנינו ...

67. *Ibid.* p. 304 — מי שהפר ברית תחלה והעמיד ישראל בערכאות של
גוים בלי רשות קהלו או הרב של עירו וישוב וניחם המפר ברית הנ״ל ויבקש אח״כ
להעמיד חבירו בד״י לא יאבה לו ולא ישמע אליו שום רב או קהל ...

68. Simon b. Zemah Duran, I, 61 — ושמא היה המלכות מקפדת שידונו
ואלה הדברים הם במקום ההוא חדשים וזרים כי — Also, III, 44, 227 — ובדיני עכו״ם
לא הורגלו בדיני ממונות ולא שמעו ולא ראו באותן הארצות.

69. Ibn Adret, III, 154 — ובקש מהקהל שימנו ב״ד.

70. Simon b. Zemah Duran, II, 290, 292 — The 8th *takkanah* —
עוד תקננו שכל דין ודברים ... שיהיו בין איש לאשתו שלא יהא רשות ביד שום אחד
מהם לדון כלל בעש״ג אלא לפני דייני ישראל ... אין ספק שלדון בעש״ג ... שהיא
עבירה ... אלא שבזאת התקנה הזכירו בה בפירוש לפי שמן הידוע הוא שהאיש ידו
תקיפה על האשה ולפעמים תהיה האשה ... ורוצים לדון בערכאותיהם ע״כ באה תקנה
זו להטיל עליהם חרם בזה; also, I. Epstein, *The Responsa of R. Simon b.*

Zemah Duran, p. 65; I. Abrahams, *Jewish Life in the Middle Ages*, p. 37.

71. R. Samuel b. Simon, 439 — ואעפ"י שהאומות דינן בזה בהפך אסור לנו
לילך בחוקותיהם דבחוקותיהם לא תלכו.

72. *Ibid*. 514 — ולענין מה שרוצים לדון בדיני גוים חלילה וחס לא תהיה זאת
בישראל שאפילו היו דיניהם כדינינו הוא אסור שהרי התורה אמרה אשר תשים... כ"ש
שאם אין דינם כדינינו ואית ביה תרתי אסורי לדון לפניהם ואסור גזלה.

73. Samuel Halevy and Joseph Taitozok, quoted by Samuel de Medina,
Hoshen Mishpat, 224 — הרי בהדיא כי דיני הערכאות אינם מעלים ולא מורידין לבטל
הדינין והמשפטים הצדיקים אשר לישראל הקדושים.

74. *Ibid., Orah Hayyim*, 5 — המבלי אין תורה בישראל.

75. *Ibid., Hoshen Mishpat*, 224 — וכמו כן אין כח בערכאות לבטל דת
הערלים ודיניהם.

76. *Ibid.* — לא איירי התם אלא כגון שהוא מנמוסי המלך אבל כשהוא מצד דיני
הדת אסור לקיימו משום כי לא כצורנו צורם...

77. *Ibid., Eben ha-Ezer*, 131; S. A. Rosanes, *Dibrei Yemei Yisroel be-Tugrama*, Vol. II, p. 63-4 p. 100 quotes a manuscript of Abraham Damon of Constantinople — ביום ד' תשעה לחדש טבת שנת שי"ח נתקבצו מרביצי התורה
בק"ק ועמהם יחידי סגולה מהקהלות בבי"ה הקאטאלני ויגמרו אמר על אשר הוגד להם
כי יש אנשים אשר יצרם תקפם לצאת ממחיצת היהדות מבלי יראת שמים לבקש ירושות
ונחלות אשר לא כדת משה וישראל... בכח השותדיות והמסוריות בערכאות של הממשלה
לכן הסכימו... שלא יהיה רשאי שום בר ישראל איש או אשה לא על ידם ולא ע"י אחרים
להסב ירושה ולא נחלה אשר לא כדת... לתבוע ירושה או כתובה לא תוספות ולא נדוניא
לפני הערכאות אלא בפני הב"ד. וכל העובר על ההסכמה הזאת יהיה בכלל מוסרי ישראל...
ויבדל מתוך הקהל. וההסכמה הזאת היא שגורה ונכריו בכל שבת שלפני ראש חודש בכל
בתי הכנסיות אשר בשאלוניק כמו החרם מהמלשינים והמוסרים.

78. *Ibid.* p. 100 — איך החכם הנזכר יש לו בית ועד לדין דיני ממונות ושהוא
הכריו בכל המדינה לבלתי לכת לעש"ג כלל אלא לבוא לפניו כי עש"ג אין דיניהם דין.

79. Joseph Caro, *Abkat Rohel*, 192; Samuel de Medina, *Yoreh Deah*, 75.

80. *Ibid.* 108, 192·

81. *Ibid.* Medina quotes the Talmud, Ned. 28a and equates the situation at hand to an unlimited tax, מוכס שאין לה קצבה, or a self-appointed tax collector, מוכס העומד מאליו.

82. *Ibid.* agrees with ruling of Barfat — שיש להחרים ולנדות המחזיק ביד
ההולך לדון בדיני גוים.

83. *Ibid.*

84. *Kenesset Hagedolah, Hoshen Mishpat*, 140; S. A. Rosanes, *op. cit.*
Vol. III; *Zion*, I, p. 266 — מימי עולם ושנים קדמוניות היתה הסכמה קדומה אל
כללות הק"ק יצ"ו אשר פה קושטנדינא בענין החזקות של הבתים והחצרות והחנויות אשר
גבלו ראשונים החכמים השלמים... וגדרו גדר... שלא ישיג איש את רעהו וישלח ידו
להחזיק במקום שהחזיק בו חברו.

85. *Ibid.* — ומדי יום ויום מתחדשים בין דין לדין בין איש לרעהו דברי ריבות
בדיני החזקות.

86. *Ibid.* — והוא להסיר תלונות אדוני הארץ הישמעאלים מעלינו האומרים שאנו
מחלישים כח קרקעותם.

87. *Ibid.* — ההסכמה הזאת נחתמה מכל הקהלות היהודים בקושטנדינא בשנת
שלז... הסכמנו שלעולם יהיו מחויבים... למנות ולהעמיד ממונים הגונים אנשי חיל
יראי אלקים לדון בדיני ריבות החזקות...

88. *Ibid.* p. 264 — שכל בר ישראל לא יכול להעזר בכח הישמעאלים ולהביא
מליצים בעדו מהם אל הממונים ולא לגלות להם שיש ממונים שומעים ודנים דיני חזקות
כדי להתרעם מהם ולא על ידם ולא עי מינים ומלשינים ומשומדים וכל העובר על פרט
מאלה יחרם ויופרש ויובדל מעדת ישראל ויאבד כל זכותו.

89. *Shibhei Jerusalem*, p. 24b; Graetz, *Geschichte*, Vol. 9, p. 25; A.
S. Rosanes, *op. cit.* p. 131 — תקנות והסכמות שיש לקק ירושלים והם כתובים
על לוח בבית הכנסת... שלא יוכל שום אדם להביא חבירו בערכאות שלהם אם לא יתרה
בו שלשה פעמים ולא ציית דינא.

90. Joseph Caro, *Abkat Rohel*, 72.

91. *Ibid., Hoshen Mishpat*, 388:5.

92. Moses b. Joseph Trani, III, 208 — ואני אומר כי מנהג זה הרע מבטל
הלכה טובה כי באיזה עסק שיש בין ישראל לאחיו חייבין לדון בדי...

93. *Ibid.* 100 — וכיון שבדיניהם היה לו דין אעפ שבדיננו לא היה לו דין
הוה ליה כמלך שכעס על א' מעבדיו ולקח שדהו שאינה גזל ואין בעבלים מוציאין אותה
מיד ישראל שלקחה מן המלך ולא גרע זה שהיה יכול להוציאו בדיניהם החקוקים להם מן
המלך שאין לו דין אלא מצד ד"ד.

94. B.K. 113b — האי בר ישראל דידע סהדותא לכותי (ולא... מכריז רבא...
תבעו מיניה) ואזל ואסהיד ליה בדיני דכותי על ישראל חבריה משמתינן ליה.

95. *Ibid.* — מ"ט דאינהו מפקי ממונא אפומא דחד.

96. *Ibid.* — ולא אמרן אלא חד אבל בתרי לא.

97. R. Tam quoted by Mordecai, B.K. (177) — וה"מ ... פסק ר"ת
להוציא ממון מישראל אבל להעמיד ממון ביד עובד כוכבים כגון שיישראל תובע את
העכו"ם וישראל זה מעיד שאין העכו"ם חייב לו כלום משמתי' ליה דהא בדינינו גמי
מעמידין ממון ביד בעליו [אפילו] בלא עד דהמע"ה. Also Isserles, 52.

98. *Ibid.* 52, 86 — ועוד גראה דכשהישראל דן עם הגוי אז מותר להעיד אבל
בישראל דן עם חבירו אה"נ דאסור להעיד אעפ"י שהוא כדין משום דמסייע לעוברי עבירה.

CHAPTER VIII

DOCUMENTS OF A GENTILE COURT

1. Mishneh Gittin 10 b; Tosefta *ibid·*, I, 9.
2. Gittin, *ad. loc.*
3. *Ibid.* — אמר שמואל דד"ד.
4. *Ibid.* — תני חוץ מכגיטי נשים.
5. Above chapter II.
6. Alfasi, Gittin *ad. loc.* is always cited. Yet, the wording of Alfasi really tells little concerning his opinion in this matter. Alfasi's general principle in organizing his code was to include only such parts of state- ments of the Talmud which he considered to be the binding opinions. In this case, Alfasi records both conclusions. The early Spanish sages, who like the Geonim, ruled according to the second conclusion, interpreted Alfasi's choice to mean that he, too, ruled in the traditional manner; namely, according to the last conclusion or else why mention it at all. However, in the 13th century, when a change occurred and the authorities no longer thought the two conclusions to be conflicting opinions, they cited Alfasi's choice of including both answers as agreeing with their premise or else why include the first answer. Comp. also Maimonides, *Malveh ve'Loveh,*

27:1 — אבל כל השטרות שחותמיהן עכו"ם הרי אלו פסולין חוץ משטרי מקח וממכר ושטרי חוב... וכן שטרי [חוב] והודאות ומתנות ופשרות ומחילות שהן בעבדים שלהן אע"פ שיש' בהן כל הדברים שמגינו הרי הן כחרסים.

7. *Ibid.* — והורו רבותי שאפילו שטרי חוב שלהן שנתנו המעות בפניהם פסולין ולא הכשירו אלא שטרי מקח וממכר שנתנו המעות בפניהם ואין אני מודה בזה.

8. Abraham Ibn Daud of Posquires, *ibid. glosses* — א"א יפה הורו רבותיו.

9. Ibn Adret, I, 895; II, 2, 211 — יש מרבותינו אומרים כן דכל שטר שהוא עצמו עשוי לקנייה הוי ליה כגט שאינו כשר בגופן של נכרים כמו ששנינו בפ"ק דגיטין כל השטרות... ואקשינן עלה בגמ' קא פסיק ותני ואפי' שטר מתנה בשלמה שטרי מכר אי לאו דיהיב זוזי... אלא שטר מתנה במאי קנה בהאי שטרא האי שטרא חספא בעלמא הוא ופריקו תני חוץ מכגיטי נשים אלמא כל שטרא קנייה... אינן כלום ומיהו יש פוסקים בלישנא אחרינא... כדשמואל דאמר שמואל דד"ד... ודעתי נוטה לזה דהלכה כשמואל ומאחר שאין בינינו ד"ד בדבר — Also, VI, 140. ודוקא היכא דאיכא הרמנא דמלכא Torat ha-Bayit, 211; III, הזה כל השטרות הכתובים בגוים... אין עושין בהם דין 63, 66, 69, 79; VI, 218; *Novellae,* Gittin 10b; R. Yom Tob b. Abraham Ibn Ashvilla, 38 — אבל כל שאין עליו עדים ישראלים אין השטר כלום אלא במקום שיש בו הרמנא דמלכא דד"ד... quotes Nahmanides and *Ittur* as agreeing; Asher, Gittin *ad. loc.;* Mordecai *ad. loc.;* Nissim Gerondi *ad. loc.;* Barfat, 51, 142, 203, 478, 493; Samuel b. Simon Duran, 219, 233, 461 and also quotes Simon b. Zemah Duran as ruling similarly, I, 158, III, 325 — ... שלא פסל שטרי מתנה אלא באתרא דליכא הרמנותא דמלכא בערכאות שכיון שגילה דעתו ז"ל במקומות אחרים דד"ד ממילא יש לנו לומר דכשרין בההוא אתרא דאית ביה הרמנותא ארכאות ולא בא אלא ללמדנו מהו דין שטרות העולים בעש"ג מחמת הדין

193

‎‏…ד״ד מחמת לא ‏בעצצמו‎; Joseph Colon, 18, 121, 161 — ‎שהוא ‏…מתנה שטר וגם‎
‎‏…ד״ד מכח לא אם ‏ממש‎ ‎בו אין וגם אנשים של ‏בערכאות עשוי שטר‎ David b. Abi
Zimra, I, 67 — ‎דשייך ‏במלתא ‏דד״ד ‏לאשממעינן אי ‏קמא לישנא ‏כתב אמאי ‏ק״ל ‏ואני‎
Contrast ‎‏בערכאותיהם ‏העול׳ השטרות דכל ‏דמתנית׳ עלה ‏לאיתויי ‏ה״ל לא ‏למלכות‎;
with I, 541 — ‎תריץ הא ‏מתנות שטרי אפי׳ ומשמע השטרות כל ‏במתנ׳ ‏דתנן ‏ואע״ג‎
‎עומדים ‏שהם להם והדומה נשים מגטי חוץ ‏פי׳ ‏החו״ץ בכלל הו מתנות ‏דשטרי ‏תלמודא לה‎
‎לראיה ‏ולא ‏לקנין‎; Samuel de Medina, Hoshen Mishpat, 304, 305; Joseph
Caro, Abkat Rohel, 72 — ‎לפני ‏אלא שטר יעשו שלא המלך ‏הנהיג אם ‏לישנא דתרי‎
Shiltei Gib- ‎‏…העולים שטרות ‏והיינו ‏…עד השטר על העדים יחתמו ‏ושלא ‏הערכאות‎;
borim, Gittin ad. loc.

It is interesting to note that this dispute concerning the two answers
in the Talmud took place in the Spanish centers. There is no mention of
it by the Franco-German rabbis. Only when we reach the Polish centers
in the 16th century is there mention of it again. Thus, Isserles, Hoshen
Mishpat, 68:1 and Solomon Luria, Yam Shel Shlomo, Gittin 22 rule that
the two conclusions do not conflict and when there is a specific royal
decree demanding the recognition of documents issued by the Gentile
courts then such documents are legal. Luria records that in his day there
was no such royal demand; consequently, Dina D'Malkhuta Dina applies
to bills of sale or indebtedness only. — ‎ומקפיד הדת מנהג המלך ‏שאין היכא אבל‎
‎האידנא ‏וא״כ ‏…לקנות ‏שיהא ‏מהני חכמים תקנו דלא ‏פשיטא עשויה השטר ‏יה׳ ומה ‏בהיך‎
‎שטר ‏להכשיר ‏תמצא לא ‏א״כ בערכאות עשוין דוקא השטרות כל ‏שיהיו ‏להקפיד ‏ד״ד שאין‎
‎דתינו נגד יהא ‏שלא רק ‏…והלוואה מכר שטר אלא ‏ערכאות‎. We do see that in his
day, Jews made use of such documents issued by the secular tribunals.
Luria found it necessary to warn that we are not bound by documents
issued by them when they result from intentional wrong doing of an individual who prefers Gentile law to Jewish without being forced to do so.
Such documents are valid only when Jewish scribes are not available, when
it concerns deeds to real-estate in places where it is the custom to register
them in the Gentile courts, or else is done out of fear of coercion. It is
only then that these are recognized. — ‎לאכשורי ‏רבנן תקינו ‏דלא נותנת ‏הסברא ‏א״כ‎
‎ישראל ‏סופרי למצוא יכול היה שלא היכא אלא ישראל ‏בדיני עליהם ‏ולדון ‏ישלהו שטרות‎
‎מן ‏שמתיירא סיבה הוא ‏או ‏…שלהן בערכאות לכתוב הוא ‏שדרך קרקעות ‏ענין הוא או‎
‎צורך ‏מבלי ‏ושטריהם ‏דתיהם בוחר לבו שברוע היכא אבל ‏…מכשירין ‏כה״ג ‏…פלוני‎
‎השטר ‏אותו שנזקקים חלילה השיאו לבו זדון ‏אלא‎.

10. Mordecai, Gittin (325); Or Zarua, III, ed. Jerusalem 1887, p. 4—
‎‏…[מועיל] ‏בעיר ‏בערכאות ‏העכו״ם פה לפני בעל וגם בלע״ז ‏ושנ״א ‏בהנ״ט בזה״ז ‏נ״ל וכן‎
11. Asher, 18:2 — ‎בערכאות ‏ולא ישראל בדיני רגילין אין הזה שבזמן ‏גראה אבל‎
‎של בערכאות כשרים כלהו ‏הלכך ‏…במתנה ‏ולא במכר לא בשטר ‏לקנות ‏ישמעאלים של‎
‎ישמעאלים‎; Adret, III, 15, 16, 79; VII, 148, 250; ha-Meyohosot, 74; Comp.
with Tur, 68 — ‎…המלך הנהיג אם הרא״ש א״א ‏וכתב‎ ‎האידנא אבל‎ ‎ד״ד דליכא כיון‎
‎חספא בערכאות הגעשים מתנות שטרי הגי בערכאות נעשים שלו השטרות כל ‏שיהו‎
‎הוא ‏בעלמא‎. Obviously, a difference existed between the lands under Moslem
and under Christian rule.

194

12. Barfat, 51.

13. *Ibid.* 142, 478, 493.

14. Ibn Adret, I, 946 — וכ״ש אם תדינם בחק המלך לחדש לו שטר וכדקיימו
‫לן דד״ד‬.

15. Nahmanides, 52 (175) — הרי הוא ... שאם השטר כשר כגון בערכאות
... ‫וכשטר של ישראל יש בו שעבוד‬; *ibid.* 71 (193) based on Hai Gaon —
ונשאל הגאון והשיב חייכם אחינו שגם אצלינו כך הוא איכא דגרסי בני חרי ואיכא דגרסי
ממשעבדי מיהו רובא דרבנן דעליהון דגרסי סמכא מפום רבוותא דעליהון סמכי דשמעתא
‫גרסי ומגבי ביה ממשעבדי‬. Comp. Nahmanides, *Novellae*, Gittin 10b.

16. *Ibid.* — אבל אם השטר פסול בדינינו אע״פ שהגוים נוהגין בו כיון שאם בא
... ‫הגוי לדון בדיני ישראל לא משתעבד ליה כלל בשטר זה הוית ליה מלוה על פה‬.

17. *Ibid.* 70 (192); *Teshubat ha-Geonim,* Harkavy, 239, 278; *Teshubat
ha-Geonim,* Coronel, 51; Nahmanides, *Novellae,* Gittin 10b; *Tur, Hoshen
Mishpat, 68 end; Barfat, 51, 203.

18. *Ibid.* — שהרי מה שאמרו חז״ל דשטרות העולות בערכאות של עכו״ם כשרים
ואפי׳ שטרי מתנה משום ד״ד... היינו לומר שהשטר כשר ויש תורת שטר עליו כאלו
נעשה ונחתם ע״י ישראל אבל לא לומר שנדין בדיניהם לגמרי כמו שנא׳ על דרך משל
שאם הקנה בשטר העשוי בעש״ג דשלבל״ע ... שיועיל הקנין כיון שנעשה בשטר העשוי
... ‫בערכאותיהן ובדיניהם מועיל הקנין אפי׳ בדשלבל״ע‬.

19. *Ibid.* — שזה אינו בכלל דד״ד שאין המלך מקפיד אלא שהשטר הנעשה ע״י
סופריו שיש להם הורמנותא דמלכא שיועיל ושנדין בו כדין שטר כשר הנעשה ע״י סופרי
... ‫ישראל‬.

20. *Ibid.;* the translation is taken from A. Neuman, *op. cit.,* pp. 213-14.

21. Barfat, 305.

22. *Ibid.* 143, 145 — דבר ברור הוא שלא נכשיר אנחנו שטרות שלהם יותר
‫מהם עצמם ואם בדיניהם אין השטר מועיל הן כלו או מקצתו לא נכשירנו אנחנו יותר מהם‬.

23. Samuel de Medina, *Eben ha-Ezer,* 200.

24. David Ibn Zimra, I, 542; II, 634 — וכי עדיף שטר העולה בערכאותיהם
... ‫משטר הנעשה בדיני ישראל‬; Samuel b. Simon Duran, 215, 394, 461; *Shiltei
Gibborim, Gittin 10b; Joseph Caro, *Hoshen Mishpat,* 68.

25. David Ibn Zimra, *ibid.* — ולא תקשה ד״ד שאין דין של מלכים אלא
‫להכשיר שטרותיהן אבל לענין דרכי הקנאה לא עדיפי משטרות שלנו‬.

26. Kolonymus b. Elazar Montino, Moses b. Hezekiah Halevy, and
Eliezer b. Moses Yaffa; recorded by Meir Katzenellenbogen, *Responsa,* 46:
אחר היות השובר הנעשה בעש״ג פסול כי העדים הם קרובים לתרח ולאברהם ולא עדיפי
‫משטרות הנעשים בסופרים שלנו ..‬.

27. *Ibid.* 47, 60 — כי מה שכתבו הרמב״ן דלא עדיפי שטרות שלהם משטרות
שלנו לא דברו רק כשחסר דבר אחד מדרכי הקנאה... אבל בנ״ד אם נאמין לסופר
שהמלוה הודה באמת היותו פרוע מה לנו אם העדות פסולה לפי דינינו הלא לא אברו
סהדי אלא להודיע האמת האמת בדברים הזה ומאחר שהמלכות מקפדת להאמין לסופרים כמאה
עדים כשרים שלנו א״כ גם בנ״ד נאמין לסופר... והלא כל עידי נכרים הם פסולים ואפילו
הכי כי נכתב ע״י נוטארי״ה הממונים מן המלכות או בערכאות אנו מכשירין השטר מאחר
‫כי בדיניהם כשר כי על נאמנות הסופרים אנו סומכין ... דד״ד‬.

28. We must again point out that the rabbis of France and Germany

during the Middle Ages did not discuss the relative status of documents issued by the Gentile courts.

29. Solomon Luria, *Yam Shel Shlomo,* Gittin 22 — וא"כ האידנא שאין ד"ד להקפיד שיהיו כל השטרות עשוין דוקא בערכאות א"כ לא תמצא להכשיר שטר ערכאות אלא שטר מכר והלוואה... רק שלא יהא נגד דתינו. Also, R. Menahem Mendel of Lubavitz, *Zemah Zedek, Hoshen Mishpat,* 11.

30. Isserles, 51, 86 — ואף לדברי הרא"ש דכתב דוקא במקום שהמלכות מקפדת שלא לכתוב ושטר רק במקום הערכאות כולו נראה דבמקום זה נמי מקרי מלכות מקפדת שם. Solomon Luria, *ibid.* — שאין שם רק משפט הערכאות ואין ישראל נמצאים שם א"כ הסברא נותנת דלא תקינו רבנן לאכשורי שטרות שלהן ולדון עליהן בד"י אלא היכא שלא היה יכול למצוא סופרי ישראל...

31. Isserles, 109. A century later, Joel Sirkes ruled (*Responsa, Ye-shonot,* 26) that two creditors, holding separate notes upon the same non-Jewish debtor, may foreclose their liens only in accordance with the sequence of the notes they hold. The creditor whose note was issued earlier has preference. However, in Poland, the law of the kingdom was not concerned with the time the notes were issued but rather regarded the dates notes were due. "The law of the kingdom is the law," and even if a note was issued at a later date but is a short-term loan, it takes precedence over a note of earlier issue but of longer term. — הדבר צריך בירור דאם בדיניהם נמי המוקדם טורף מן המאוחר אפי' כבר גבה המאוחר... אבל מ"מ בדיניהם אין מחליטין הבית למאוחר כיון דידע דאיכא מוקדם א"כ פשיטא דהדין עם ראובן דאין זה ד"ד אלא גזילה... אבל אם בדיניהם כך הוא המשפט להגבות למאוחר כשזמן פרעון שלו קודם... א"כ הדין עם שמעון... אבל בנ"ד דכיון דעשה שמעון ע"פ דיניהם הדד"ד אין זה מזיק שיעבודו של חבירו.

32. B.B. 147b; Ket. 85b; B.K. 89a; B.M. 20a; Kid. 48a — אמר שמואל המוכר שטר חוב לחבירו וחזר ומחלו מחול.

33. *Hakam Zevi,* 147-8 — ובח"כ אפי' הא נמי ליתא שהרי מכר ח"כ וחזר ומחלו בודאי אינו מחול בד"י וכוזה אנו דנין... Meir b. Gedaliah of Lublin, *Meir Einei Hakamim,* 22.

34. *Hoshen Mishpat,* 69:2; Isserles, *ibid.;* Siftei Kohen, 69:10; Comp. Ibn Adret, *ha-Meyohosot,* 22.

35. Ezekiel b. Judah Landau, *Nodai be-Yehuda, Hoshen Mishpat,* 10: נ"ל לומר שבנדון זה הוא נאמן לומר פרעתי דהא הטעם הוא שבזמן הזה פוסקים שאינו נאמן לומר פרעתי הואיל ודי"ד הוא כן שלא יהי' נאמן כל זמן שהשטר הוא ביד מלוה וא"כ שטר שנכתב בנוסח התיקון המדינה אמרינן... אבל בנ"ד שזה השטר הוא מאוחר על תשרי הבע"ל וא"כ מאוחר הוא פסול לגמרי בד"י והמלוה חייב בקנס בדיניהם וא"כ אין לנו לדון בזה הכ"י כד"י וצריכין אנו לאוקמי אדין תורה ולא הוי אלא כסתם כ"י ונאמן לומר פרעתי. Contr. with Ibn Adret, VI, 149 — A note written in a Gentile court that went past its due date could not be re-written should the debtor claim that it was paid. This ruling held true even if the king ordered that it be re-written. This does not fall under the category of a royal decree but was considered royal theft. — שאלו בא שמעון עם טענת

196

פירעון אז הדין עמו שאין בזה ד״ך דגזלה היא זו דכל שטר העומד לגבות ועבר זמנו
.ואמר פרעתי נאמן מן הדין והמלך שאמר שאינו נאמן כעין גזילה היא

36. *Ibid.* 11 — במה שפלפלת אם יכול לומר פרעתי נגד כ״י כזה שעפ״י ד״ך
אין לו תוקף פשיטא שיפה אמרת...

37. *Ibid.* The questioner felt that Jewish law recognized the validity
of such a note but honored the claim of the debtor when he stated that
he had paid the note. Landau considers the note חספא בעלמא — a scrap
of paper without any validity. It is worthless because *Dina D'Malkhuta*
had rendered it valueless. The two would arrive at different conclusions
in a case where a promissory note was post-dated and the debtor refuses
to pay. The questioner, who accepts the note on face value according to
Jewish law, would demand payment. The respondent would disqualify the
note on the grounds that a post-dated promissory note is rendered void
by "the law of the kingdom."

38. R. Yeruham, *Sefer Mesharim;* Samuel de Medina, *Hoshen Mishpat,* 350.

39. Asher, 18:2.

40. Above chapter VII; J. Caro, *Bet Joseph, Hoshen Mishpat,* 26;
Isserles, 369.

41. Barfat, 51; *Abkat Rohel,* 75; *Hoshen Mishpat,* 68 — אפילו לדעת
הרמב״ם הדבר ברור דשטרי צוואה כשרים כשטרי מכר ישהרי אין השטר עושה קנין אלא
דבור ׳המצו׳ עושה קנין דדבריו ככתובים וכמסורים דמי... Of interest is the case
cited by Joseph Caro, *Bet Joseph,* 26; *Hatam Sofer, Hoshen Mishpat,* 142,
of a husband who presented his wife with a house which he registered in
her name with the secular courts. His wife, in turn, wrote a will leaving
the house to her heirs and cutting the husband off without allowing him
any share at all in this house. Adret ruled that *Dina D'Malkhuta Dina* is
not operative or else you void all the laws of the Torah. Caro disagrees
in this instance and cites three reasons to prove his point: (1) The husband,
himself, turned the house over to his wife; (2) According to "the law of
the kingdom," the wife's heirs have possession (מוחזקים); (3) *Dina D'Malkhuta Dina* is applicable in this instance since there is a direct benefit to
the king. The king shares in the inheritance of the king's property left to
the heirs. It is to the king's benefit that the husband should not inherit.

Joseph Caro rules that the will is valid. Comp. *Hatam Sofer, Hoshen
Mishpat,* 142 who takes each of the above mentioned reasons and arrives
at another conclusion. (1) a husband who registers a house in his wife's
name does not thereby relinquish his right to inherit the house. After all,
he would inherit a home which was hers all the time. (2) Why should
the law of the Gentile courts render the wife's heirs "in possession"? The
law of the Torah should make her husband the "possessor." (3) The king
shares in the inheritance no matter who inherits, the heirs or the husband.
Therefore, there is no benefit to the king if the will is or is not valid. See
R.M.M. of Lubavitz, *Zemah Zedek, Hoshen Mishpat,* 38.

197

42. Samuel de Medina, *Eben ha-Ezer,* 131; see also above chapter VII. However, when a will upholds Jewish law it was recognized as valid even if it was drawn up by a Gentile court. Thus, when a daughter destroyed a document which allowed her brother to inherit their father's estate while cutting her off without anything, Trani ruled, that the document was valid whether a Bet Din or a Gentile court had issued it and the daughter must make good any loss her brother sustained. In this instance the document, if valid, upheld Jewish law for without it, the daughter could inherit as well by merely applying to a non-Jewish court. Trani, I, 130 — ולא שנא בין שטר שנעשה בגופן שלנו לנעשה בגופן שלהן דשטרות ישלהן כה״ג הוא כשטרות של ישראל וכ״ש שלא נעשו כי אם לקיום דיני ישראל שלא יזכו הבנות בירושה במקום הבן.

43. Yom Tob b. Abraham Ibn Ashvilla, 53.

44. *Hatam Sofer, Hashmatot le-Hoshen Mishpat,* 198 — ואותן ד׳ מאות Comp. .זהובים נגבין בשיין הנהוגין במדינותינו כי כן צוה הקיר״ה בפקידו שלו דדד״ד *ibid., Eben ha-Ezer,* 149, 165.

45. Trani, I, 309.

46. Barfat, quoted by Joseph Caro, *Abkat Rohel,* 80 — דשטרי כתובות הנעשי׳ בעש״ג היו כשטר מכר והלוואה שהם כשהם כשרים לכ״ע דכיון שעיקר השטר של כתובה שכותבים בפניהם הוא כמו שטר חוב...

47. *Ibid.* — ...הוא כשר גם התנאים שהם כתובים באותו שטר כתובה שלהם .שתקח היא חצי נכסיו לאחר מותו

48. Trani, I, 390.

49. Barfat, 5, 6 invalidated a marriage performed by Gentile authorities. *Abkat Rohel, ibid.* cites these responsa and states that Barfat recognized the *Ketuba* issued as a result of such a marriage. לענין ממון תנאיהם קיימים. The quote could not be traced.

50. Trani, I, 309 and quoted by Joseph Caro in *Abkat Rohel,* 81 who disagrees. Caro felt that if a marriage is contracted in a Gentile court and is not considered valid, then the *Ketuba* issued by the same court at the same time can neither be considered legal. The *Ketuba* is a document given by a husband to his wife. If a marriage is not legal, neither can the *Ketuba* be legal. דכיון דקידושין ונשואין אין כאן תנאי נישואין אין כאן. Caro differentiated between the Christian and Moslem countries. In Christian countries there was no demand on the part of the king for Jews to make use of the Gentile courts for such documents. As a consequence, these instruments were but as bits of paper. In Moslem countries, since there was a definite royal decree demanding the acknowledgment of all instruments drawn up in a Gentile court, these documents are *eo ipso* valid.

Caro's arguments would be valid if everyone would agree that a concubine is not to receive a *Ketuba.* It would be an indication that the *Ketuba* is inexorably tied in with marriage. However comp. P. T. Ket. V — .ר׳ מאיר אומר פלגש אין לה כתובה רבי יהודה אומר יש לה כתובה אבל לא תנאי כתובה א״ר יהודה אמר רב נשים בכתובה ובקידושין פלגשים בלא כתובה — Contr. Sanh. 21a ובלא קידושין. The above is the reading as found in the talmudic text before us. However, see the reading of Rashi, Genesis 25:6 which obviously stated that a concubine was קידושין בלא כתובה.; In North Africa, deeds and documents drawn up in a Jewish court were not recognized by the authorities. Jews were ordered to make use of the Moslem courts. See Barfat, 102 — והערכאות לא יחושו לעדים יהודים ולא לשטר העשוי בגופן שלנו. Also, 148 — ואין עושין הצדא״ק אלא ליפוי כח שתוכל לגבותו בדיני ישמעאל. Comp. also Samuel b. Simon Duran who advised Jews to stay clear of so doubtful an act. One should not write a *Ketuba* in a Gentile court since there is ample doubt as to the validity of such a document. Anyone who does so saddles himself with a *Ketuba* of dubious value which in turn raises the question of whether or not it is permissible for him to have relations with his wife. See Duran, 293.

51. Barfat, 102, 148, 174; Simon b. Zemah, III, 94, 219, 278; Samuel b. Simon Duran, 417 — שכך המנהג באלו הארצות שנוהגין בצדא״ק שהכתובה והצדא״ק הכל אחד ואין עושין הצדא״ק אלא ליפוי כח שתוכל לגבותו בדיני ישמעאל ומחיים אבל כל שנפרע מן הצדא״ק גם שעבוד הכתובה נמחל כנגדו.

52. Barfat, 148 — וכן כשגובה כתובתה בד״ד מחייבין אותה להחזיר גם הצדא״ק וכן אנו דנין בכל יום...

53. Ibn Adret, II, 244 — ;ומסרו בערכאותיהם עם חבורתו והוצרך לפזר ולשחד III, 75 — ...; V, 287; ;ועל הצ' דינרים השיב שעכבם לעצמו מחמת הוצאות ושחדים Asher, 89:8.

54. Maimonides, *Malveh ve-Loveh*, 27:1 — והוא שיהיו עשויים בערכאות שלהן אבל במקום קיבוץ פליליהם בלא קיום השופט שלהן לא יועילו לו כלום וכן צריכין שיעידו עדי ישראל על אלו העכו״ם שהן עדי השטר ועל זה השוטר או השופט שקיים השוחד; עדותו שאין ידועים בקבלות; Mordecai, Gittin (324) quoting *Sefer ha-Hakma* and R. Yakkar.

55. Asher, Gittin 10b — ולא מסתבר לי דא״כ נפל פיתא בבירא דמי יעיד עליהם בזה דסתם עכו״ם מקבלי שוחדא כדאמר בפ' כל כתבי (קטז:); Samuel de Medina, *Hoshen Mishpat*, 304; *Shiltei Gibborim*, Gittin *ad. loc.*

56. Asher, *ibid.* — וסמכינן עלייהו דאי לא יהיב זוזי קמייהו לא הוי מרעי; Adret, IV, 126; VII, 148 — ולפי מה שקבלו מרבותינו סתם; נפשייהו לצוות לחתום ערכאות לא מקבלי שוחדא.

57. *Ibid. ha-Meyohosot*, 78 — דחזקה דערכאי לא משקר.

58. Barfat, 143.

59. Asher, Gittin, *ad. loc.* — ואפי' אי נפיק קלא עלייהו דשקלי שוחדא לאצלויי דינא לעדות שקר לא מרעי נפשייהו. Contr. de Medina, *Hoshen Mishpat*, 350 who considered Asher to be far too lenient in this matter. — אלא הרא״ש שהפליג להקל בזה עד מאד עד שכתב דאפי' נפק עלייהו קלא דמקבלי שוחדא להטות הדין מסתמא לא מסהדי שקרא. It is difficult to determine the view of Alfasi who merely states: ודוקא ערכאות דלא מקבלי שוחדא. Whether or not he demands specific proof as did Maimonides is not evident.

60. Ps. 144:8.

61. *Ibid.* 26:10.

62. Samuel b. Simon Duran, 477 — לפי שסתם גוים מקבלי שוחד הם ומקרא
מלא הוא אשר פיהם דבר שוא וימינם מלאה שוחד ואעפ״כ הכשירו חז״ל שטרות העולים
בערכאותיהם משום דד״ד...

63. *Abkat Rohel,* 73 — ובפרט אלו השופטים... ובודאי דלא מקבלי שוחדא
וידוע ומפורסם הוא זה דלא מקבלי שוחדא וכבר ניסוהו בזה כמה פעמים ולא מקבלי
שוחדא...

64. Gittin 11a — רבינא סבר לאכשורי בכנופייא דארמאי שאינן ערכאות א״ל
רפרם ערכאות תנן; see Maimonides, *Malveh ve-Loveh,* 27:1; de Medina,
Hoshen Mishpat, 304.

65. Adret, V, 168 in the name of Zerahiah Halevi — האחד שיהיה לכותב
רשות מפאת המלך להתנהג במלאכת הספרות והשני שיהיה כעין ערכאות רצונו שיהיה
ידוע אצלינו שאינו מקבל שוחד ואז יש לו דין ערכאות משום ד״ד.

66. *Ibid. Torat ha-Bayit,* 111 — סוף... וכ״ש סופר העיר שהעמידוהו לכך
דבר כל דבר שבממון הולך אחר הסכמ׳ המדינה למנהג׳.

67. Nahmanides quoted by M. Katzenellenbogen, 54; *Shiltei Gibborim,*
Gittin; Isserles, *Hoshen Mishpat,* 68:1 — שטרות העשויין בגוטרי״ן של מלכים
פירוש ע״י סופרי המלך ואפי׳ אין עדים חתומים בו אלא אחד ממוני׳ ע״פ המלך כשר
ובזה״ז סופר — ולא מן הדין אלא משום ד״ד. See also Nissim Gerondi, Gittin 10b
הממונה מן המלך יש לו דין עש״ג.

68. *Ibid., Tur,* 68:1; Joseph Colon, 18; de Medina, *Hoshen Mishpat,*
304 — דברי הכל אלו השטרות שכותבין הסופרים אין להם דין ערכאות אע״פ שהם ממונין
מפי השופטים כיון שאין נעשים בפני השופטים; David Ibn Zimra, I, 541 agrees
with *Tur* that scribes do not have the status of a court. — בנ״ד מודו דלית
חששא בהאי שטרא... דלא נעשה בפני שופטים see Katzenellenbogen who states:
דסופרים אשר דבר בו הטור היינו הנוטירי הממונים מן השופטים... וסופרים אשר דבר
בו הרמב״ן ר״ל סופר מתא נאמן המלך או המושל כמו הקנצלי״ל... כי עליהם שייך לומר
יותר ד״ד כי המלך מקפיד על אמונתם.

69. Adret, *ha-Meyohosot,* 65 — ועכשיו רצו הצבור לחוש לתקלות אלו ולתקן
שיהא סופר מתא כותב עיקר המקח ותנאיו בפנקסו ושיהא אותו הפנקס נאמן כשני עדים
כדרך שנוהגים בפנקסי ערכאות שלהם.

CHAPTER IX

KINGS OVER ISRAEL

1. B.B. 119a — אלמא א״י מוחזקת היא.
2. See S. Zeitlin, "Responsa of the Tosaphists," *JQR*, 1954-5, p. 75; also L. Löw, *Gesammelte Schriften*, III, p. 353 — *"Darum kommt auch Samuel's Princip im Palästinensischen Talmud gar nicht vor"*; A. N. Z. Roth, *Hasoker*, Vol. V, p. 110 — במקומות שונים נמצא בתלמוד בבלי ולא בתלמוד ירושלמי; I. Herzog, *The Main Institution of Jewish Law*, I, p. 24; Asher Gulak, *Yesodei Hamishpat ha-Ivri*, IV, 28-29.
3. *Ibid*. pp. 110-115.
4. B.K. 113a — אלא להבריח בו את המכס מי שרי והאמר שמואל דינא דמלכותא דינא.
5. *Ibid*.
6. Comp. J. Caro, *Kessef Mishneh, Gezelah*, 5:11 who states that Maimonides' view that *Dina D'Malkhuta Dina* is operative with a Jewish or a Gentile king is based upon the same reasoning.
R. Akiba could not be dealing with a Jewish king. There were no Jewish kings in Judea in his day. Furthermore, Maimonides speaks of a Gentile king in the diaspora and when he equates a Jewish king with a Gentile king, he means that *Dina D'Malkhuta Dina* is binding when a Jewish king rules outside of the land of Israel.
7. Gittin 10b. See also, R. Hayyim Volozin, *Hut Hameshulosh*, 17 who states — וכן דמשקלי וטרי הנך אמוראי לשנויי דלא תקשי אמתניתין מהא דאמר שמואל דד״ד... The Mishneh needs no explanation.
8. J.T. B.K. 3c — א״ר יוחנן ותשמע מיניה... הדין אכסניי פרכא עד דלא ייתון רומאי שרי מיחשדוניה ומן דייתון רומאי אסור.
9. *Ibid*. The correct interpretation of the text is that the matter deals with the collection of taxes from transients of a city. Until the tax collector assesses the residents of the city, a transient may bribe the collector to exempt him from tax payments, a thing he no longer may do once the assessment has been levied upon the townspeople.
10. Gittin 10 b; Ned. 28a.
11. *Ibid*. — תני חוץ מכגיטי נשים.
12. Comp. with the discussion in chapter I.
13. Roth, *op. cit*. — אבל לאמתו של הדבר כל הטעמים שזכרנו בדויים הם מלבם של החוקרים כי ביחסם את הדין הזה לתקופת שמואל התיגעו והתחבטו להסביר את הורתו... אולם גולם מעיניהם שהדין הזה נוצר עוד מלפני שמואל... מעולם לא נתכוון שמואל להמציא דין חדש באמרו את הדין הזה ולא בא אלא לזרז את בני דורו שיזהרו בחוק הישן; ,,דד״ד"; D. Hoffman, *Mar Samuel*, p. 41 — *"Samuel, der von der Überzeugung durchdrungen war, dass es eines yeden Bürgers unabweisbare Pflicht sei, die Staatsgesetze heilig zu halten und dies ausserdem schon in einer alten Mischna ausgesprochen fand . . . (Gittin 10b)."* Ibid.

ft. note 4 — *"Graetz, Gesch. II, s. 287 behauptet dass der Samuel'sche Grundsatz im Widerspruche mit ältern Halacha's sich befinde und vergisst zu erwähnen, dass er in einer Mischna eine feste Stütze hat, während der Widerspruch mit einer ältern Halacha von Samuel hinreichend ausgeglichen ist!"*

14. Roth, *ibid.*; D. Hoffman, *ibid.* — ואם נאמר שדינו של שמואל הוא דין

חדש ולא היה נוהג מקודם שאמרו מן הנגמע הוא לפרש על ידו את המשנה אשר נשנית זמן רב קודם שמואל...; נוכל לראות בפירוש שגב חכמי התלמוד כן חשבו שאין דין הנזכר דין מחודש אלא היה קיים כבר לפני זה וע״כ הקשו איך יובנו דברי המשנה.

15. מזיק לאחרים. See also correct interpretation of this passage as cited above ft. note 9.

16. *Teshubat ha-Geonim*, quoted by Rashi; *Teshubat Rashi*, 255, ed. Elfenbein and by Ibn Adret, VII, 428 — שהרי גוים שהחזיקו בה ולכדוה אין להם חזקה דקיי״ל קרקע אינה נגזלת ואינה נחמסת לעולם ואי״י בחזקתינו עומדת (רשב״א — היא) לעולם ואעפ״י שאין לנו (רשב״א — היום שום) שם שולטנות.

17. Comp. Maimonides, *Commentary to Mishneh*, Ned. 28a — אבל אם העמידו המלך הנה העיקר אצלנו דד״י ואין מותר לו לברוח מן המכס ואיך ישבע ולא עוד שהוא — *Gezelah*, V, 11; עליו ואין הפרש בזה בין מלך עכו״ם ומלך ישראל עובר המבריח ממכס זה מפני שהוא גוזל מנת המלך בין שהיה המלך עכו״ם בין שהיה המלך ישראל. It is evident that Maimonides was aware of the problem concerning a Jewish king but equated his powers with those of a Gentile king insofar as *Dina D'Malkhuta Dina* is concerned. However, in both instances, it cannot be determined whether Maimonides speaks of the land of Israel or the diaspora.

18. Tosafists, quoted by Nissim Gerondi, Ned. 28a. See above Chapter III.

19. Tosafot, Ned. 28a; Ibn Adret, *Torat ha-Bayit*, 134 — וא״נ בארץ ישראל דלא אמרינן בה דד״י כדעת קצת רבותינו הצרפתים ז״ל לפי שא״י ירושה היא לנו מאבותינו להדיוט כמלך; cf. A. Neuman, *op. cit.* pp. 8-9.

20. Ibn Adret, I, 637 — ואף במלכי ישראל בחוצה לארץ ודוקא בארץ שהיא Hayyim, *Or Zarua*, 110 — ירושה לכל ישראל הוציאו רבותינו הצרפתים בנדרים למלכי ישראל אין דיניה דין שא״י אחד ואחד ואיניה של מלך אבל באומות העולם כך לפי שא״י כל ישראל — Ibn Adret, *Commentary*, Ned. 28a — דינם שכל הארץ למלך שותפין בה ואין בה למלך יותר מלאיש אחר; Joseph Habbib, *Nemukei Joseph ad. loc.* — והסכימו רוב המפרשים ז״ל דדוקא במלכי אומות העולם... ומלכי ישראל אין דנין דין אלא על פי תורה...

21. R. Samuel b. Meir, B.B. 54b; see Chapt. III.

22. Comp. *Hatam Sofer, Hoshen Mishpat*, 44 who maintains that the opinions of Samuel b. Meir and the Tosafists are not mutually exclusive. On the contrary, the Tosafists agree that in all matters which the populace accepts freely, *Dina D'Malkhuta Dina* applies to a Jewish king in Palestine as well. However, taxes which people usually do not accept freely upon themselves are the point wherein differences between a Jewish king and a Gentile king arise. The Gentile king who owns the land has the power to

coerce payment whereas the Jewish king has no claim to the land. —
ולפ״ז אין לחלק בין מלך או״ה למלך ישראל שאפי׳ מלך ישראל שאין הארץ שלו כ״א
לשבטים נתחלקה מ״מ כל נימוסיו וחקיו מקבלים עליהם ברצונם ומחילה גמורה הוא...
ומ״מ נ״ל דלא פליג אלא במסים ומכס שמטיל על כרחם ס״ל לא שייך לומר בני מדינה
ניחא להו אלא משום שהוא אדון הארץ וא״כ יש׳ לחלק בין מלכי ישראל למלכי או״ה אבל
במנהגי׳ ונימוסי׳ כמו ב״ב נד: מודה ר״ן דהטעם משום דניחא להו ואין לחלק בין מלכי
ישראל לאו״ה. This opinion narrows the scope of R. Samuel b. Meir's view.
It limits the process to individual items, laws, and/or ordinances. It no
longer sees R. Samuel b. Meir's view as a major change in the philosophy
of kingship, that is, rule by the will of the people, but sees it as a type
of retail approval necessary for each and every law. R. Samuel b. Meir
stipulated that "free will acceptance" was necessary. It is the king, so
accepted, who then rules. It has nothing whatever to do with whether
taxes are or are not pleasing to the public.

23. Samuel 8:11.

24. Tosefta, Sanhedrin 4:3; Sanhedrin 20b — ר׳ יוסי אומר כל האמור
בפרשת המלך המלך מותר בה; רב יהודה אמר שמואל כל האמור בפרשת המלך המלך
מותר בה.

25. *Ibid.* — ר׳ יהודה אומר לא נאמרה פרשה זו אלא בשביל לאיים עליהם; ורב
אמר לא נאמרה פרשה זאת אלא לאיים עליהם.

26. Maimonides, *Melakim*, 4:1 — ;שכל האמור בפרשת המלך מלך זוכה בה
Meiri, quoted by Bezalel Ashkenazi, B.K. 113a — כל מה שאמרנו בדין המלכות
שהוא אצלינו דין גמור הוא... מצד המלכות על הדרך האמור במלכי ישראל כל האמור
בפרשת המלך מלך מותר בו. And also *Bet ha-Behira*, Ned. 28a; Yom Tob b.
Abraham Ibn Ashvilla, B.B. 54a; Joseph Habbib, *Nemukei Joseph ad. loc.;*
Joseph Caro, *Bet Joseph, Hoshen Mishpat*, 162; *Kessef Mishneh, Melakim*,
4:1; David Ibn Zimra, *ad. loc.; Migdal Oz, ad. loc.;* Samuel b. Meir, B.B.
69b — *Semag*, שהמלך פורץ בתים וגדר מלפגיו לעשות לו דרך ולא יטה ימין ושמאל
positive 115; *Zohar, Vayesheb* — ותו מ״ט אתענש עליה אחאב דינא דאורייתא דשוי
שמואל קמייהו דישראל הרי הוא דכתיב שדותכם... קח ואי אחאב נטל כרם מנבות
דינא הוא. Comp. this with *Tosafot*, Sanh. 20a; However the following disagree with this ruling: Mordecai, B.K. — ובמלכי ישראל לא אמרי׳ דד״ד כדאמרי׳
בפ׳ כ״ג דלא נאמר פ׳ המלך אלא כדי לאיים עליהם אבל המלך אסור בכל האמור בפ׳ המלך;
Ibn Adret, *Novellae*, Ned. 28a attributes similar reasoning to the Tosafists;
Gersonides, Samuel 8:11 — והנה הודיע שמואל לישראל את משפט המלך ר״ל...
ואחשוב שאין המלך מותר באותם העניינים שזכר אבל רצה שמואל ליראם ולבהלם והודיעם
מה שיעשה המלך כשיתחזק על ממלכתו...

27. Ibn Adret, *ibid.* attributes to the Tosafists, who exclude a Jewish
king from *Dina D'Malkhuta Dina*, the decision that מלך אסור בו. Contrari-
wise, if מותר בו, then *Dina D'Malkhuta Dina* is operative with Jewish kings
as well; Comp. Meiri quoted in ft. note 26; Ibn Zimra, *Melakim*, 4:1 —
פרק כ״ג פלוגתא דתנאי ואמוראי ופסק כדר׳ יוסי ושמואל שאמרו כל האמור בפ׳ המלך
וכמה מקומות בתלמוד — *Migdal Oz, ad. loc.* ;מלך מותר בו ואמרי׳ בכמה דוכתי דד״ד
הלכה רווחת דד״ד.

28. Ibn Zimra, *ad. loc.* — ואמרי׳ בכמה דוכתי דד״ד ואפי׳ מלכי הגוים אמרי׳ בהן דד״ד.

29. The dispute in the Tosefta between R. Jose and R. Judah should be decided in favor of R. Jose. Similarly the talmudic disputation between Rab and Samuel should affirm the opinion of Samuel. Thus, the king should be granted full powers as enumerated in the Bible — המלך מותר בו.

30. Comp. the following:

(a) Gersonides, Samuel 8:11, quoted in ft. note 26 with his commentary to Deut.;

(b) Joseph Habbib, *Novellae,* Ned. 28a, *ibid.* B.B. 54b;

(c) Ibn Adret, *Novellae,* Ned. 28a; *Responsa,* I, 637;

(d) Don Isaac Abrabanel, *Commentary,* Samuel 8:11 who agrees with Maimonides that מותר בו, and then concludes: דלא הותר למלך דברים הללו ;ועושק וגזל הוא בידו ולא נאמר פ׳ זאת אלא לאיים שהתורה לא זכרה דבר מזה בפ׳ המלך

(e) Hayyim b. Isaac, *Or Zarua,* 110 who rules אסור בו and stipulates that if מותר, then only those enumerated in Samuel are permitted but nothing else.

31. Interesting is the comment made by Simon b. Zemah Duran, IV, 14 who claims that Jewish kings must obey the laws of the Torah and these are naturally binding upon all Israel. It must then always be said that the "law of a Jewish king in the Holy Land is the law"; i.e., *Dina D'Malkhuta Dina* — כי המלך ישראל מחוייב להנהיג כפי חקי התורה ולדינא אין נ״מ בזה כי לעולם אמרינן דד״ד...

32. Isserles, 123 — נראה דודאי אמרי׳ (דד״ד)... וראייה מעזרא ונחמי׳ בן. Isserles who חכלי׳ שהיו מושלים ע״פ כורש מלך פרס וכן שאר מלכי ישראל בבית שני based his view upon Barfat, failed to distinguish between the Exilarchs, to whom Barfat attributed *Dina D'Malkhuta Dina,* and the kings of Judea. Barfat, 271; Samuel b. Simon Duran, 533, 637 — וכן הוא מלך צרפת היות במלכותו כשאר המלכים במלכותם כמו מלך פרס בימים ההם בארצות ההם.

33. Trani, III, 78 — ועוד מד״ד שמחייב את אלו שהולכו לציפורי לפרוע עם בני טבריה ודה״ה ואינו דין שיפרעו בשני מקומות כמו שכתב הרשב״א ז״ל ובכי האי אזלינן בתר דינייהו כמו שכתב בתרומת הדשן...

34. Samuel de Medina, *Hoshen Mishpat,* 369 — שיצאו מטברי׳ לדור בציפורי וכתב וז״ל מ״מ אם היה עושה כך למס הקצוב בכל השנה הוי גזילה דמלכותא...

35. *Ibid., Yoreh Deah,* 194; Joseph Ibn Leb quoted by Trani, II, 199.

36. *Ibid.* does not accept that such a law existed. He shows how Jews openly purchased slaves everywhere in the Turkish Empire including Palestine. Jews would not dare do so were it an open violation of royal decrees. At best, he concludes, the law might have originated from a number of Gentile judges but was not "the law of the kingdom." — ובמלחמת גיפרי שכבשה אחד מעבדי המלך יר״ה בחיל שנתן לו המלך שבו ערלים מהם לעבדים ולשפחות ומכרו מהם פה ובדמשק בפירסום ואפי׳ יהודים קנו מהם. ואם היה ד״ד שאינם מניחים ליהודים להיות אצלם עבדים ושפחות... לא היה ליהודים ליקנות מהם בפירסום...

204

שהיו מענישי׳ את הקונים היהודים. Note the word פה which refers to his own land, Palestine.

37. *Ibid.* — דד״ד היינו הדינים הקבועים בכל מלכותא.

38. *Ibid.* — דלא שייך דד״ד אלא בדברים שהם עסקי המלך ולא בדברים שהם עסקי ישראל עם ישראל.

39. Comp. *ibid.* III, 17 — וא״כ במלכות המלך אדונינו יר״ה אשר כל הארץ וכל הכרכים ועיירות הם תחת ידו ורשותו ועבדיו הם עומדים במקומו הכל נקרא מושל אחד... ויש רשות מן המלך לכל מי שפורע מס גולגלתו שיסחר במקום שירצה וזהו כמו ד״ד ואינם יכולים לעכב עליו... See also *ibid.* II, 64 wherein Trani permitted a Jew to till his fields during the Sabbatical year *(Shemittah)* because the king demanded a great share of the crops. Trani reasoned that no Jew may violate even rabbinic *(Shemittah* in their day was only a rabbinic prohibition) law when it involved a common Gentile. However rabbinic law was waived when a king's decree demanded it. — א״נ דשביעית בזמן הזה דרבנן ואע״ג דמדרבנן.

אסור לגוי אחר גבי מלך התירו. — It seems logical to assume that the leniency with regard to the crown is based upon Samuel's law. It must be stated, however, that Trani might have recognized the great powers of the kings and knew that practical conditions would force the Jew to till his soil during the Sabbatical year in order to fulfill the demands of the king. It may be the greater threat of force that the king wields rather than Samuel's precept which prompted Trani to waive rabbinic law.

40. Sanh. 49a.

41. Joshua 1:18.

42. Sanh. *ad. loc.* — יכול אפי׳ ד״ת ת״ל רק חזק ואמץ.

43. Rashi, *ibid.* — רקין מעוטין שאם בא המלך לבטל ד״ת אין שומעין לו; Maimonides, *Melakim,* 3:9 — המבטל גזרת המלך בשביל שנתעסק במצות אפי׳ במצוה קלה הרי זה פטור דברי הרב ודברי העבד דברי הרב קודמין ואין צריך לומר אם גזר המלך לבטל מצוה שאין שומעין לו.

44. The evidence is not too convincing, yet Barfat, 272 does interchange the terms. This may very well be due to the fact that he did not discuss their differences and as such was not too careful in his choice of words.

45. *Hatam Sofer, Hoshen Mishpat,* 44 — ותו ממ״נ אי נימא דאיירי באופן שאין קפידא כלל א״כ פשיטא שמצוה לשמוע למלך ולא למרות פיו ואין זה נוגע כלל לענין ד״ד כיון שאינו נגד דין תורה...

46. *Ibid., Orah Hayyim,* 208 — אחר שהסכימו ישראל ואמרו ליהושע וה״ה לכל מלך כל איש אשר ימרה את פיך לכל אשר תצונו יומת הרי החרימו כל העובר על מצות מלך ישראל אפי׳ אינו משבט יהודה... However, *Dina D'Malkhuta Dina* is operative only to Gentile kings. They may exercise the death penalty. מלכותא דקטלי חד משיתא בעלמא לא מיענשא (Sheb. 35b). This was only true as long as it was not rampant destruction. לאפוקי כרצחן וחמסן בעלמא דגזלנותא דמלכותא לאו דינא אלא ד״ד... Contr. Samuel Edels, *ad. loc.* who states that Samuel applies this to Jewish kings not to Gentile kings.

47. Interesting, although homiletic in quality, is the remark made by

Ben Dov, *Talpioth* 1961, who refers to the term *Malkhuta* in its Aramaic form and claims that this proves that Samuel's law is applicable to the diaspora only or else *Malkhut,* the Hebrew would have been employed to connote Israel as well. He points to the similar use of *Haga* which refers to non-Jewish holidays and *Hag* which refers to the Jewish ones.

May we point out that *Malkhut* in rabbinic literature has the con-notation of either Jewish or non-Jewish kingdoms. The phrase גזירת המלכות will suffice as but one of many examples that might be cited.

CHAPTER X

CIVIL AND RELIGIOUS LAW

1. Jellinek, "Neuzeit," 1862, Nr. 1 — ". . . *Samuel habe schon zu Anfang des dritten Jahrhunderts den Grundsatz proclamirt, dass die Staats gesetze in civil-und criminalrechtlicher Beziehung Geltung für den Juden haben . . .;*" L. Löw, *Gesammelte Schriften,* pp. 348-352; B.M. Shohet, *op. cit.* pp. 112-113; S. W. Baron, *op. cit.;* A.N.Z. Roth, *Hasoker,* vol. V, pp. 110-115 — כי בזה הכל מודים שאין חייב לכבד את דיני הממשלה ופקודיו אם רצונם לשנות את הדת או לבטל איזו מצוה; Holdheim, *Ueber die Autonomie der Rabbinen und das Prinzip der Jüdischen Ehe,* pp. 137-165; Z. Frankel, *ibid.;* I. Agus, *Teshubot Ba'alei Tosafot, Responsum* 3 states that R. Tam is the only one to make the clear distinction that *Dina D'Malkhuta Dina* is only applicable to civil matters *(Dinei Mamanot)* but excludes all religious laws *(Issur ve'Hetter).* The evidence presented here shows quite clearly that R. Tam was not the first nor the only one who explicitly makes such a distinction.

2. Gittin 10b.

3. B.B. 54b.

4. Ned. 28a; B.K. 113a.

5. B.K. 113b; Yeb. 46a.

6. Assaf, *Teshubat ha-Geonim* (תש"ב) p. 75 — כי כן היתה מאמר שמואל כי כאשר השליט הקב"ה את המלכויות בעולמו כך השליטן על, ממון בני אדם לשלוט בו כרצונם.

7. Rashi, Gittin 10b — דד"ד ואע"פ שהגוותן והמקבל ישראלים הם חוץ מגיטי נשים דלאו בני כריתות נינהו הואיל ולא שייכו בתורת גיטין וקידושין אבל על הדינין נצטוו בני נח.

8. Samuel b. Meir, B.B. 54b — ומנהגות של משפטי ... כל מסים וארנוניות מלכים...

9. I. Agus, *op. cit.,* responsum 3 — דהפקיעו חכמים ממון במנהג המלכות. See also כדרך שהפקיעו מפני תקנת השבים ומפני תקון העולם ומפני דרכי שלום. Mordecai, B.K. 113a (215); Maimonides, *Commentary to Mishneh,* Ned. III, 3.

10. Maimonides, *Zekhiya u-Mattanah,* 1:15 — עושין כפי משפט המלך שזה דין המלכים כולם כל — *Gezelah,* 5:13 — שכל דיני המלך בממון על פיהן דנין ממון שמשיהם.

11. Ibn Adret, *Torat ha-Bayit,* III — סוף דבר כל דבר שבממון הולך אחר הסכמ' המדינה ומנהג'...

12. *Ibid.* VI, 254 — וא"נ במה שישראל עושה עם ישראל חבירו מדעת עצמו כאותה שאמרו ... כל השטרות העולות בערכאות... כיון שזה מדעתו עשה מתנתו בערכאות הרי קבל עליו לילך בזה בדיני המלכות ... ובדבר שבממון יכול לשעבד עצמו מן הדין שלא משלו ונתן. See also Yom Tob Ibn Ashvilla, Yeb. 46a; Joseph Habbib, *Nemukei Joseph ad. loc.* — ...ומסתברא דבדיני ממונות בהקנאות וחיובין; Solomon b. Simon ...ומיהו אם דין המלכות הוא שיהא קונה ומקנה כעכו"ם דד"ד...

ובממונא הוא דמכשרי׳ שטרות העולים בערכאות שלהם אבל באיסורא׀ — Duran, 520
;לא שהרי משנה שלימה ׀שנינו כל השטרות... ובממונא טעמא דמכשירין להו משום דד״ד
Asher, *Novellae*, B.B. 54b — כל משפט חרוץ שתקן והנהיג המלך על כל בני מדינתו
ואין בו משום גזל המחזיק בממון ע״פ המלך.

13. *Tosafot*, Bekorot 4b; Simon b. Zemah, I, 158 — מלתא פשיטא היא
שבכל דבר שיש בו איסור א״א לומר דד״ד להתירו דבעניין ממון הוא דאמרי׳ הכי אבל
דבר שיש בו איסור ׀זה לא אמרו אדם מעולם... ושאני איסור גזל (שבו אומרים דד״ד)
שהאיסור שבו אינו אלא מחמת ממון.

14. The concept of איסור בעד אחד יוחזק, e.g., if meat was determined
to be non-kosher by the testimony of one witness which is acceptable by
Jewish law, then, he who eats such meat is subjected to flagellation, a
punishment which usually requires two witnesses. However, in this instance,
the single witness merely determines the status of the meat. What happens
afterwards is not the direct result of his testimony. The nature of the meat
in question was his only concern.

15. Two opinions are recorded in one responsum by Nissim Gerondi
(40), concerning a Jew who purchased grape juice from a Gentile ere it
fermented into wine. The Jew left the wine in the domain of the Gentile
with proper precautions, but no actual guard was standing. The question
arose, was the wine permissible for use or was it ritually unfit (*S'tam
Yaynom*)?

One opinion prohibited Jews from partaking of the wine since it was
purchased without the proper methods of acquisition necessary according
to Jewish law. Even though, according to secular law a transfer of ownership was properly effected, this opinion stated that *Dina D'Malkhuta Dina*
was not applicable in this matter. The wine was forbidden unless a guard
was stationed to properly supervise it. — שזה היין יינו של נכרי הוא לפי שהקנין
העשוי עליו אינו מועיל כיון שלא נעשה בו אחד מדרכי ההקנאה ואעפ״י שהקנין מועיל
משום דד״ד אינו עניין בזה... וכיון ׀שהוא יינו של נכרי צריך בו שמירה.

However, another authority ruled that *Dina D'Malkhuta Dina* does
apply, and the method of acquisition has validity and as such the wine
belongs to the Jew. The wine is permissible since according to Jewish law
wine owned by a Jew, albeit in the domain of a non-Jew, is permissible
when proper precautions are taken even if a guard is not stationed. —
שזה היין יינו של ישראל הוא לפי שהקנין העשוי בו מועיל מצד דד״ד.

Those who deny the effectiveness of *Dina D'Malkhuta Dina* in this
matter do so because the case fails to satisfy the requirements whereby
Dina D'Malkhuta Dina may be invoked. However, both decisions agree that
Dina D'Malkhuta Dina does not directly determine the religious status of
this wine. It is not *Dina D'Malkhuta Dina* that rules whether or not the
wine is permissible for use. *Dina D'Malkhuta Dina* openly declares who
the rightful owner of the wine is, the Jew or the Gentile. Subsequently, the
status of the wine is not decided by *Dina D'Malkhuta Dina,* but by religious law. Thus, according to the first opinion, since *Dina D'Malkhuta Dina*

is not invoked, the wine belongs to the Gentile. Henceforth, all requirements necessary in order to allow such wine to be used must be fulfilled. Equally so is the situation if *Dina D'Malkhuta Dina* rules the wine to be owned by the Jew. Then, the more lenient requirement must be fulfilled. The indirect consequences of *Dina D'Malkhuta Dina,* even if they be part of religious law, may be determined by Samuel's maxim.

16. David Ibn Zimra, I, 514 — 'ונמצא כל המחזיק בקרקע כדין מחזיק ואפי
תאמר שגזל אותו הוא או אבותיו מ"מ כיון שיש בידו מכתב הרי הוא שלו דדד"ד ומלכא
אמר שכל מי שיש בידו מכתב יהיה הקרקע ושלו הלכך אין כאן גזל ומותר לישראל ללקט
האתרוגים בידו לצאת בהם.

17. J. Caro, *Abkat Rohel,* 47, for the complete responsum see above Chapter V.

18. *Ibid.* — המלך יש לו רשות להשתמש בכל בית ובית שבעיר כשירצה ומשתמש
בשעה שצריך א"כ יכולים היהודים לקנות רשות כל העיר ממנו שהרי ד"ד.

19. Ibn Adret, III, 34, 40 — ומ"מ אם יש מאמר המלך בזה שיגזור במה יתן
הלוה למלוה בהתחלף המטבע נראה שהדין כמו שיגזור המלך... וכיון שכן קיי"ל דד"ד..

20. *Ibid.* V, 198 — אף בזה דינו דין שהתוספות הזה שלא בתנאי ושלא ברצון
הבעלים הוא נפרע ואלמלא דינו של מלכות אינו בכלל רבית אלא בכלל גזל אלא שדינו
של מלך דין והפקרו הפקר ואין כאן גזל ואין כאן רבית .Comp. with Nahmanides, 46; *Sefer ha-Terumot,* 46; contr. Joseph Caro, *Abkat Rohel,* 6 who disagrees. Caro feels that all the laws of the Torah could be voided because of *Dina D'Malkhuta Dina* — דאם לא כן בטלתה כל התורה כולה בד"ד.

21. Mordecai b. Hillel, B.K. (154) in the name of Isaac b. Peretz — המלוה לישראל חבירו על המשכון אין המלוה זקוק לשומרו יותר משנה למוכרו ולגבות
הלואתו כד"ד גבי מלוים לעובד כוכבים בריבית ועשה מעשה כזה באחד שמשכן... ואחר
שנה שלא פרע בא הישראל ומכר המשכון... ותבעו חבירו לדין ופסק דאין לו עליו כלום
וי"א דבמקום שהמנהג .משום ד"ד... See also Isserles, *Hoshen Mishpat,* 73:14 — שהמלוה לעכו"ם לא יכול למוכרו בפחות משנה דנין כן גם בישראל שהלוה לחבירו על
המשכון דאזלינן בזה אחר המנהג. Contr. with J. Caro, *Abkat Rohel,* 6 who disagrees and feels that any amount above and beyond the amount of the loan must be returned to the debtor. — שזה דוקא במקח וממכר אבל לותר ממון
ישראל לישראל חבירו כנ"ד לא .Also, Shabbatai ha-Kohen, *Siftei Kohen, Hoshen Mishpat ad. loc.* — האיך גלמד מדיני עכו"ם לבטל דין תורה ח"ו לא תהא כזאת
בישראל.

22. Ibn Adret, V, 244 — דאין חרם מבוטל ע"י כך שאין ביד שום אדם לבטל
שבועות ונדרים וחרמות של אחרים ולא להתיר זולתו איש לאשתו ואב לבתו.

23. *Ibid.* — ואי"ת שאין השבועות ונדרים וחרמות חלים על דבר מצוה ומצוה לקיים
דבר המלך ושלטון דברים בגו. Comp. Nissim Gerondi, 65 who states three separate times — ועתה בזה"ז ע"פ ד"ד אין מקום לדיני חרם ונדוי. This does not refer to the technical term, signifying Samuel's law. It means that the law forbade the issuing of the *herem.* Furthermore, the term *herem* in Gerondi's statement refers to the punitive *herem* and not to a type of vow. See also Samuel de Medina, *Yoreh Deah,* 156 who also forbids a community to violate its

oath even if it be in opposition to the law of the kingdom. "The law of the kingdom is the law," but it may not dismiss an oath which is in the category of religious law.

24. Joseph Habbib, *Nemukei Joseph,* Yeb. 46a — ולפי״ז עבדים ישמעאלים שלנו אינם יכולים להתגייר אלא לדעת רבן ואם נתגיירו שלא לדעת רבן אין טבילתן כלום...

25. The opinion of *Tosafot,* Rashi, *ad. loc.,* Maimonides, *Abadim,* 9:4 that the talmudic passage refers to a non-Jewish slave. However, Joseph Habbib, *Nemukei Joseph, ad. loc.* maintains that the slave in question was a Jew.

26. Yeb. 46a, see also above Chapter I.

27. *Tosafot,* Yeb. 46a — מספקא ליה אי דד״ד או לא ואע״ג דלא קני גופיה הכא קני או דלמא הכא נמי לא קני אלא קני למעשה ידיו ובנכריותן מיירי אם היו באין להתגייר.

28. Rashi, *ad. loc.* — הלכך מכר הוא ובעי גיטא דחירותא אי בעי לאיגיורי ולאשתרויי בבת ישראל.

29. The Egyptian communities were presided over by a *nagid,* similar to the head of the Exile (*Resh Galuta*) in the East. The origin of this office is somewhat obscure. It is thought to have begun in the 10-11 century.

30. David Ibn Zimra, I, 67 — וכיון שמנהג המדינה מימי הנגידים הראשונים אשר שמענו שמעם לדון ע״פ השטרות העולות בערכאותיהם בין בשטרי הודאות ומתנות ושוברים חוץ מגיטי נשים ושחרורי עבדים דאיסורא ניגהו.

31. J. Caro, *Abkat Rohel,* 134 — ודאי כיון דמטעם דד״ד מקני גופיה ל״ש אם השבאי הוא גוי או ישראל.

32. Samuel de Medina, *Yoreh Deah,* 194 — והשתא בזה״ז שמד״ד אין שום אדם חוץ מדתם יכול ליקח עבד או שפחה אם לא דרך שכירות נמצא א״כ שעבד או שפחה הלוקח ישראל מגוי לא חל עליו שם עבד כנעני ולא שייך ביה איסור עבד וא״כ תיכף ומיד כשמתגייר מותר בבת ישראל.

33. Comp. Trani, II, 199 who denied the existence of the law forbidding Jews from owning slaves.

34. Yeb. 120a — אין מעידין אלא עד שתצא נפשו ואפי׳ ראוהו מגוייד וצלוב והחיה אוכלת בו...

35. Ezekiel Landau, *Nodei be-Yehuda, Eben ha-Ezer,* 46 quotes Joel Sirkes. Landau merely disputes the conclusion that "the law of the kingdom" demands the breaking of the neck. He feels that this was left to the discretion of the hangman who is subject to bribery. If there were no doubt that it was a specific demand of the authorities, Landau would concur with Sirkes. — ומה שרצה מעל׳ להמציא דבהרוגי מלכות דרכם לשבור מפרקתו בשעה שצולבין אותו אומר אני אפי׳ נימא שדרכם בכך מ״מ אין זה מצד ד״ד ואין פוסקים זה בפסק דינם דנימא דבתר... אלא התליין עושה זה מעצמו והברירה בידו וא״כ בידו לקבל שכר שלא לעשות דבר זה...

36. *Ibid.* 52 — אבל כאן שבא המושל לבדוק את ההרוג וזה חקו ונימוסי המלכות לבדוק את כל גוף הנהרג וליראות כיצד נרצח והם פושטים בגדיו כולם לבדוק כל גופו... והמושל עם הרופאים המיוחדים לזה בא לשם קודם שבא הר׳... ולכן הוי כמו שהי׳ מלובש בהם וא״כ יש היתר מצד הבגדים...

37. *Hatam Sofer, Eben ha-Ezer,* 43. See also Naphtali Zevi Judah Berlin, *Meshib Dabar,* IV, 23 who released a woman to be remarried when her husband was reported drowned in the Thames River in London, England. The identity of the deceased was established by the testimony of a policeman who had attempted to rescue the victim. Since this testimony was the result of the policeman fulfilling his duty, it was considered "indirect" testimony (מסל״ת). A photograph of the drowned man taken three days after he drowned was also accepted as valid documentary evidence. It was regarded as a document of a Gentile court; Also, Isaac Elhanan Spector, *Ayn Yitzchak, Eben ha-Ezer,* 31; *Beer Yitzchak, Eben ha-Ezer,* 5:4; also, Joseph Saul Nathanson, *Shoel u'Meshib,* I, 10 recognized a death certificate even when the name of the deceased was not quite accurate. He checked other pertinent facts, e.g., the rank, branch of service, and duration of service of the deceased, and permitted the widow to remarry. —

ורק יראו לחקור בשם אם אייזק קאטץ הי׳ צוגם פיהרער בייא דער זיבענטער קאמפאניע וכמה שני עבודתו שעבד אצל המיליטער... .Also, Hayyim Ozer Grodzensky, *Ahiezer,* III, 10 — ומסיק כן להלכה דבכתב מהריגימענט יש לסמוך עליו במלחמה.

38. *Ibid., Yoreh Deah,* 338.

39. *Ibid.*

40. *Ibid., Eben ha-Ezer,* 65 — וגם בד״ד כל שקראוהו ע״י צייטונג ולא בא אחר יב״ח נחשב אבד זכרו ש״מ דאינהו בקיאין דבזמן הזה יכול להודיע ע״י דואר אפי׳ ברחוק מקום.

42. *Ibid., Hoshen Mishpat,* 187 — משא״כ פדיון בכור הוא להקב״ה בעצמו .Comp. *ibid. Yoreh Deah,* 134 — והקב״ה נותנו במתנה לכהן ואין ד״ד דארעא לגבי גבוה כלום אבל גדר מטבע הוא שגזר המלך עליו ושתצא ומי שממאן מלמכור ולקח באותו מטבע יחייב ראשו מלכותא וד״ד דין אמת ומשפט צדק הוא בזה ולא מלכותא דארעא לחוד גזר עליו אלא גם מלכותא דרקיעא ית״ש... והיינו מטבע שגופו ממון ואין חילוק אם יהי׳ זהב או כסף או נייר... והנה לפ״ז אין ספק אצלי דהני באנק״א המה כסף גמור אפי׳ לקדש אשה. Contr. Isaac Elhanan Spector, *Ayn Yitzchak, Yoreh Deah,* 30 who honors banknotes even to the extent that they may be used for the redemption of first born.

42. Boruch Frankel, quoted by *Hatam Sofer, Orah Hayyim,* 113 — מעשה שהלשינו מלשיני אצל שרי המדינה דמעהרין שהיהודים מוכרים חמצם בשטרות מבלי שטעמפל חותם הקיר״ה וכשבא הדבר לפני החסיד קיר״ה אמר הדבר ידוע שאין זה מו״מ של תגר אלא ענין דת רעליגיאהן ע״כ אין בו זה בחיוב שטעמפל ועי״ז נולד קצת ספק בלב הגאון זצ״ל הנ״ל דמשמע ד״ד פסול השטר ההוא. Also, J. S. Nathanson, *Shoel u'Meshib,* I, 211 — באן ע״פ ד״ד ודאי אינה מכירה גמורה ותדע שהרי אינה לוקח השטעמפל.

43. *Ibid.* — ולבבי לא כן ידמה כי השטר כשר הן בדין ישראל... הן בדאו״ה אלא כשיתבענו בדאו״ה צריך לשלם תחלה השטעמפל אך הקיר״ה בחסדו וישרנותו אמר שעל כיוצא בזה לא תטיל עול השטעמפל... .See also, Jacob b. Joseph Reischer, *Shebut Yaakob, Orah Hayyim,* II, 15 — ביש עכו״ם המעות ומכרו כדינו דודאי נקנה החמץ... ;Isaac Elhanan מיד לישראל מחק ודין המלכות אליבא דכ״ע מקרי חמץ של ישראל... Spector, *Ayn Yitzchak, Orah Hayyim,* 22; *Masat Benjamin,* 97; *Magen*

Abraham, 448:5; Abraham Shapiro, *Dbar Abraham,* I, 1; Jacob b. Aaron, *Mishkenot Jacob, Orah Hayyim,* 149.

44. *Ibid.* 311, 314. See also, Abraham Shapiro, *Dbar Abraham,* I, 1; Benjamin Aaron Slonic, *Masat Benjamin,* 35.

45. Meir of Rothenburg Pr. 677: synopsis taken from I. Agus, *op. cit.* (589). Contr. this with the Sephardic view in the 16th century, Trani, I, 194, who ruled that the king has absolute power to decide in trade competition. A Jew bought a contract from the king to mine; another Jew outbid the first. The king may award the contract to whomever he chooses and the other has absolutely no recourse. *Dina D'Malkhuta Dina* overrules the Jewish laws of trade competition. Comp. J. Caro, *Orah Hayyim,* 539; David Halevy, *Turei Zahab, ibid.* 3 in name of Solomon Luria; Joel Sirkes, *Bet Hodosh* quoted by Joseph Saul Nathanson, *Shoel u'Meshib,* I, 41.

46. See next chapter on modern views on this subject.

Chapter XI

MODERN QUESTIONS OF DINA D'MALKHUTA DINA

1. Italics are the author's.
2. Italics are my own.
3. Letter of M. Berr-Isaac-Berr, 1791. Translation taken from M. D. Tama, *Transactions of the Parisian Sanhedrin or Acts of the Assembly*.
4. *Ibid.* p. 152 ff.
5. Comp. *Talpioth,* 1945-46, articles on גירות ונישואין אזרחיים. The articles debate whether a civil marriage between Jews can be dissolved by a civil divorce alone. See also *ha-Pardes,* 1941, נישואי אזרחים, wherein the view is quoted that a Kohen may marry such a woman because no *Get* is required.

6. From a manuscript found at the Dropsie College Library, as yet unpublished, written by C. Adler, second copy, translated from the original document found in the National Archives A. F. IV Brief 2156.

7. See — תשובות ר׳ ישמעאל ב״ר אברהם יצחק הכהן רבה של מודינא על י״ב
דשורת — J. Rosenthal, *Talpioth,* 1949, pp. 571-2; השאלות של הקיסר נאפוליאון
הדין נותנת שחייבים אנו להרכין ראשינו לכל חוק המלכות... דאמר שמואל דד״ד וכמ״ש
כל הפוסקים דכל כמה שאין הד״ד נגד דיני התורה אנו חייבים לקיימם... ומעתה דאם
הדבר מוכרח מדין תורה שאיש אחד יתן גט לאשתו צריך שילך תחילה לפני הערכאות
שלהם ויעשה לפניהם מאי דצריך... ואח״כ ילך לפני המורה צדק... ויתן גט לאשתו
ע״פ תורתינו הקדושה וכמו שנוהגים לעשות לענין הנשואים שהולכים יחד החתן והכלה
לפני הערכאות להודיע להם שהם מתחתנים זה עם זה... ואח״ז עושים הנישואים עפ״י
הדין תורה בקידושין ובחופה... ומאחר עלות שצריכים אנו לקיים חוק המלכות... א״כ
כל... מי שיתן גט לאשתו לפי תה״ק קודם שישיג הגט מדיני בערכאות כפי הד״ד הגט
בטל [ובכ״י נמצאת הערה: חלילה לומר כן] Contr. with Jacob b. Joseph Reischer, *Shebut Yaakob, Orah Hayyim,* I, 20. In a mixed marriage, where the Jewish husband retained all other practices and the Gentile woman observed her customs, would the leavened products the wife has, be permissible for use by the husband after Passover or do all things belonging to a wife automatically become the property of her husband. R. Reischer replied that although Jews do not recognize such a marriage, nonetheless, since the secular law recognizes the husband as the legal owner of all property, then *Dina D'Malkhuta Dina* is applied and the leavened products are the husband's. He would not be permitted to make use of them. — דכל שהוא מחוק
ודין המלכות באחריות ישראל חייב לבער... וא״כ ה״ה בנד״ד מחקי ודין המלכות כמלכות
אחשורוש להיות כל איש שורר ושליט על אשתו המיוחדת לו ועל נכסיה דהוי בכלל חמץ
של ישראל שעבר עליו הפסח.

8. M. Friedlander, *The Jewish Religion,* p. 488 ff.; D. W. Amram, *American Hebrew,* 1903, p. 179 in his article "The Jewish Law and the Law of the State in Matters of Divorce." Today, Orthodox and Conservative Jews follow the same procedure.

9. Yeb. 90b; Git. 33a, 73a; B.B. 48b; Ket. 3a — כל המקדש אדעתא דרבנן מקדש.

10. A. Geiger, *Wissenschaftliche Zeitschrift*, 1837.

11. S. Holdheim, *Ueber die Autonomie der Rabbinen und das Princip der Jüdischen Ehe*, p. 59-60; . . . *führte der aus Tiberias zurückgekehrte Lehrer Samuel in Naharadea . . . den Grundsatz durch: dass im Civilrechte das Landesgesetz anerkannt werden müsse*. Again p. 66 — "*. . . und das Landesgesetz auch für alle civilrechtlichen Verhältnisse der Juden einge-führt ist, da tritt der jüdische Rechtsgrundsatz: dass in Civilrecht die Ver-fügungen der Staatsregierungen vom Juden anerkannt werden müssen . . .*"

12. *Ibid.* p. 87 — "*Hat aber der Staat die Machtvollkommenheit, die Jüdische Autonomie aufzuheben und das Landesgesetz an deren Stelle zu lassen, so kann das religiöse Gewissen sich dabei volkommen beruhigen, da in keinem Fall die religiösen, sondern die privaten Rechtsverhältnisse dabei . . .*"

13. *Ibid.* p. 138 — "*Die Jüdische Ehe in ihrem Bestande und während der ganzen Dauer derselben ist ein religiöses, auf sittlich religiöser Grund-lage basirendes Verhältniss; geworden und zu Stande gekommen ist sie durch die Mitwirkung juristischer Elemente, nämlich: durch die Entäus-serung und Erwerbung einer Sache . . .*"

14. Kid. I:1.

15. Holdheim, *op. cit.* p. 138 ft. note 107 — "*Die drei Erwerbsarten welche schon formell viel Analoges mit jenen bei der Erwerbung von Grundstücken getenden* כסף, שטר *haben, während statt der dritten, dort* חזקה *Besitzergreifung, die in dem Gebrauch . . . hier charakteristisch* ביאה *substituirt wird . . .*"

16. Kid. 2b — ניקנית לשון דאורייתא מקדש לשון דרבנן.

17. *Ibid.* — אין קיחה אלא בכסף.

18. *Ibid.* 5a; Ket. 57b — ארוסה בת ישראל אוכלת בתרומה שנ' וכהן כי יקנה נפש קנין כספו והאי קנין כספו הוא.

19. *Ibid.* 6a.

20. Holdheim, *op. cit.* — this entire process of thought is found in the cited passages.

21. Kid. 9a; comp. S. Zeitlin, *An Historical Study of the Canoniza-tion of the Hebrew Scriptures*, 1933; *The Rise and Fall of the Judean State*, pp. 303-305 who clearly showed that in olden times it was the father who wrote the "instrument of cohabitation" as seen in the "Book of Tobit." Comp. also J. A. Frankel, *Literaturblatt des Orients*, 1840, 21. This was against the *Halakha* as proposed in 65 CE and thus the Book of Tobit was excluded from the religious canon. This also disproves the theories of Holdheim.

22. Holdheim, *op. cit.* p. 141.

23. *Ibid.* quoting Nissim Gerondi, Ned. 30a — מכיון שהיא מסכמת לקדושי

האיש היא מבטלת דעתה ורצונה ומשוי נפשה אצל הבעל כדבר של הפקר והבעל מכניסה
לרשותו הלכך אין אנו דנין בקדושין מצד האשה אלא מצד הבעל.
24. Bezah 37 — אין מקדשין בשבת ויו״ט.
25. Comp. N.Z.Y.B., *Meshib Dabar*, IV:49 — ומזה אנו למדין שקנין
אשת ישראל לבעלה אינו כקנין שאר חפצים שב״ד יכולים להפקיר ולהפקיע שלא ברצון
בעלים אלא כהקדש וכמו שא״א לב״ד הגדול להקדיש בהמת האדם בלי רצונו ודיבורו
שיאמר רוצה אני להקדיש כך א״א לב״ד הגדול להפקיע קדושת אשה לאיש.
26. Comp. I. Herzog, *op. cit. vol.* I, p. 27.
27. See Z. Frankel, *Zeitschrift;* S. R. Hirsch, *ibid.* p. 275 ff; L. Löw,
Gesammelte Schriften, III, 348; A N. Z. Roth, *Hasoker*, p. 116; Kaufman
Kohler, *CCAR Yearbook*, 1915, Vol. XXV, "The Harmonization of the
Jewish and Civil laws of Marriage and Divorce," p. 341; M. Mielziner,
*The Jewish Law of Marriage and Divorce in Ancient and Modern Times
and its relation to the law of the State.*
28. K. Kohler, *op. cit.* p. 343. Statements such as one made by Leon
Harrison, *CCAR Yearbook*, Vol. XXIII, 1913, p. 355 — "There is only
one valid divorce in America, the divorce that is issued by an American
court of law. Indeed the spirit of Orthodox Judaism itself tacitly admits
this fact in the well-known talmudic maxim, "Dino D'Malchuso Dino"
(the law of the land is the law), may be ignored.
29. See J. A. Fränkel, *Literatureblatt des Orients*, 1840, 21, "Uber
das Princip der Jüd. Ehe," who gives an accurate account of the talmudic
attitude towards marriage.
30. N.Z.Y.B., *Meshib Dabar*, IV:8 — משא״כ בשהתה עשר שנים ולא ילדה
אין עליה שום חוב לקבל גט פטורין ממנו כי מה פשעה היא בדבר אם הוא לא זכה להבנות
ממנה אלא בזמן המשנה היה אפשר מד״ת לגרש בע״כ אבל עתה שא״א בכך מצד המלכות
אין לב״ד לכופה לקבל ממנו ג״פ מרצון.
31. I. Hoffman, *Der Orient*, 1842, 50 — *"Im Talmud wird nämlich
an mehren Stellen die bestimmte Lehre ausgesprochen, dass, wenn der
Staat, in welchem wir leben, nicht aus Religionszwang, sondern ein allge-
meines Gesetz zum besten seiner Unterthanen erlässt, der Israelit sich
unbedingt nach diesem Gesetz richten darf und soll . . . Aber wir haben
uns nur nach dem Landesgesetze zu richten, welches mehr Verbindlichkeit
und Verpflichtung für uns hat, als selbst ein mosaisches Gesetz; wir dürfen
daher jedes Amt annehmen und am Sabbat jede Amtsverrichtung, jede
Arbeit, jeden Waffendienst vornehmen, welche der Staatsdienst oder die
Bürgerpflicht uns auflegt . . .* See also, S. W. Baron, *A Social and Religious History of the Jews,* Vol. II, p. 252.
32. Z. Frankel, *ibid.* — *"wir wollen nicht hervorheben wie es möglich
war, einen solchen falschen Schluss aufzustellen, dass, weil der Jude den
Landesgesetzen da, wo es die Unterthanen treue und das unmittelbare Wohl
des Vaterlandes erheischt, Gehorsam zu leisten hat (in diesem Sinne spricht
es der Talmud aus), er sich auch berechtigt fühle, die Vorschriften seines
Glaubens da aufzugeben . . .*

215

33. Holdheim, *op. cit.* p. 92-93, footnote 62 — *"Er hat freilich kein Geschäft, das am Sabbath verboten, aber auch keines, das an ihm geboten, verrichtet; nichts gethan, was der Heiligkeit des Tages zuwider, aber auch nichts, was ihr angemessen ist . . . Das stimmt mit dem Buchstaben überein, der nur das Schreiben als Melachah verbietet. Dem Geiste nach aber ist der Schulbesuch an und für sich . . . an sich ein Geschäft . . .*

34. Letter of M. Berr-Isaac-Berr, 1791, M. D. Tama, *op. cit.*

35. J. George Fredman and Louis A. Falk, *Jews in American Wars.*

36. J. A. Fränkel, *"Unsere Religion erlaubt uns im Dienste des Königs und des Vaterlandes das Ceremonialgesetz ausser Acht zu lassen," Literaturblatt des Orients,* 1842, 21.

37. Erub. 45a — א״ר יהודה אמר רב נכרים שצרו על עיירות ישראל אין יוצאין עליהם בכלי זיינן ואין מחללין עליהן את השבת... בד״א כשבאו על עסקי ממון... ובעיר הסמוכה לספר אפילו לא באו על עסקי נפשות אלא על עסקי תבן וקש׳ יוצאין עליהן בכלי זיינן ומחללין עליהן את השבת.

38. Maimonides, *Shabbat,* 2:23 — ומצוה על כל ישראל שיכולין לבוא ולצאת ולעזור לאחיהם שבמצור ולהצילם מיד עכו״ם בשבת ואסור להן להתמהמה למוצאי שבת.

39. *Ibid.* — וכשיצילו את אחיהן מותר להן לחזור בכלי זיין שלהן למקומם בשבת כדי שלא להכשילן לעתיד לבוא.

40. Joseph Caro, *Bet Joseph,* 329; *Orah Hayyim,* 329:6-7 — יש מי שאומר שבזה״ז אפי׳ באו על עסקי ממון מחללין שאם לא יניחנו ישראל לשלול ולבוז ממנו יהרגנו והוי עסקי נפשות.

41. Israel Meir ha-Kohen, *Mishneh Berurah, ad. loc.* — ודע דהיום כשבאו מהאומות שחוץ לגבולינו לשלול ולבוז בז בודאי מחוייבים אנו לצאת בכלי זיין אפי׳ על עסקי ממון וכדינא דמלכותא... וכבר נפסק בגמ׳ דד״ד. The above was quoted in the name of *Agudah* and *Rokeah.*

42. Shab. 19a — אין צרין על עיירות של נכרים פחות מג׳ ימים קודם לשבת ואם התחילו אין מפסיקין.

43. Hulin 17a; Maimonides, *Melakim,* 8:1 — חלוצי צבא כשיכנסו בגבול העכו״ם... מותר להן לאכול נבלות וטרפות ובשר חזיר וכיוצא בו אם ירעב ולא מצא מה יאכל אלא מאכלות אלו האסורים וכן שותה יין נסך...

44. Joseph Caro. *Kessef Mishneh, ad. loc.* — ואין כוונתו במי שהוא מסוכן מחמת רעבון דהא פשיטא ואפי׳ אינו מחלוצי צבא נמי אלא כשתאב לאכול ולא שכיח ליה היתרא...

45. David Ibn Zimra, *ad. loc.* — ולא איירי שהם מסוכנים אצל הרעב אלא שאינם צריכין לטרוח לבקש מאכל היתר כיון שנכנסו לגבול העמים...

46. J. A. Fränkel, *op. cit.* p. 326 — *"Allein sowohl im Talmud als in den spätern an den Talmud sich ängstlich halten den Schriften werden Gesetze über den sein jüdisches Vaterland vertheidigenden Soldaten vorgeschlagen, welche wir für uns in unserm Staate in Ausspruch nehmen müssen und können. Sollte also den Juden, als sie noch selbst einem politischen Staat . . . erlaubt gewesen sein für ihren König, für ihr Vaterland und für ihre Brüder am Sonnabend oder an den Festtagen zu kämpfen und im Kampfe die Speisegesetze und andere Gebräuche und Satzungen zu über-*

treten; so werden auch wir für unsern König . . . dieselbe Dispensation vom Gesetze nicht nur beansprüchen können, sondern selbst beansprüchen müssen. See also *ibid.* Abraham Tiktin, chief rabbi in Breslau and Meyer Weil of Berlin; Hillel Posek, *Hillel Omer, Orah Hayyim,* 137, *Yoreh Deah,* 225, *Hoshen Mishpat,* 22.

47. The same appears to have been the case in Germany, where the maxim *Dina D'Malkhuta Dina* was not always necessary since the government made exceptions and provisions to release soldiers for holidays and made allowances for special food. See J. A. Fränkel, *op. cit.* p. 328.

48. Elijah Mizrachi, *Responsa,* 45; Rosanes, *op. cit.* p. 134 — התאספו
...ויעשו תקנה שלא להתעסק בשום אופן בממכר הכרכום שלא לקנות מן הגנבים.

49. *Ibid.* — ובכל ערב ר"ה היה לחדשה אמנם התקנה בשלמותה... לא נתרצו
...לחדשה

50. *Ibid.* — וגם נמצא סוחר עני שבא מחוצה לארץ ושמו יהודה... הלך בחברת
גנבים... עד אשר נתפס בידי המלכות ונחרץ משפט מות עליו.

51. *Ibid.* — אם כונתכם לשמים כמו שאתם אומרים היה לכם לעשות תקנה שלא
...יקנו כרכום שהיא גזלת (גזרת) המלך ודד"ך גם מלקנות גנבות שהוא אסור.

52. *Ibid.*

53. J. Caro, *Hoshen Mishpat,* 369:1, 356-359 — אסור לקנות מהגנב החפץ
שגנב ועון גדול הוא ושהרי מחזיק ידי עוברי עבירה וגורם לו לגנוב גניבות אחרות שאם
לא ימצא לוקח גונב אינו גונב. Translation from I. Abrahams, *Jewish Life in the Middle Ages,* pp. 107-108.

54. See above Chapter VII.

55. *Mafteah,* p. 182.

56. *Ibid.* p. 191.

57. No Jew is permitted to directly hide a fellow Jew who is sought by the authorities but it is permissible to advise him. *Dina D'Malkhuta Dina* is not applicable even if it forbid such an act. See Jair Hayyim Bachrach, *Havat Jair,* 176 — ועוד אפשר לומר נהי דלטמרו בידים אסור מ"מ להשיאו עצה
ולהראותו לו מקום נהי דמצד ד"ד אסור מצד דין תורה מותר.

58. Comp. Semahot II, 9.

59. J. S. Nathanson, quoted by I. Herzog, *op. cit.* p. 135.

60. Solomon b. Simon Duran, 212 — ע"כ אני אומר אם המלך רוצה לחדש
שכל יהודי שיעשה יין לשתייתו יתן כך וכך לחבית לא ד"ד הוא לפי שדיניהם נותן כיון
שיהודי נותן מכס דהיינו כסף גולגולתא| שיכול לעשות יין כרצונו לשתייתו אבל אם הוא
מטיל על המוכרים אותו לישמעאלים דינו דין כי יכול הוא לענוש למוכרו לישמעאלים מפני
איסור דתם.

61. J. Henkin, "Be'Inyan Dina D'Malkhuta Dina," *ha-Pardes,* Vol. 31, April 1957, pp. 3-5 — חוק הדירות של הממשלה הוא ישר מתוקן ומקובל בפרט
בערים הגדולות... ואף שלפעמים נראה כעול נגד בעלי בתים... הכונה כשמפלה בין
עם לעם משום רשעות כגון שגוזרים גזירות על ישראל ח"ו... אבל כשיש חוק להתקנות
עניים... כ"ש דאזלינן בתרי'...

BIBLIOGRAPHY

Abarbanel, Don Isaac, Commentary to Samuel.

Abraham Ben David De Portaleone, Shiltei Gibborim, Mantua, 1612.

Abraham Ben Isaac of Narbonne, Ha-Eshkol, Mekize Nirdamim, Jerusalem, 1938.

————, Seforim Shel Rishonim, ed. S. Asaf, Jerusalem, 1935.

Abraham Ibn Daud, Sefer ha-Kabbala, ed. A. Neubauer, Oxford, 1887.

Abraham Ibn Daud of Posquieres, Rabad, glosses to Maimonides', Mishneh Torah and to Alfasi's Halakot.

Agus, Irving, R. Meir of Rothenburg, Philadelphia, 1947.

————, Teshubot Baalei Tosafot, New York, 1954.

Ahai, Rab, Sheiltot, Venice, 1546; Vilna, 1867.

Alexander Ha-Kohen Süsslein, Sefer Agudah, Cracow, 1571.

Alfasi, Isaac Ben Jacob, Halakot in Vilna edition of the Babylonian Talmud.

————, Responsa, ed. Leiter; Leghorn, 1781.

Altmann, Berthold, "Studies in Medieval German Jewish History." *Proceedings of the American Academy for Jewish Reserach*, X, (1940).

Amram, D. W., "The Jewish Law and the Law of the State in Matters of Divorce," *American Hebrew*, New York, 1879.

Aryeh Leib Ben Asher, Shaagat Aryeh, Warsaw, 1879. Frankfurt on the Oder, 1756.

Asaf, Simha, Teshubat ha-Geonim, Jerusalem, 1928 and 1942.

Asher Ben Yehiel of Toledo, She'elot u-teshubot, Venice, 1607; Constantinople, 1517.

Auerbach, B. H., Brit Abraham.

Baal Halakot Gedolot.

Bachrach, Jair Hayyim, Havat Yair, Frankfort on the Main, 1699.

Baer, Fritz, Die Juden im Christlichen Spanien, Berlin, 1929.

Bahye Ben Asher, Kad ha-Kemah.

Bamberger, B. J., "Individual Rights and the Demands of the State: The position of Classical Judaism," *CCAR Yearbook*, Liv., 1944.

Barfat, Isaac Ben Sheshet, She'elot u-teshubot, Lemberg, 1805; Constantinople, 1546; Riva di Trenta, 1559.

————, Yeshonot, Munkacs, 1901.

Baruch Ben Isaac of Worms, Sefer ha-Terumah, Zolkiev, 1811.

Ben Dov, *Talpioth*, 1961.

Benjamin of Tudela, The Itinerary of Rabbi Benjamin of Tudela. Transl. and ed. by A. Asher, London and Berlin, 1840-1.

Berlin, N. Z. J., Meshib Dabar, Warsaw, 1894; New York, 1958.

Bezalel Ben Abraham Ashkenazi, Shittah Mekubezet, Venice, 1762.

Caro, Joseph, Shulhan Aruk,

————, Kessef Mishneh, to most editions of Maimonides' Mishneh Torah.

————, Abkat Rohel, Salonica, 1791.

218

Bibliography

————, She'elot u-teshubot le'Dinei Nashim, Mantoua, 1730.

Colon, Joseph, She'elot u-teshubot, Sudzilkow, 1834; Warsaw, 1884.

David Ben Solomon Ibn Zimra, She'elot u-teshubot, Leghorn, 1651; Vol. III, Fürth, 1781; Sudzilkow, 1836.

————, Lilshonot le'ha-Rambam, Venice, 1749.

Duran, Simon Ben Zemah, Tashbetz, Amsterdam, 1738.

Duran, Solomon Ben Simon, Tashbash, Leghorn, 1742.

Duran, Zemah Ben Simon, Yakin u'Boaz, Leghorn, 1782.

Edels, Samuel Eliezer Ben Judah, Maharsha, Amsterdam, 1755.

Elfenbein, I., R. Solomon b. Isaac of Troyes, New York, 1943.

Eliezer Ben Joel Halevi, Sefer Rabiah, ed. Aptowitzer, Vol. I-III, Berlin, 1913; Jerusalem, 1935.

Eliezer Ben Nathan of Mayence, Sefer Raban, Prague, 1610.

Eliezer of Worms, Sefer ha-Rakeach, ed. Warsaw.

Epstein, Isidore, The Responsa of R. Solomon ben Adreth of Barcelona, London, 1925.

————, The Responsa of R. Simon b. Zemah Duran, London, 1930.

Falk, Joshua, Sefer Meirat Enayim.

Finkelstein, Louis, Jewish Self-Government in the Middle Ages, New York, 1924.

Friedlander, M., The Jewish Religion, London, 1913.

Geiger, A., *Wissenschaftliche Zeitschrift*.

Gersonides, Commentary to Samuel.

Gerondi, Nissim Ben Reuben, She'elot u'teshubot, Rome, 1545; Metz, 1786; Warsaw, 1907.

Ginzberg, Louis, Geonica, Vol. I and II, New York, 1909.

————, Ginzei Schechter, New York 1928-9.

Graetz, Heinrich, Geschichte der Juden von den ältesten Zeiten bis auf die Gegenwart, Leipzig, 1853-76.

————, History of the Jews, J.P.S., Philadelphia, 1891-98.

Grodzensky, Hayyim Ozer, Ahiezer, Jerusalem, 1945; Vilna 1946.

Gulak, Asher, Yesodei Hamisphat ha-Ivri, Berlin, 1922.

Gumbiner, Abraham Abelle Ben Hayyim, Magen Abraham, commentary found in Joseph Caro's Maginei Eretz, Amsterdam, 1720.

Habbib, Joseph Ibn, Nemukei Joseph, Commentary found in most editions of Alfasi's Halakot.

Habib, Levi Ibn, Ralbach, Venice, 1565; Lemberg, 1865; Brooklyn, 1962.

Hakmei Zorfat Ve'Lotir, see Mueller, Joel.

Halakot Pesukot, Versailles. 1886.

Halevy, David, Turei Zahab, commentary to Joseph Caro's Shulhan Aruk.

Hananel, Novellae, found in most editions of the Talmud.

Hapardes, "Nissuei Esrohim,," 1941; Vol. 31, April 1951.

Harkavy, Abraham Y., Teshubat ha-Geonim, Berlin, 1887.

————, Zikkaron la'Rishonim ve'Gam la'Acharonim, Berlin, 1887.

BIBLIOGRAPHY

Harrison, Leon, *CCAR Yearbook*, Vol. 23, 1913.

Henkin, J., "Be'Inyan Dina D'Malkhuta Dina," *Hapardes*, Vol. 31, April, (1951).

Hershman, A. M., R. Isaac b. Sheshet Perfet and his Times, New York, 1943.

Herzog, I., The Main Institutions of Jewish Law, London, 1936.

Hesronot Ha-Shas.

Hoffman, David, Mar Samuel, Leipzig ,1873.

Holdheim, Samuel, Autonomie der Rabbinen und das Princip der jüdischen Ehe, Schwerin, 1843.

Isaac Ben Abba Mari, Sefer ha-Ittur, ed. Schönblum; Warsaw, 1801.

Israel Ben Pethahiah, Isserlein, Terumat ha-Deshen, Venice, 1519.

Israel Meir ha-Kohen, Mishneh Berurah, ed. Shulsinger Bros., New York, 1943

Israel of Krems, Hagohot ha-Ashri, found in text of R. Asher's commentary to the Talmud.

Issachar Baer Ben Noah, Riban, Warsaw, 1867.

Isserles, Moses, Mapat ha-Shulhan, inserted into the text of Joseph Caro's Shulhan Aruk.

——, Darkei Moshe, Sulzbach, 1692.

——, She'elot u'teshubot, Amsterdam, 1711; Hanau, 1710.

Jacob Ben Aaron, Mishkenot Jacob, Vilna, 1837.

Jacob Ben Asher, Turim, Warsaw, 1882; Venice, 1475.

Jacob Ben Meir, Tam, Sefer Hajaschar, ed. Rosenthal, Berlin, 1898.

Jacob Ben Moses Halevi Molin, Sefer Maharil, Cremona, 1558; Lublin, 1590.

Jaffe, Mordecai Ben Abraham, Lebushim, Cracow, 1594; Berdichev, 1818-1821.

Jellinek, A., *Neuzeit*, 1862.

Joseph Ben Meir Halevi Ibn Migash, She'elot u'teshubot, Warsaw, 1870.

Josephus, Wars, Loeb Classical Library edition.

Judah he-Hasid, Sefer Hasidim, ed. Wistinetzki, Frankfort, 1924.

Katzenellenbogen, Meir, She'elot u'teshubot, Cracow, 1882.

Kaufmann, D., "Jewish Informers in the Middle Ages," *J.Q.R.* (OS) Vol. 8, (1895).

Kenesset Hagedolah, ed. Soblesky, Warsaw, 1890.

Kisch, Guido, "Jewish and Christian Courts," *Historia Judaica*, Vol. XXI.

Kohler, Kaufman, "The Harmonization of the Jewish Civil Law of Marriage and Divorce," *CCAR Yearbook*, Vol. 25, (1915).

Landau, Ezekiel Ben Judah, Nodei be'Yehuda, Prague, 1776; Warsaw, 1880; Wilna, 1928.

Landau, Sol, Christian-Jewish Relations, New York, 1959.

Lauer, C., "R. Meir Halevy aus Wien und der Streit um das Grossrabinat

Bibliography

in Frankreich," *Jahrbuch der Jüdisch-Literarischen Gesellschaft*, Vol. XVI, (1924).

Lauterbach, J. Z., Rabbinic Essays, HUC Press, Cincinnati, 1951.

Lewin, B. M., Ozar Hageonim, Jerusalem, 1939.

Literaturblatt Des Orients.

Löw, L., Gesammelte Schriften, Szegedin, 1881.

Luria, Solomon, Yam Shel Shlomo, Lublin, 1616; Prague, 1616;

————, She'elot u'teshubot, ed. Lemberg, 1859.

Maaseh ha-Geonim, ed. Freiman, Mekize Nirdamim, 1909.

Maimonides, Moses, Mishneh Torah, Amsterdam, 1702;

————, Commentary to Mishneh, found in most editions of the Talmud.

————, She'elot u'teshubot, ed. Freiman, Jerusalem, 1934; ed. Sasportas.

Mann, Jacob, "The Responsa of the Babylonian Geonim as a Source of Jewish History," *JQR*, Vol. VII-XI, (1916-21).

Marx, A., "R. Joseph Arli and R. Johanan Treves," *Studies in Memory of Moses Schorr.*

Meir Ben Baruch of Rothenberg, She'elot u'teshubot, Cremona, 1557; Prague, 1608; Sdilkow, 1835; ed. Bloch, 1891; Budapest, 1895; Lemberg, 1860; Berlin, 1891.

Meir Ben Gedaliah, Meir Einei Hakamim, Fürth, 1737; Vilna and Grodno, 1833.

Meiri, Menahem Ben Solomon. Bet Habehira, Vienna, 1934.

Melziner, M., The Jewish Law of Marriage and Divorce in Ancient and Modern Times and its relationship to the Law of the State.

Menahem Mendel of Lubavitz, Zemah Zedek.

Meshal ha-Kadmoni, ed. Venice and Zamora.

Mintz, Judah, She'elot u'teshubot, Venice, Cracow, 1882.

Mizrahi, Elijah, She'elot u'teshubot, Jerusalem, 1938.

Mordecai Ben Hillel Ashkenazi, Sefer Mordecai, Riva di Trenta, 1559, printed with Alfasi.

Moses Ben Jacob of Coucy, Sefer Mitzvot Gadol (Semag), Kopost, 1807.

Mueller, Joel, Hakmei Zorfat ve'Lotir, Vienna, 1881.

————, Mafteah, Berlin, 1891.

Nahmanides, Moses, Novellae, Lisbon, 1489.

————, Torat ha-Adam, Venice, 1595.

Nathanson, Joseph Saul, Shoel u'Meshib, Lemberg, 1865.

Neuman, Abraham, The Jews of Spain, Philadelphia, 1942.

Or Zarua, Hayyim Ben Isaac, She'elot u'teshubot, Leipzig, 1860.

Or Zarua, Isaac Ben Moses of Vienna, She'elot u'teshubot, Vol. I, II, Zhitomir, 1862; Vol. III, Jerusalem, 1887; Vol. IV, Jerusalem, 1890.

Ozar Tov, Hebrew section of Magazin für die Wissenschaft des Judenthums, Berlin, 1874-1892.

Plato, Republic, translated by H. Davis, New York, and London, 1901.

Posek, Hillel, Sefer Hillel Omer, Tel-Aviv, 1955.

Bibliography

Rabinowitz, L., The Jews of Northern France in the 12-14 Centuries, London, 1938.

Reischer, Jacob Ben Joseph, Shebut Yaakov, Lemberg, 1897.

Rosanes, S. A., Dibrei Yemei Yisroel be-Tugrama, Husiatyn-Sofia, 1907-1937; Tel-Aviv, 1930.

Rosenthal, J., *Talpioth*, (1949).

Roth, A. N. Z., "Dina D'Malkhuta Dina," *Hasoker*, V, (1937-8).

Rousseau, Jacques, The Social Contract and Discourses, London, 1930.

Samuel Ben Meir, Commentary to tractate Babba Batra printed with editions of the Talmud.

Samuel De Modena, She'elot u'teshubot, Salonica, 1595.

Shaarei Teshuba, ed. Moses Mordecai Meyuhas, Salonica, 1802.

Shaarei Zedek, ed. Nissim b. Hayyim Modai, Salonica, 1792.

Shabbatai ha-Kohen, Siftei Kohen, commentary printed with many editions of Joseph Caro's Shulhan Aruk.

Shapiro, Abraham, Dbar Abraham, Kedaini, 1930; New York, 1946.

Sherira, Letter, ed. Hyman, London, 1910.

Shohet, D. M., The Jewish Court in the Middle Ages, New York, 1931.

Sirkes, Joel, Bet Hodosh ha-Hadoshot, Koretz, 1785.

————, Bet Hodosh ha-Yeshonot, Ostrog, 1834.

Slonik, Benjamin, A., Maasot Benjamin, Sidlikow, 1833; Vilna, 1894.

Sofer, Moses, Hatam Sofer, Orah Hayyim, Pressburg, 1879; Yoreh Deah and Hoshen Mishpat, Vienna, 1883; Eben Haezer, Vienna, 1877; Vol. VI, Vienna, 1883.

Solomon Ben Abraham ha-Kohen, She'elot u'teshubot, Salonica, 1586.

Solomon Ben Abraham Ibn Adret, She'elot u'teshubot, Vol. I Bologna, 1539; Vol. II Leghorn, 1657; Vol. III Leghorn, 1778; Vol. IV Vilna, 1881; Vol. V Leghorn, 1825; Vol. VI Warsaw, 1868;

————, Toldot ha-Adam, Lemberg, 1811;

————, Teshubot ha-Rashba ha-meyuhasot le'ha-Ramban, Warsaw, 1883;

————, Torat Habayit ha-Aruk, Venice, 1607.

Solomon Ibn Verga, Shebet Yehuda, ed. M. Wiener, Hanover, 1924.

Spector, Isaac Elhanan, Beer Yitzchak, Königsberg, 1858;

————, Ayn Yitzchak.

Starr, Joshua, "Jewish Life in Crete under the Rule of Venice," *PAAJR*, Vol. 12.

————, The Jews in the Byzantine Empire, Athens, 1939.

Tama, M. D., Transactions of the Parisian Sanhedrin or Acts of the Assembly, London. 1807.

Teshubat ha-Geonim, ed. Coronel Vienna, 1871.

Teshubat ha-Geonim, ed. Halberstam, Deva, 1927.

Teshubat ha-Geonim, ed. Jacob Mosafya, Mekize Nirdamim, Lyck, 1864.

Teshubat ha-Geonim, ed. Rabinowitz, Vilna, 1885.

Teshubat ha-Geonim ha-Ketzorot.

Bibliography

Teshubat ha-Geonim Kadmonim, collected by Yom Tob Elem, ed. D. Cassell, Berlin, 1848.

Toraton Shel Rishonim.

Tosefta, ed. Zuckermandel, Pasewalk, 1881.

Trani, Moses Ben Joseph, She'elot u'teshubot, Venitia, 1629.

Volozin, Hayyim, Hut Hameshulosh, New York, 1956.

Weil, Jacob, She'elot u'teshubot, Venice, 1549; Cremona, 1556.

Weiss, I. H., Dor Dor ve'Dorshav, Vienna, 1871; Berlin, 1924.

Yaari, A., Igrot Eretz Yisroel, Tel-Aviv, 1943.

Yeruham Ben Meshullam, Sefer Mesharim, Constantinople, 1516.

Yom Tob Ibn Ashvilla, She'elot u'teshubot, Mosad haRav Kook, Jerusalem, 1959.

Zacuto, Abraham Ben Samuel, Sefer Yohasin, ed. Shulem.

Zeitlin, Solomon, "An Historical Study of the Canonization of the Hebrew Scriptures," *PAAJR*, (1931-2).

————, "The Herem Hayyishub," *J.Q.R.*, Vol. 37, (1947).

————, "Opposition to the Spiritual Leaders Appointed by the Government," *J.Q.R.*, Vol. 31 January (1941).

————, "Rashi and the Rabbinate," *J.Q.R.*, Vol. 31, July (1940).

————, "Responsa of the Tosafists," *J.Q.R.*, (1954).

————, The Rise and Fall of the Judean State, J.P.S., Philadelphia, 1964.

Zevi Hirsch Ben Jacob Ashkenazi, Hakam Zevi.